DYSLIPIDEMIA ESSENTIALS

Third Edition

Christie M. Ballantyne, MD
Clinical Director, Section of Atherosclerosis
Professor of Medicine
Baylor College of Medicine
Director, Center for Cardiovascular Disease Prevention
Methodist DeBakey Heart Center
Houston, Texas

James H. O'Keefe, Jr., MD
Director, Preventive Cardiology
Mid-America Heart Institute
Professor of Medicine
University of Missouri School of Medicine
Kansas City, Missouri

Antonio M. Gotto, Jr., MD, DPhil
The Stephen and Suzanne Weiss Dean
Professor of Medicine
The Weill Medical College of Cornell University
New York, New York

PHYSICIANS' PRESS

Innovative Medical Publishing

ABOUT THE AUTHORS

Christie M. Ballantyne, M.D., is Director of the Center for Cardiovascular Disease Prevention, Methodist DeBakey Heart Center; Associate Chief and Clinical Director of the Section of Atherosclerosis, Department of Medicine; Director of the Maria and Alando J. Ballantyne, M.D., Atherosclerosis Laboratory; Professor of Medicine and Pediatrics, Baylor College of Medicine; and Co-Director, Lipid Metabolism and Atherosclerosis Clinic, The Methodist Hospital, Houston, Texas. His postgraduate training included an American Heart Association/Bugher Foundation Fellowship at the Howard Hughes Medical Institute and Institute for Molecular Genetics at Baylor. Dr. Ballantyne has been the recipient of numerous study grants, including an American Heart Association Established Investigator Award, and he has several NIH grants to study leukocyte–endothelial adhesion molecules and novel markers for atherosclerosis. He is Editorial Director for www.lipidsonline.org and www.cardiometabolicrisk.org. Dr. Ballantyne has published extensively and speaks nationally and internationally on lipids, atherosclerosis, and inflammation. Dr. Ballantyne's research interests include the pathophysiology of atherosclerosis, with an emphasis on monocyte function.

James H. O'Keefe, Jr., M.D., is Director of Preventive Cardiology at the Mid America Heart Institute and Professor of Medicine at the University of Missouri in Kansas City. His postgraduate training included a cardiology fellowship at Mayo Clinic in Rochester, Minnesota. Dr. O'Keefe has contributed more than 110 publications and books on cardiovascular medicine. He lectures extensively on the role of therapeutic lifestyle changes and drug therapy in cardiovascular risk reduction, and he is actively involved in patient care.

Antonio M. Gotto, Jr, MD, DPhil, is the Stephen and Suzanne Weiss Dean of Weill Medical College of Cornell University in New York, New York. He is also Professor of Medicine and Provost for Medical Affairs. Previously, at Baylor College of Medicine in Houston, Texas, he was the Bob and Vivian Smith Professor and Chairman of the Department of Medicine, Scientific Director of the DeBakey Heart Center, and held the JS Abercrombie Professor Chair for Atherosclerosis and Lipoprotein Research. He also served as Chief of the Internal Medicine Service at The Methodist Hospital in Houston. Dr. Gotto's postgraduate work included doctoral studies at Oxford University in England, as a Rhodes Scholar, and residency training at Massachusetts General Hospital in Boston, Massachusetts. He has been National President of the American Heart Association; President of the International Atherosclerosis Society; a member of the National Heart, Lung, and Blood Advisory Council and the National Diabetes Advisory Board; and a reviewer of the National Cholesterol Education Program's Third Report on Detection, Evaluation, and Treatment of High Blood Cholesterol in Adults. Dr. Gotto speaks nationally and internationally on cardiovascular disease and has contributed more than 500 scholarly articles and books. He and his associates were the first to achieve complete synthesis of a plasma apolipoprotein (apo C-I). They also determined the complete cDNA and amino acid sequence of apo B-100, one of the largest proteins ever sequenced and a key protein in atherosclerosis. His research interests include clinical disorders of lipid transport and the structure, metabolism, and function of lipoproteins and apolipoproteins and their relationship to atherosclerosis.

Printed in the United States of America   ISBN: 1–890114–65–0

DEDICATION

*We dedicate this volume to our patients
and to all individuals who volunteered
to be in the clinical trials that have
provided us the evidence upon
which we practice prevention*

Christie M.
Ballantyne, MD

James H.
O'Keefe, Jr., MD

Antonio M.
Gotto, Jr., MD, DPhil

TABLES, FIGURES, TRIALS

TABLE OF CONTENTS

ABBREVIATIONS

ACC	American College of Cardiology	HDL	high-density lipoprotein
ACE	angiotensin converting enzyme	HDL-C	HDL cholesterol
ACLS	advanced cardiovascular life support	IDL	intermediate density lipoprotein
ACS	acute coronary syndrome	IV	intravenous
AHA	American Heart Association	kg	kilogram
ATP	Adult Treatment Panel (National Cholesterol Education Program)	L	liter
		LDL	low-density lipoprotein
BAS	bile acid sequestrants	LDL-C	LDL cholesterol
BID	twice daily	Lp(a)	lipoprotein(a)
BMI	body mass index	LPL	lipoprotein lipase
BP	blood pressure	Lp-PLA$_2$	lipoprotein-associated phospholipase A$_2$
BUN	blood urea nitrogen		
CABG	coronary artery bypass grafting	LV	left ventricular; left ventricle
CHD	coronary heart disease (prior MI, evidence of clinically-significant silent ischemia, history of angina pectoris, prior CABG, prior coronary angioplasty or stent)	LVEF	left ventricular ejection fraction
		LVH	left ventricular hypertrophy
		max	maximum
		mcg	microgram
		mcL	microliter
CHD risk equivalent: peripheral artery disease, including abdominal aortic aneurysm; carotid artery disease (TIA or stroke of carotid origin, asymptomatic carotid stenosis > 50%), other vascular disease of atherosclerotic origin (e.g., renal artery stenosis), diabetes mellitus, or 2 or more risk factors conferring a 10-year CHD risk > 20%		mg	milligram
		MI	myocardial infarction
		min	minute
		mL	milliliter
		NCEP	National Cholesterol Education Program (Adult Treatment Panel)
		NHLBI	National Heart, Lung, and Blood Institute
CI	contraindication	NPO	nothing by mouth
CK	creatine kinase	NRT	nicotine replacement therapy
CNS	central nervous system	NYHA	New York Heart Association
COPD	chronic obstructive pulmonary disease	O$_2$	oxygen
CrCl	creatinine clearance	PCI	percutaneous coronary intervention
DHA	docosahexaenoic acid	PE	pulmonary embolism
dL	deciliter	PO	per os - by mouth; oral
ECG	electrocardiogram	PPAR	peroxisome proliferator-activated receptor
Echo	echocardiogram; echocardiography		
EF	ejection fraction	q__h	every __ hours
e.g.	for example	q__d	every __ days
EPA	eicosapentaenoic acid	qmonth	once a month
FDA	Food and Drug Administration	qweek	once a week
FH	familial hypercholesterolemia	TG	triglyceride
FIB	fibrates	TLC	therapeutic lifestyle changes
g	gram	TID	three times daily
GI	gastrointestinal	TSH	thyroid stimulating hormone
gm	gram	ULN	upper limit of normal
		VLDL	very low density lipoprotein

ACKNOWLEDGMENTS

To accomplish the task of presenting the data compiled in this reference, a small, dedicated team of professionals was assembled. We wish to acknowledge Kerrie Jara for editorial assistance, Monica Crowder-Kaufmann for typing and formatting, Norman Lyle for cover design, and Mark S. Freed, MD, President and Editor-in-Chief of Physicians' Press, for his vision, commitment, and guidance.

Christie M. Ballantyne, MD
James H. O'Keefe, Jr, MD
Antonio M. Gotto, Jr, MD, DPhil

NOTICE

Chapter 1

Dyslipidemia Essentials

Atherosclerotic vascular disease is the leading cause of morbidity and mortality in the United States, accounting for more than one-third of all deaths each year. At any one time, 13 million Americans have coronary heart disease (CHD), almost 5 million have had strokes, and millions have significant claudication from peripheral artery disease. Dyslipidemia is the most prevalent and important modifiable risk factor for atherosclerosis, affecting one in two U.S. adults. Proper treatment reduces the risk for cardiac death, nonfatal myocardial infarction (MI), stroke, revascularization procedures, and peripheral artery disease by 25-50%. Despite these benefits, only 20% of adults meet national guidelines for cholesterol control, and hundreds of thousands of lives are lost each year from failure to implement established measures.

Dyslipidemia Essentials integrates the latest clinical guidelines and trials into a concise, authoritative, and practical step-by-step guide to cardiovascular risk reduction and the management of dyslipidemia. These measures form the basis for a management strategy aimed at halting the progression of atherosclerosis, stabilizing rupture-prone plaques, preventing arterial thrombosis, and improving cardiovascular prognosis.

Overview of Dyslipidemia

A. **Definition.** Dyslipidemia is defined as an abnormal plasma lipid status. Common lipid abnormalities include elevated levels of total cholesterol, low-density lipoprotein (LDL) cholesterol, lipoprotein(a), and triglyceride; low levels of high-density lipoprotein (HDL) cholesterol; and a preponderance of small, dense LDL particles. These abnormalities can be found alone or in combination.

B. **Prevalence.** Approximately 50% of U.S. adults have an elevated total cholesterol level, and the vast majority of patients with atherosclerotic vascular disease have some form of dyslipidemia, even though their total cholesterol may not differ significantly from those without atherosclerosis;

35-40% of all cases of CHD occur in patients with "normal" total cholesterol levels (< 200 mg/dL). Despite marked benefits of lipid therapy, 70-80% of individuals with dyslipidemia fail to meet LDL cholesterol targets established by the National Cholesterol Education Program Adult Treatment Panel III (ATP III).

C. **Risk Factors.** Elevated levels of total cholesterol and LDL cholesterol and low levels of HDL cholesterol are major modifiable lipid risk factors for CHD and other forms of atherosclerotic vascular disease. It has been estimated that for each 1% decrease in LDL cholesterol and for each 1% increase in HDL cholesterol, the risk for cardiovascular events is reduced by 2% and 3%, respectively. Other important modifiable risk factors for CHD include elevated levels of triglyceride, lipoprotein(a), small dense LDL particles, homocysteine, C-reactive protein (CRP), fibrinogen, and lipoprotein-associated phospholipase A_2 (Lp-PLA$_2$).

D. **Screening.** Routine lipoprotein analysis is recommended by the ATP III for all adults aged 20 years and older, as dyslipidemia is usually an asymptomatic condition and early recognition and treatment improves prognosis.

E. **Lipid Therapy and the New CHD Paradigm.** It has now been established that the most dangerous (i.e., rupture-prone) atherosclerotic plaques are not necessarily those causing the most severe narrowing, and that most acute coronary syndromes are caused by lesions that were less than 70% stenotic (nonobstructive) prior to ulceration and thrombosis. Nonobstructive plaques with extensive inflammation (stimulated by oxidized lipoproteins in the vessel wall), lipid-rich cores, and thin fibrous caps are more prone to ulceration and rupture than long-standing obstructive lesions with extensive calcification and thick fibrous caps comprised of dense collagenous tissue.

Moderate reductions in LDL cholesterol slow the progression of coronary disease in most patients, and lesion regression is more frequent with LDL cholesterol reduction. Nevertheless, the beneficial effects of lipid therapy are due more to plaque stabilization than to changes in stenosis severity, which are generally modest and disproportionate to the 25-50% reduction in major cardiovascular events. Plaque stabilization, which can be accomplished in weeks to months with aggressive treatment of dyslipidemia, may be related to resorption of macrophage and extracellular lipid deposits, a decrease in neointimal inflammation, and maintenance of fibrous cap integrity. Effective treatment transforms the inflamed, friable plaque into a stable, fibrotic plaque that is less prone to ulceration, rupture, and thrombosis. In addition, lipid-modifying drug therapy improves endothelial dysfunction caused by dyslipidemia, resulting in additional vasodilatory, antithrombotic, and anti-inflammatory effects. For patients with CHD, treatment of dyslipidemia and other concomitant risk factors is essential to improve long-term cardiovascular prognosis.

F. **Effect of Therapy.** Several large, randomized, placebo-controlled trials of statin therapy have shown reductions in cardiovascular morbidity and mortality and all-cause mortality with lipid therapy in both primary and secondary prevention (Table 11.1, pp. 113-127). A meta-analysis of more than 30 interventional trials that used diet, drugs, or surgery to lower cholesterol has shown that for every 1% total cholesterol is lowered, total mortality is reduced by 1.1% and cardiovascular mortality is reduced by 1.5% (Circulation 1995;91:2274-82; Circulation 1998;97:946). A number of trials have used serial angiography to assess atherosclerotic lesion progression or regression in response to aggressive lipid therapy or placebo (Table 11.2, pp. 128-145). In these trials, the increase in percent diameter stenosis was 1-3% less per year in aggressively treated patients than in placebo patients. Despite minor improvements in lesion severity, lipid-lowering therapy results in marked (25-50%) reductions in major cardiovascular events primarily due to plaque stabilization.

Intensive Statin Therapy and
Cardiovascular Prognosis: Lower is Better

A. **Overview.** Dramatic results from recent, large-scale, randomized trials have demonstrated improved cardiovascular prognosis through intensive lowering of LDL cholesterol (LDL-C), prompting the ATP III and AHA/ACC to issue guideline updates recommending expanded and more intensive use of lipid-modifying drug therapy, particularly statins (Circulation 2004;110:227-239, Circulation 2006;113:2363-2372).

   1. **Relationship Between LDL Cholesterol and CHD.** Data from epidemiological studies and clinical trials have shown that for every 1 mg/dL reduction in LDL-C, the relative risk for CHD is reduced by 1%

(Figure 1.1). Benefits extend to LDL-C levels of 50-70 mg/dL, well below the previously recommended LDL-C target of < 100 mg/dL for high-risk patients. Average cholesterol levels in the U.S. are nearly twice the normal physiological level (Figure 1.2).

2. **Statin vs. Placebo Trials.** Statins are overwhelmingly the drug class of choice for improving dyslipidemia and cardiovascular prognosis. In addition to lowering LDL cholesterol levels by 18-55%, they also reduce the number of small, dense (atherogenic) LDL particles, raise HDL cholesterol levels by 5-15%, and lower triglycerides by 7-30%. When CHD event rates are plotted against LDL cholesterol levels, a direct relationship is apparent, without a lower threshold, in both primary and secondary prevention trials (Figures 1.3, 1.4). In the Heart Protection Study (HPS), the largest statin study to date, 20,536 patients with arterial occlusive disease or diabetes were randomized to simvastatin 40 mg/d or placebo. At 5 years, simvastatin reduced the risk for coronary death by 18% (5.7% vs. 6.9%, p = 0.0005). Importantly, patients with baseline LDL cholesterol levels < 100 mg/dL (~ 70 mg/dL or less on treatment) had the same relative risk reduction in CHD as patients with baseline LDL cholesterol levels > 100 mg/dL (p. 120). Likewise, in the Anglo-Scandinavian Cardiac Outcomes Trial (ASCOT, p. 116) and the Collaborative Atorvastatin Diabetes Study (CARDS, p. 117), statin therapy reduced the risk for CHD by 25-37% compared to placebo, with benefits extending to patients with baseline LDL cholesterol levels < 116 mg/dL (~ 80 mg/dL or less on treatment). In these studies, statin therapy was well tolerated and extremely safe: muscle and liver adverse effects were no different than placebo, and rhabdomyolysis was very rare.

3. **Statin vs. Statin Trials.** The first direct evidence to support the "lower-is-better" hypothesis comes from the Pravastatin or Atorvastatin Evaluation and Infection Therapy (PROVE IT) trial, which randomized 4162 patients with an acute coronary syndrome to in-hospital initiation of intensive LDL cholesterol lowering with atorvastatin 80 mg/d (median LDL cholesterol 62 mg/dL) or standard LDL cholesterol lowering with pravastatin 40 mg/d (median LDL cholesterol 95 mg/dL). At 2 years, atorvastatin reduced the primary endpoint of death, MI, unstable angina requiring hospitalization, revascularization after 30 days, and stroke by 16% (22.4% vs. 26.3%, p = 0.005) (p. 124). Additional evidence that more intensive statin therapy provides greater

event reduction than moderate statin therapy has been provided by the Treating to New Targets (TNT) trial (p. 126), which compared atorvastatin 80 mg/d vs. 10 mg/d, and the Incremental Decrease in Endpoints through Aggressive Lipid Lowering (IDEAL) trial (p. 121), which compared atorvastatin 80 mg/d vs. simvastatin 20-40 mg/d. The ongoing Study of the Effectiveness of Additional Reduction of Cholesterol and Homocysteine (SEARCH), comparing simvastatin 80 mg/d vs. 20 mg/d, is expected to define further the role of intensive LDL cholesterol lowering on cardiovascular events. Intensive LDL cholesterol lowering has also been shown to prevent/delay the progression of atherosclerosis compared to moderate LDL cholesterol lowering.

4. **Atherosclerosis Imaging Trials.** In the Reversal of Atherosclerosis with Aggressive Lipid Lowering (REVERSAL) trial, pravastatin 40 mg/d (on-treatment LDL cholesterol 110 mg/dL) led to progression of atherosclerosis, whereas atorvastatin 80 mg/d (on-treatment LDL cholesterol 79 mg/dL) did not (p. 144). Similar results using carotid intima-media thickness as an endpoint were obtained in the Atorvastatin vs. Simvastatin Atherosclerosis Progression (ASAP, p. 130) and Arterial Biology for the Investigation of the Treatment Effects of Reducing Cholesterol (ARBITER, p. 129) trials. No statin has an indication in the package insert for stabilization or reversal of atherosclerosis.

B. **Implications.** Multiple lines of evidence now indicate a role for expanded and more intensive use of lipid-modifying drug therapy, prompting the ATP III to issue a guideline update recommending optional lower LDL cholesterol targets for patients at very high risk for CHD (LDL cholesterol target < 70 mg/dL) or moderately high risk for CHD (LDL cholesterol target < 100 mg/dL) (Circulation 2004;110:227-239) (pp. 18-22). More recently, based on two trials published subsequent to the ATP III update further supporting the cardiovascular benefit for intensive LDL lowering — Treating to New Targets (TNT, p. 126) and Incremental Decrease in Endpoints through Aggressive Lipid Lowering (IDEAL, p. 121) — the AHA/ACC issued a 2006 update to their secondary prevention guidelines stating that it is reasonable to treat patients with CHD or other clinical forms of atherosclerotic disease to an LDL cholesterol < 70 mg/dL (Circulation 2006;113:2363-2372). These results have immediate and profound implications on patient care. There are an additional 13 million individuals in the United States and many millions more worldwide at high risk for CHD but without high levels of LDL cholesterol who should now be considered for lipid-modifying drug therapy. Conservative estimates indicate that appropriate use of statin therapy in these patients could prevent 67,000 coronary deaths, 78,000 strokes, 117,000 nonfatal myocardial infarctions, and 146,000 revascularization procedures each year. For the physician managing 1000 high-risk patients, appropriate use of lipid-modifying drug therapy plus implementation of other risk reduction measures (smoking cessation, control of hypertension, diabetes, obesity) could prevent one death, MI, or stroke every 12 days.

C. **Implementation.** Despite the enormous benefits of statins (and other lipid-modifying drug therapy), less than 40% of patients with CHD are being treated with a statin, and less than 20% of treated patients have LDL cholesterol levels below 100 mg/dL. Furthermore, more than 50% of patients discontinue lipid-modifying drug therapy on their own. To optimize cardiovascular prognosis, it is essential to initiate lipid-modifying drug therapy in all appropriate individuals, starting with a dose of a statin sufficient to achieve at least a 30-40% reduction in LDL cholesterol, and to titrate the dose upward at 6-week intervals until LDL cholesterol targets are achieved, using combination therapy as needed. For patients with CHD, diabetes, or CHD risk equivalents with an optional LDL cholesterol target of < 70 mg/dL, initial therapy that provides the > 50% reduction usually required should be considered (see Table 2.5). Patient compliance should also be reinforced at every visit.

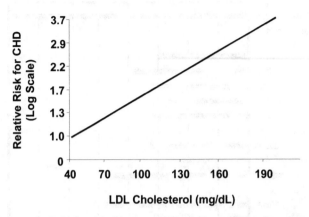

Figure 1.1. Relationship Between LDL Cholesterol Levels and Relative Risk for CHD

The log-linear relationship between LDL cholesterol and CHD risk is consistent with a large body of data from epidemiological studies and clinical trials. For every 30 mg/dL change in LDL cholesterol, the relative risk for CHD is changed in proportion by about 30%. The relative risk is set at 1.0 for LDL cholesterol = 40 mg/dL. From: NCEP ATP III guideline update (Circulation 2004;110:227-239).

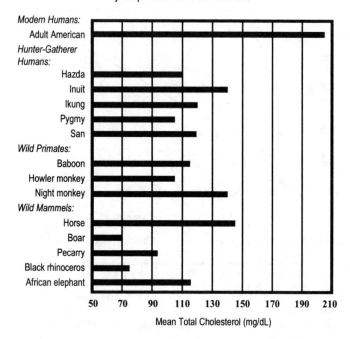

Figure 1.2. Total Cholesterol Levels in Various Populations

Total cholesterol levels for hunter-gatherers, wild primates, and wild mammals generally range from 70-140 mg/dL (LDL cholesterol 35-70 mg/dL). In modern Westernized humans, mean total cholesterol levels (208 mg/dL; LDL cholesterol 130 mg/dL) are almost twice these normal values, and atherosclerosis is present in up to 50% of individuals by age 50 (Arterioscler Thromb Vasc Biol 2002;22:849-54). In contrast, evidence from hunter-gatherer populations following their indigenous lifestyle indicate average total cholesterol levels of 100-150 mg/dL (LDL cholesterol 50-75 mg/dL) and no evidence for atherosclerosis, even in individuals living into the eighth decade of life (Eur J Clin Nutr 2002;56:S42-52).

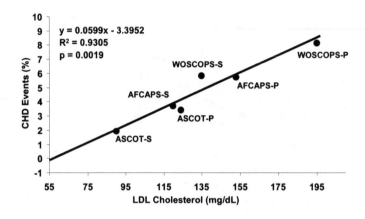

Figure 1.3. Relationship Between LDL Cholesterol and CHD Event Rates in Primary Prevention Trials

CHD event rates in primary prevention trials (4-5 years' duration) are directly proportional to LDL cholesterol levels. P = placebo, S = statin. From: J Am Coll Cardiol 2004;43:2142-6. See pp. 113-127 for trial names, design, and results.

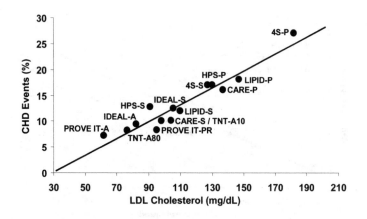

Figure 1.4. Relationship Between LDL Cholesterol and CHD Event Rates in Secondary Prevention Trials

CHD event rates in secondary prevention trials (5 years' duration except PROVE IT [2 years]) are directly proportional to LDL cholesterol levels. A = atorvastatin, A80/A10 = atorvastatin 80 mg/10 mg, P = placebo, PR = pravastatin, S = statin. Adapted from: J Am Coll Cardiol 2004;43:2142-6. See pp. 113-127 for trial names, design, and results.

Chapter 2

Approach to Management of Dyslipidemia

Step 1: Identification of Dyslipidemia

A. **Lipoprotein Analysis**. A fasting lipoprotein profile, consisting of total cholesterol, LDL cholesterol, HDL cholesterol, and triglyceride should be obtained in all adults over age 20 and repeated at least once every 5 years. Blood samples should be drawn after a 9-12 hour fast while the person is in a steady state—absence of active weight loss, acute illness, recent trauma or surgery, pregnancy, or recent change in diet.   To ensure reliable measurements, blood samples should be sent to a laboratory recognized by an established standardization program.

B. **Exclusion of Secondary Causes.** Once a dyslipidemia is identified, a history, physical examination, and basic laboratory tests are performed to screen for secondary causes of dyslipidemia, including diet, medications, alcohol abuse, diabetes, hypothyroidism, nephrotic syndrome, chronic renal failure, and obstructive liver disease (Appendix 2, pp. 165-167).

C. **Identification of Genetic Dyslipidemia.** If severe hypercholesterolemia is present (total cholesterol > 300 mg/dL) or a genetic disorder is discovered (Appendix 1, pp. 163-164), a family history and measurement of cholesterol in other family members are needed.

Step 2: Risk Stratification

A. **Overview of Risk Categories.** The need for and intensity of lipid therapy is related to a person's risk for vascular events; those at highest risk require the most aggressive therapy. ATP III recognizes recommends stratifying patients into one of four risk categories — high risk, moderately high risk, moderate risk, and lower risk — based on 10-year risk for major coronary events (coronary death or nonfatal MI).

1. **High risk: CHD and CHD risk equivalents.** These persons have a 10-year risk for major coronary events > 20%. Included in this group are individuals with one or more of the following characteristics: established CHD (prior MI, silent ischemia, angina pectoris, prior CABG or coronary angioplasty/stent); peripheral artery disease, including abdominal aortic aneurysm; carotid artery disease (TIA or stroke of carotid origin, asymptomatic carotid stenosis > 50%); other vascular disease of atherosclerotic origin (e.g., renal artery stenosis); diabetes mellitus (fasting plasma glucose ≥ 126 mg/dL or 2-hour plasma glucose after a standard 75-mg glucose load ≥ 200 mg/dL); or multiple risk factors conferring a 10-year CHD risk > 20% (Table 2.1). Diabetes is a "CHD risk equivalent" in ATP III, as diabetic patients without CHD have the same risk for coronary death or MI as nondiabetic individuals with CHD. For patients at high risk, ATP III recommends an LDL cholesterol target < 100 mg/dL. For patients at <u>very high risk</u> due to the presence multiple high risk characteristics, ATP III recognizes the benefits of more intensive LDL lowering and identifies an optional LDL cholesterol target of < 70 mg/dL. Included in this group are individuals with established cardiovascular disease *plus* one or more of the following: (1) multiple major risk factors (especially diabetes); (2) severe and poorly controlled risk factors (especially continued cigarette smoking); (3) multiple risk factors of the metabolic syndrome (especially elevated triglyceride ≥ 200 mg/dL plus non-HDL cholesterol ≥ 130 mg/dL with low HDL cholesterol < 40 mg/dL); and (4) acute coronary syndrome. Based on trial evidence published subsequent to the ATP III update (TNT, IDEAL), the 2006 AHA/ACC secondary prevention guideline update states that it is *reasonable* to treat patients with CHD or other clinical forms of atherosclerotic disease to an LDL cholesterol target of < 70 mg/dL.

3. **Moderately high risk:** Multiple (≥ 2) risk factors (Table 2.2) and 10-year CHD risk of 10-20% (Table 2.1). For patients at moderately high risk, ATP III recommends an LDL cholesterol target < 130 mg/dL; an optional LDL cholesterol goal < 100 mg/dL is suggested in the ATP III update.

4. **Moderate risk:** Multiple (≥ 2) risk factors (Table 2.2) and 10-year CHD risk < 10% (Table 2.1). For patients at moderate risk, ATP III recommends an LDL cholesterol target < 130 mg/dL.

5. **Lower risk:** 0-1 risk factors. These individuals are at lower risk for major coronary events, with a 10-year event rate < 10%. Framingham risk assessment is not required in these cases. For patients at lower risk, ATP III recommends an LDL cholesterol target < 160 mg/dL.

B. **Emerging Risk Factors.** Emerging risk factors are not used to determine LDL cholesterol goals but can be helpful in evaluating the need for and intensity of drug therapy in patients at intermediate risk. Therefore, measurement of high-sensitivity C-reactive protein (hs-CRP), lipoprotein(a), Lp-PLA$_2$ (if available), and homocysteine should be considered in patients at intermediate risk for atherosclerosis or with strongly positive family histories. Hs-CRP is a nonspecific systemic marker of inflammation; lipoprotein(a) is an LDL-like particle with the addition of a unique plasminogen-like glycoprotein, apo(a); Lp-PLA$_2$ is an enzyme primarily transported on LDL that may induce vascular inflammation; and homocysteine is a by-product of protein (methionine) metabolism. Elevated levels of these markers are associated with increased risk for future cardiovascular events and may help determine the need for aggressive risk factor modification and lipid therapy in borderline cases; noninvasive assessment of atherosclerosis by carotid ultrasound and electron beam computed tomography (EBCT) of the heart can also be used for this purpose. In January, 2003, the AHA/CDC issued clinical guidelines for use of hs-CRP, a nonspecific marker of systemic inflammation, in global CHD risk assessment (Circulation 2003;107:499-511). Recommendations were based on strong evidence linking inflammation to atherosclerosis, plaque instability/rupture and cardiovascular events, and prospective and nested case-control studies indicating a moderate-to-strong independent relationship between hs-CRP and CHD risk. Acknowledging the need for additional studies, conclusions/recommendations included:

- hs-CRP is an independent marker of risk and, in those judged at intermediate risk by global risk assessment (i.e., 10-year CHD risk of 10-20%), measurement of hs-CRP may help direct further evaluation and therapy in the primary prevention of cardiovascular disease. The benefits of such therapy based on this strategy remain uncertain.

- In patients with stable coronary disease or acute coronary syndromes, hs-CRP measurement may be useful as an independent marker of prognosis for recurrent events, including death, MI, and restenosis after percutaneous coronary intervention (PCI). The benefits of therapy based on this strategy remain uncertain.

- hs-CRP levels, using standardized assays, should categorize patients into one of three relative risk categories: low risk (< 1 mg/L); average risk (1.0-3.0 mg/L); and high risk (> 3.0 mg/L). Measurement of hs-CRP should be done twice (averaging results), optimally two weeks apart, fasting or nonfasting in metabolically stable patients. If hs-CRP level is > 10 mg/L, the test should be repeated and the patient examined for sources of infection or inflammation.

- The entire adult population should not be screened for hs-CRP for cardiovascular risk assessment, nor should hs-CRP levels be used to determine preventive measures for secondary prevention or for patients with acute coronary syndromes.

Highlighting the need for further investigation, and in contrast to previous studies, a large, prospective study (and accompanying meta-analysis) found that compared to other established risk factors (increased total cholesterol, cigarette smoking, etc), CRP was a relatively moderate predictor of CHD risk and added only marginally to the prediction of CHD risk based on established risk factors (N Engl J Med 2004;350:1387-97). However, the upper quartile for CRP in this study was ~ 2 mg/L, whereas levels > 3 mg/L are considered elevated by the AHA/CDC guidelines. Further studies are under way, including a randomized trial of rosuvastatin 20 mg/d vs. placebo in ~ 15,000 healthy individuals with low LDL cholesterol and high CRP levels in the Justification for the Use of statins in Primary prevention: an Intervention Trial Evaluating Rosuvastatin (JUPITER; Circulation 2003;108:2292-97).

C. **LDL Cholesterol and Non-HDL Cholesterol Goals.** LDL cholesterol lowering is the primary goal of therapy for persons with dyslipidemia, resulting in marked reductions in the risk for coronary death, nonfatal MI, revascularization procedures, and stroke. LDL cholesterol goals vary inversely with CHD risk: persons at highest risk have the lowest LDL cholesterol targets. Non-HDL cholesterol (LDL cholesterol + VLDL cholesterol, calculated by subtracting HDL cholesterol from total cholesterol) is a secondary goal of therapy in persons with triglycerides ≥ 200 mg/dL. LDL and non-HDL cholesterol goals from the 2004 ATP III update and the 2006 AHA/ACC secondary prevention update are shown in Tables 2.3 and 2.4, respectively.

D. Metabolic Syndrome. Many persons have a constellation of major and emerging risk factors, referred to as the metabolic syndrome, that increases the risk for coronary events at any level of LDL cholesterol. These individuals benefit from specific therapeutic measures beyond LDL cholesterol lowering (see atherogenic dyslipidemia, p. 33). Clinical diagnosis of the metabolic syndrome, as defined in the ATP III guidelines and subsequent AHA/NHLBI scientific statement (Circulation 2005;112:2735-52), requires ≥ 3 of the following risk factors:

- Abdominal obesity (waist circumference): men ≥ 102 cm (40 in); women ≥ 88 cm (35 in)
- Elevated triglycerides: ≥ 150 mg/dL or drug treatment for elevated triglycerides
- Reduced HDL cholesterol: men < 40 mg/dL; women < 50 mg/dL; or drug treatment for reduced HDL cholesterol
- Hypertension: ≥ 130/85 mmHg or drug treatment for hypertension
- Impaired fasting glucose: ≥ 100 mg/dL or drug treatment for elevated glucose

Table 2.2. Major Risk Factors That Modify LDL Cholesterol Goals

- Cigarette smoking
- Hypertension (BP ≥ 140/90 mmHg or on antihypertensive medication)
- Low HDL cholesterol (< 40 mg/dL)
- Family history of premature CHD (CHD in male first-degree relative < 55 years; CHD in female first-degree relative < 65 years)
- Age (men ≥ 45 years; women ≥ 55 years)

HDL cholesterol ≥ 60 mg/dL counts as a negative risk factor and removes one risk factor from the total count. Since diabetes mellitus is considered a CHD risk equivalent, it is not counted as a risk factor.

Table 2.1. Framingham Risk Score: 10-Year Risk for Coronary Heart Disease Events (Death or Nonfatal MI)

Step 1: Calculate Point Total				
Age (years)		**Points (men/women)**		
20-34		-9 / -7		
35-39		-4 / -3		
40-44		0 / 0		
45-49		3 / 3		
50-54		6 / 6		
55-59		8 / 8		
60-64		10 / 10		
65-69		11 / 12		
70-74		12 / 14		
75-79		13 / 16		
HDL Cholesterol (mg/dL)		**Points (men/women)**		
≥ 60		-1 / -1		
50-59		0 / 0		
40-49		1 / 1		
< 40		2 / 2		
Systolic BP (mmHg)		**Untreated**		**Treated**
< 120		0 / 0		0 / 0
120-129		0 / 1		1 / 3
130-139		1 / 2		2 / 4
140-159		1 / 3		2 / 5
≥ 160		2 / 4		3 / 6
Total Cholesterol	**Age: 20-39**	**40-49**	**50-59**	**60-69**	**70-79**
< 160	0 / 0	0 / 0	0 / 0	0 / 0	0 / 0
160-199	4 / 4	3 / 3	2 / 2	1 / 1	0 / 1
200-239	7 / 8	5 / 6	3 / 4	1 / 2	0 / 1
240-279	9 / 11	6 / 8	4 / 5	2 / 3	1 / 2
≥ 280	11 / 13	8 / 10	5 / 7	3 / 4	1 / 2
Tobacco	**Age: 20-39**	**40-49**	**50-59**	**60-69**	**70-79**
Nonsmoker	0 / 0	0 / 0	0 / 0	0 / 0	0 / 0
Smoker	8 / 9	5 / 7	3 / 4	1 / 2	1 / 1
TOTAL POINTS:	Man _____		Woman _____	

Table 2.1. Framingham Risk Score: 10-Year Risk for Coronary Heart Disease Events (Death or Nonfatal MI) (cont'd)

Step 2: Determine 10-Year Risk for CHD		
	10-year risk (%)	
Point Total (previous page)	Men	Women
< 0	< 1	< 1
0	1	< 1
1	1	< 1
2	1	< 1
3	1	< 1
4	1	< 1
5	2	< 1
6	2	< 1
7	3	< 1
8	4	< 1
9	5	1
10	6	1
11	8	1
12	10	1
13	12	2
14	16	2
15	20	3
16	25	4
17	≥ 30	5
18	≥ 30	6
19	≥ 30	8
20	≥ 30	11
21	≥ 30	14
22	≥ 30	17
23	≥ 30	22
24	≥ 30	27
≥ 25	≥ 30	≥ 30

Table 2.3. LDL/Non-HDL Cholesterol Goals from ATP III Guidelines¶

Risk Category	Description	LDL-C Goal (mg/dL)	Non-HDL-C Goal* (mg/dL)
High/ Very high	CHD or CHD risk equivalent† (10-yr risk for CHD > 20%)	< 100 optional < 70‡	< 130 optional < 100‡
Moderately high	≥ 2 risk factors§ with 10-yr risk for CHD 10-20%‖	< 130 optional < 100#	< 160 optional < 130
Moderate	≥ 2 risk factors§ with 10-yr risk for CHD < 10%‖	< 130	< 160
Lower	0-1 risk factor§	< 160	< 190

*   Non-HDL cholesterol = total cholesterol minus HDL cholesterol. Non-HDL cholesterol (LDL cholesterol + VLDL cholesterol) is a secondary goal of therapy after LDL cholesterol for persons with triglycerides ≥ 200 mg/dL
†   See footnotes, Table 2.7 (p. 21), for description of CHD/CHD risk equivalent.
‡   An optional lower target of < 70 mg/dL should be strongly considered for patients at very high risk for MI or death, as described on page 12.
§   See Table 2.2 (p. 15) for major risk factors that modify LDL cholesterol goal
‖   As determined by the Framingham risk score (Table 2.1, pp. 16-17)
An optional LDL cholesterol goal < 100 mg/dL should be strongly considered for all moderately high risk patients, particularly those with: advancing age; ≥ 2 risk factors; severe risk factors (e.g., continued cigarette smoking, strongly positive family history of premature atherosclerotic cardiovascular disease); elevated triglycerides ≥ 200 mg/dL plus elevated non-HDL cholesterol ≥ 160 mg/dL; low HDL cholesterol < 40 mg/dL; the metabolic syndrome; and/or the presence of emerging risk factors (e.g., hs-CRP > 3 mg/L or coronary calcium > 75th percentile for a person's age and sex)
¶   Adapted from NCEP ATP III guideline and update (Circulation 2002;106:3143-3421, Circulation 2004;110:227-239)

Table 2.4. LDL and Non-HDL Cholesterol Goals from 2006 AHA/ACC Guideline Update for Secondary Prevention*

Description	LDL-C Goal (mg/dL)	Non-HDL-C Goal (mg/dL)‡
CHD or other clinical athero-sclerotic vascular disease†	< 100; it is reasonable to treat to < 70	< 130; it is reasonable to treat to < 100

† Peripheral artery disease, atherosclerotic aortic disease, carotid artery disease
‡ For triglycerides 200-499 mg/dL. * From: Circulation 2006;113:2363-2372

Step 3: Initiation of LDL-Lowering Therapy

Therapeutic lifestyle changes (diet modification, increased physical activity, weight control, smoking cessation) are considered first-line therapy for all patients with dyslipidemia. In most patients this will improve lipid levels only modestly (< 10% total cholesterol lowering). Drug therapy should be started on the initial visit concurrently with lifestyle changes in higher-risk persons and in those in whom lifestyle changes alone are unlikely to achieve the LDL cholesterol goal (Table 2.3). When indicated, drug therapy should be sufficient to reduce LDL cholesterol levels by *at least 30-40%* (Table 2.5). Very high risk patients frequently require LDL reduction of 50% (Table 2.6). Use of minimal drug therapy to produce a small reduction in LDL cholesterol to barely attain LDL cholesterol goal is not recommended. The general time-frame and sequence of intensification of diet and drug therapy is shown in Figure 3.2.

Table 2.5. Statin Doses Required to Attain an Approximate 30-40% Reduction in LDL Cholesterol Levels (Standard Doses)

Drug	Dose (mg/d)	LDL Reduction (%)
Rosuvastatin	5-10	39-45
Atorvastatin	10	39
Simvastatin	20-40	35-41
Pravastatin	40	34
Lovastatin	40	31
Fluvastatin	40-80	25-35

Estimated LDL cholesterol reductions were obtained from US Food and Drug Administration package inserts for each drug. For every doubling of the dose above the standard dose, an approximate 6% decrease in LDL cholesterol levels can be obtained. Rosuvastatin is available in doses up to 40 mg; atorvastatin, simvastatin, pravastatin, lovastatin and fluvastatin are available in doses up to 80 mg. From: NCEP ATP III guideline update (Circulation 2004;110:227-239)

Table 2.6. Drug Doses Required to Attain ≥ 50% Reduction in LDL Cholesterol Levels

Drug	Dose (mg/d)	LDL Reduction (%)
Rosuvastatin	20*-40†	52-59
Atorvastatin	80†	51-54
Ezetimibe/simvastatin	10/20‡-10/80†	52-60

Estimated LDL cholesterol reductions were obtained from Am J Cardiol 1998;81:582-7; Am J Cardiol 2003;92:152-60; Mayo Clin Proc 2004;79:620-9; Am Heart J 2004;148:e4.

* Optional starting dose

† Not recommended as starting dose per US Food and Drug Administration package inserts

‡ Recommended usual starting dose

Table 2.7. LDL Cholesterol Lowering in High Risk Individuals*

LDL	Treatment
LDL ≥ 100 mg/dL (or ≥ 70 if LDL target < 70 mg/dL is chosen†)	Initiate statin therapy‡ simultaneously with TLC, with subsequent therapy based on follow-up LDL: **Follow-up LDL > 100 mg/dL.** Options include: (1) intensify statin therapy (2) intensify diet therapy by adding plant sterols/stanols (2 gm/d) and increasing soluble fiber to 10-25 gm/d (3) consider adding ezetimibe, a bile acid sequestrant, or niacin (4) if LDL had been lowered by at least 30-40% and is near 100 mg/dL (or near 70 mg/dL if target < 70 mg/dL is chosen), consider maintaining current regimen **Follow-up LDL < 100 mg/dL:** Maintain current regimen, or consider further LDL lowering to reasonable goal < 70 mg/dL in select high risk patients,† using steps above. If elevated triglyceride or low HDL cholesterol is present, consider adding nicotinic acid, a fibrate, or fish oil to statin therapy
LDL < 100 mg/dL (or < 70 if LDL target < 70 mg/dL is chosen†)	Initiate TLC and consider further LDL lowering to reasonable goal < 70 mg/dL in select high risk patients,† using steps above.

Table 2.7. LDL Cholesterol Lowering in High Risk Individuals (cont'd)

TLC = therapeutic lifestyle changes (diet, weight control, increased physical activity, smoking cessation)

* High risk = CHD or CHD risk equivalent. CHD = coronary heart disease (prior MI, evidence of clinically-significant silent ischemia, history of angina pectoris, prior CABG or coronary angioplasty/stent); CHD risk equivalent = peripheral artery disease, including abdominal aortic aneurysm; carotid artery disease (TIA or stroke of carotid origin, asymptomatic carotid stenosis > 50%), other vascular disease of atherosclerotic origin (e.g., renal artery stenosis), diabetes mellitus, or ≥ 2 risk factors conferring a 10-year CHD risk > 20%.

† A minimum LDL cholesterol goal < 100 mg/dL is indicated for all patients. In addition, based on compelling evidence from recent clinical trials demonstrating benefit for more intensive LDL lowering, and as stated in the 2006 AHA/ACC secondary prevention guideline update, it is reasonable to treat patients with CHD or other clinical forms of atherosclerotic vascular disease to an LDL cholesterol < 70 mg/dL.‡ Reducing LDL cholesterol from 100 mg/dL to 70 mg/dL will further reduce the risk for CHD by 20-30%, based on HPS (p. 120).

‡ Statins should be dosed to reduce LDL cholesterol levels by *at least* 30-40% (Table 2.5, p. 19). Use of minimal drug therapy to produce a small reduction in LDL cholesterol to barely attain LDL cholesterol goal is not recommended. To achieve LDL < 70 mg/dL in very high risk patients, ≥ 50% reductions in LDL cholesterol are frequently required (Table 2.6, p. 20).

Adapted from NCEP ATP III guideline (Circulation 2004;110:227-239) and update (Circulation 2002;106:3145-3421), and from AHA/ACC guideline update for secondary prevention (Circulation 2006;113:2363-2372).

Table 2.8. LDL Cholesterol Lowering in Moderately High Risk Individuals*†

Baseline LDL	Treatment
LDL ≥ 130 mg/dL	Initiate statin therapy‡ simultaneously with TLC. If follow-up LDL > 100 mg/dL at 6 weeks, strongly consider additional therapy to further reduce LDL to optional goal < 100 mg/dL †§
LDL < 130 mg/dL	TLC x 3 months. If follow up LDL > 100 mg/dL, strongly consider statin therapy‡ to further reduce LDL to optional goal < 100 mg/dL. If LDL > 100 mg/dL after 6 weeks on statin, strongly consider intensification of LDL-lowering therapy †§

TLC = therapeutic lifestyle changes (diet modification, weight control, increased physical activity, smoking cessation)

*   Moderately high risk = multiple (≥ 2) risk factors (Table 2.2) plus 10-year Framingham CHD risk of 10-20% (Table 2.1). LDL cholesterol goal < 130 mg/dL; optional goal < 100 mg/dL

†   ASCOT demonstrated significant reductions in CHD events using statin therapy in hypertensive patients with multiple risk factors and baseline LDL cholesterol 100-129 mg/dL. An LDL cholesterol goal < 100 mg/dL should be strongly considered for all moderately high risk patients, particularly those with: advancing age; ≥ 2 risk factors; severe risk factors (e.g., continued cigarette smoking, strongly positive family history of premature atherosclerotic cardiovascular disease); elevated triglycerides ≥ 200 mg/dL plus elevated non-HDL cholesterol ≥ 160 mg/dL; low HDL cholesterol < 40 mg/dL); the metabolic syndrome; and/or the presence of emerging risk factors (e.g., hs-CRP > 3 mg/L or coronary calcium > 75th percentile for a person's age and sex)

‡   Statins should be dosed to reduce LDL cholesterol levels by *at least* 30-40% (Table 2.5). Use of minimal drug therapy to produce a small reduction in LDL cholesterol to barely attain LDL cholesterol goal is not recommended

§   Options include: (1) intensify statin therapy; (2) intensify diet therapy by adding plant sterols/stanols (2 gm/d) and increasing soluble fiber to 10-25 gm/d; (3) consider adding ezetimibe, a bile acid sequestrant, or niacin; (4) if LDL cholesterol has been lowered by at least 30-40% and is near 100 mg/dL, consider maintaining current regimen. For elevated triglyceride or low HDL cholesterol, consider adding nicotinic acid, a fibrate, or fish oil to statin therapy

Adapted from: NCEP ATP III (Circulation 2004;110:227-239 [update]; Circulation 2002;106:3145-3421)

Table 2.9. LDL Cholesterol Lowering in Moderate Risk Individuals*

Baseline LDL	Treatment
LDL ≥ 130 mg/dL	TLC x 3 months, with subsequent therapy based follow-up LDL:
	Follow-up LDL ≥ 160 mg/dL: Initiate statin therapy.[†] For LDL > 130 mg/dL after 6 weeks on statins, prescribe additional therapy.[‡]
	Follow-up LDL < 160 mg/dL: Continue TLC, control other risk factors, and manage the metabolic syndrome. Consider statin therapy[†] to reduce LDL to < 130 mg/dL.
LDL < 130 mg/dL	Instruct on appropriate lifestyle changes, periodic follow-up, and control of other risk factors. Recommend diet for the general public and exercise regimen.

CHD = coronary heart disease; TLC = therapeutic lifestyle changes (diet modification, weight control, increased physical activity, smoking cessation)

* Moderate risk = multiple (≥ 2) risk factors (Table 2.2) plus 10-year Framingham CHD risk < 10% (Table 2.1). LDL cholesterol goal < 130 mg/dL

† Statins should be dosed to reduce LDL cholesterol levels by *at least* 30-40% (Table 2.5). Use of minimal drug therapy to produce a small reduction in LDL cholesterol to barely attain LDL goal is not recommended

‡ Options include: (1) intensify statin therapy; (2) intensify diet therapy by adding plant sterols/stanols (2 gm/d) and increasing soluble fiber to 10-25 gm/d; (3) consider adding ezetimibe, a bile acid sequestrant, or niacin; (4) if LDL cholesterol has been lowered by at least 30-40% and is near 130 mg/dL, consider maintaining current regimen. For elevated triglyceride or low HDL cholesterol, consider adding nicotinic acid, a fibrate, or fish oil to statin therapy

Adapted from: NCEP ATP III (Circulation 2004;110:227-239 [update]; Circulation 2002;106:3145-3421)

Table 2.10. LDL Cholesterol Lowering in Lower Risk Individuals*

Baseline LDL	Treatment
LDL ≥ 220 mg/dL	Initiate statin therapy simultaneously with TLC. These individuals usually have a genetic form of hypercholesterolemia, so family members should be screened. For LDL > 160 mg/dL after 6 weeks on statins, prescribe additional therapy. Early referral to a lipid specialist is recommended.
LDL 160-219 mg/dL	TLC x 3 months, with subsequent therapy based on LDL: **Follow-up LDL ≥ 190 mg/dL:** Initiate statin therapy.[†] For LDL > 160 mg/dL after 6 weeks on statins, prescribe additional therapy.[‡] **Follow-up LDL 160-189 mg/dL:** Statin therapy is optional, but is favored in patients with a severe major risk factor (heavy cigarette smoking, marked hypertension, strongly positive family history, very low HDL); multiple life habit or emerging risk factors (elevated homocysteine or C-reactive protein, high calcium score on EBCT); 10-year CHD risk approaching 10%; or the metabolic syndrome.[§] **Follow-up LDL < 160 mg/dL:** Continue TLC.[§]
LDL < 160 mg/dL	Instruct on appropriate lifestyle changes, periodic follow-up, and control of other risk factors. Recommend diet for the general public and exercise regimen.

CHD = coronary heart disease; TLC = therapeutic lifestyle changes (diet modification, weight control, increased physical activity, smoking cessation)

*   Lower risk = 0-1 risk factor (Table 2.2). LDL cholesterol goal < 160 mg/dL

†   In general, statins should be dosed to reduce LDL cholesterol levels by *at least* 30-40% (Table 2.5). Use of minimal drug therapy to produce a small reduction in LDL cholesterol to barely attain LDL cholesterol goal is not recommended

‡   Options include: (1) intensify statin therapy; (2) intensify diet therapy by adding plant sterols/stanols (2 gm/d) and increasing soluble fiber to 10-25 gm/d; (3) consider adding ezetimibe, a bile acid sequestrant, or niacin; (4) if LDL cholesterol has been lowered by at least 30-40% and is near 160 mg/dL, consider maintaining current regimen

§   For elevated triglyceride or low HDL cholesterol, consider adding nicotinic acid, a fibrate, or fish oil to statin therapy

Adapted from: NCEP ATP III (Circulation 2004;110:227-239 [update]; Circulation 2002;106:3145-3421)

Step 4: Management of Resistant Dyslipidemia

A. **Referral to a Lipid Specialist.** Referral to a lipid specialist is made on an individual basis, usually after a primary care physician finds combination drug therapy ineffective, or before such therapy is initiated when he or she is uncomfortable monitoring the metabolic impact of combination drug therapy. In general, patients with severe refractory lipid disorders and those who require complex management should meet with a lipid specialist.

B. **LDL Apheresis.** LDL apheresis may be considered for patients with: (1) homozygous familial hypercholesterolemia (FH) and LDL cholesterol >500 mg/dL despite maximal tolerated diet and drug therapy; (2) heterozygous FH without established CHD and LDL cholesterol $\geq$ 300 mg/dL despite maximal tolerated diet and drug therapy; and (3) heterozygous FH with established CHD and LDL cholesterol $\geq$ 200 mg/dL despite maximal tolerated diet and drug therapy. This option is less often needed now with use of high-dose statins combined with ezetimibe.

C. **Ileal Bypass Surgery.** Ileal bypass surgery is a therapeutic option in patients intolerant to drug therapy. In the POSCH trial, patients randomized to partial ileal bypass surgery had significant reductions in angiographic progression of atherosclerosis and CHD events (p. 142).

D. **Gene Therapy.** Gene therapy is potentially a future option for treating homozygous FH and other rare dyslipidemias caused by gene defects. Although promising, gene therapy is still experimental. Antisense oligonucleotide therapy is another experimental approach for these patients.

Chapter 3

Treatment of Specific Dyslipidemias

The primary goal of therapy for most dyslipidemias is to achieve the LDL cholesterol goal using therapeutic lifestyle changes and, if needed, LDL-lowering drug therapy (Figures 3.1-3.5). For persons with triglycerides ≥ 200 mg/dL, a secondary goal of therapy is to achieve the non-HDL cholesterol target (Table 2.3). High-risk individuals with persistently low HDL cholesterol may be considered for drug therapy to raise HDL cholesterol levels.

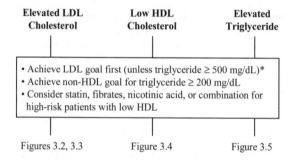

Elevated LDL Cholesterol	Low HDL Cholesterol	Elevated Triglyceride

- Achieve LDL goal first (unless triglyceride ≥ 500 mg/dL)*
- Achieve non-HDL goal for triglyceride ≥ 200 mg/dL
- Consider statin, fibrates, nicotinic acid, or combination for high-risk patients with low HDL

Figures 3.2, 3.3	Figure 3.4	Figure 3.5

Figure 3.1. Overview of Treatment of Dyslipidemia

*   For triglyceride ≥ 500 mg/dL, levels should be lowered acutely to < 500 mg/dL before achieving LDL cholesterol goal to prevent acute pancreatitis

Elevated LDL Cholesterol (Figures 3.2, 3.3)

A. **Overview**. The relationship between LDL cholesterol and CHD is well established: Intensive lowering of LDL cholesterol reduces cardiovascular morbidity and mortality and slows the progression of atherosclerotic plaques. Since the advent of statin therapy, a benefit has also been demonstrated on all-cause mortality. A curvilinear (log-linear) relationship between LDL cholesterol and relative risk for CHD has been demonstrated in epidemiological studies and clinical trials, indicating that for every 30 mg/dL reduction in LDL cholesterol, the relative risk for CHD is proportionally reduced by about 30% (Figure 1.1, p. 7).

B. **ATP III and AHA/ACC Guidelines.** ATP III recommends an LDL cholesterol goal < 100 mg/dL in patients with CHD or CHD risk equivalents, with an optional LDL cholesterol target < 70 mg/dL for patients at very high risk (Circulation 2004;110:227-239). Less stringent LDL cholesterol targets are recommended for the following patient subsets: ≥ 2 risk factors and a 10-year Framingham CHD risk of 10-20% (LDL cholesterol target < 130 mg/dL; optional target < 100 mg/dL); ≥ 2 risk factors and a 10-year Framingham CHD risk < 10% (LDL cholesterol target < 130 mg/dL); 0-1 risk factor without CHD (LDL cholesterol target < 160 mg/dL) (Table 2.3). Based on additional trial evidence published subsequent to the ATP III update demonstrating cardiovascular benefits for intensive LDL lowering (TNT, IDEAL), the 2006 AHA/ACC update to the secondary prevention guidelines recommends an LDL cholesterol target < 100 mg/dL for patients with CHD or other clinical forms of atherosclerotic disease, but in addition, states that it is *reasonable* to treat such patients to an LDL cholesterol target of < 70 mg/dL (Circulation 2006;113:2363-72).

C. **Drug Therapy**
 1. **Statins.** Statins are overwhelmingly the drug class of choice for elevated LDL cholesterol, providing safe and effective LDL cholesterol lowering by 18-55%. The effects of statins on clinical events have been studied in large placebo-controlled trials randomizing more than 90,000 patients to statin therapy or placebo for approximately 3-5 years. These trials consistently demonstrated marked clinical benefits with the use of statins, including reductions in cardiovascular morbidity and mortality,

all-cause mortality, coronary revascularization procedures (bypass surgery or coronary angioplasty), and stroke (Table 11.1, pp. 113-127). Ten-year follow-up of 4S demonstrated that statin treatment for 5 years followed by open-label statin therapy for 5 years was associated with survival benefit compared with open-label statin therapy for the past 5 years only (relative risk 0.85, p = 0.02), largely due to a 24% reduction in coronary mortality (Lancet 2004;364:771-777). Angiographic trials of statin therapy have consistently demonstrated slowed progression and increased regression of atherosclerotic lesions, and a reduction in new lesion development (Table 11.2, pp. 128-145).

2. **Ezetimibe.** Ezetimibe is a newer agent that selectively inhibits the intestinal absorption of cholesterol and is used primarily as an adjunct to statin therapy for patients requiring further reductions in LDL cholesterol. Ezetimibe lowers LDL cholesterol by 18% and triglyceride by 8% and raises HDL cholesterol by 1%. Cholesterol-lowering effects are observed when ezetimibe is given as monotherapy or as an adjunct to statins. When added to ongoing statin therapy, ezetimibe provides additional reductions of 14-25% in total cholesterol, LDL cholesterol, and triglycerides. Ezetimibe is well tolerated with few adverse effects.

3. **Niacin.** When administered at 1.5-4.5 gm/d, niacin decreases LDL cholesterol by 5-25%, increases HDL cholesterol by 15-35%, and decreases triglycerides by 20-50%. Studies using niacin in combination therapy have demonstrated reductions in cardiovascular events and slowed progression of atherosclerosis. For many patients with severe mixed dyslipidemia (i.e., elevated LDL cholesterol and triglyceride with low HDL cholesterol), combination niacin and statin therapy is the most effective way to normalize all lipid parameters.

4. **Bile acid sequestrants.** These agents are used primarily as adjuncts to statin therapy for patients requiring further reductions in LDL cholesterol. Bile acid sequestrants typically reduce LDL cholesterol by 15-30%; HDL cholesterol may increase slightly (3-5%) and plasma triglycerides are usually not affected but may increase. Compliance has been problematic with the first-generation bile acid sequestrants (cholestyramine, colestipol) because of the frequent occurrence of constipation. Colesevelam is a newer bile acid sequestrant that is well tolerated and is an option as monotherapy for isolated mild or moderate LDL cholesterol elevation or as an adjunct to statin or niacin therapy for more severe mixed dyslipidemias.

Elevated LDL Cholesterol

1.	Initiate therapeutic lifestyle changes (TLC)*	• Diet, weight control • Increased physical activity • Smoking cessation • Consider referral to a dietician

6 weeks ↓

2.	Intensify TLC if LDL goal not met	• Reinforce reduction in saturated/trans fats • Consider adding plant stanols/sterols (2 gm/d) • Increase fiber intake (10-25 gm/d) • Consider referral to a dietician

6 weeks ↓

3.	Consider adding drug therapy to achieve LDL goal*	• A statin† is the drug of choice for most patients; ezetimibe, bile acid sequestrants, and nicotinic acid are useful adjuncts to statins

6 weeks ↓

4.	Intensify drug therapy if LDL goal not met	• Increase dose of statin or add ezetimibe, bile acid sequestrant, or nicotinic acid • Add plant stanols/sterols and increase fiber intake if not done at earlier step • If elevated triglyceride or low HDL, consider adding nicotinic acid, a fibrate, or fish oil

6 weeks ↓

5.	<u>LDL goal met</u>: Monitor response/adherence to therapy every 4-6 months; achieve non-HDL goal if triglyceride ≥ 200 mg/dL; treat metabolic syndrome and other risk factors <u>LDL goal not met</u>: Titrate drugs; consider referral to a lipid specialist

Figure 3.2. Time-Frame and Sequence of LDL-Lowering Therapy

---

* Drug therapy should be initiated concurrently with therapeutic lifestyle changes in patients at higher risk for CHD (see text for description)

† Statins should be dosed to reduce LDL cholesterol by at least 30-40%

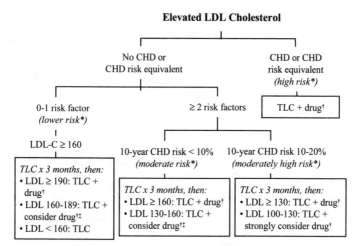

Elevated LDL Cholesterol

No CHD or CHD risk equivalent

CHD or CHD risk equivalent *(high risk*)*

0-1 risk factor *(lower risk*)*

≥ 2 risk factors

TLC + drug†

LDL-C ≥ 160

10-year CHD risk < 10% *(moderate risk*)*

10-year CHD risk 10-20% *(moderately high risk*)*

TLC x 3 months, then:
• LDL ≥ 190: TLC + drug†
• LDL 160-189: TLC + consider drug†‡
• LDL < 160: TLC

TLC x 3 months, then:
• LDL ≥ 160: TLC + drug†
• LDL 130-160: TLC + consider drug†‡

TLC x 3 months, then:
• LDL ≥ 130: TLC + drug†
• LDL 100-130: TLC + strongly consider drug†

Figure 3.3. Treatment of Elevated LDL Cholesterol (cont'd next page)

LDL cholesterol levels are expressed in mg/dL. CHD = coronary heart disease; CHD risk equivalents = cerebrovascular disease, abdominal aortic aneurysm, peripheral artery disease, diabetes mellitus, or multiple (≥ 2) risk factors with 10-year CHD risk > 20% (Table 2.1, pp. 16-17); CHD risk factors = see Table 2.2 (p. 15). TLC = therapeutic lifestyle changes (Chapters 5-6); also control hypertension and diabetes
† Initial drug therapy usually consists of standard dose of a statin to reduce LDL cholesterol levels by *at least* 30-40% (Table 2.5, p. 19). In very high risk patients, achievement of LDL cholesterol < 70 mg/dL frequently requires ≥50% reduction (Table 2.6, p. 20). Use of minimal drug therapy to produce a small reduction in LDL cholesterol to barely attain LDL cholesterol goal is not recommended. If LDL cholesterol levels at 6 weeks remain above LDL cholesterol target (Table 2.3, p. 18), options include: (1) intensify statin therapy; (2) intensify diet therapy by adding plant sterols/stanols 2 gm/day and increasing soluble fiber to 10-25 gm/d; (3) consider adding ezetimibe, a bile acid sequestrant, or niacin; (4) if elevated triglyceride or low HDL cholesterol is present, consider adding nicotinic acid, a fibrate, or fish oil to statin therapy; or (5) if LDL cholesterol has been lowered by 30-40% and is near target, consider maintaining current statin dose. Difficult-to-control patients should be referred to a lipid specialist. Also see Tables 2.7-2.10. *Footnotes continued next page.*

Figure 3.3. Treatment of Elevated LDL Cholesterol (cont'd)

---

‡ Drug therapy is optional but may be especially useful if ≥ 1 strong risk factor (severe hypertension, heavy cigarette smoker, strong family history of early CHD)

* **LDL CHOLESTEROL GOALS BY RISK CATEGORY:**

  High Risk:
  - CHD or other clinical forms of atherosclerotic disease (e.g., peripheral artery disease, atherosclerotic aortic disease, carotid artery disease): LDL cholesterol should be < 100 mg/dL. Based on important evidence demonstrating cardiovascular benefit for more intensive LDL lowering, it is reasonable to treat such patients to an LDL cholesterol < 70 mg/dL.
  - Diabetes mellitus or ≥ 2 major risk factors conferring a 10-year CHD risk ≥ 20% in the *absence* of CHD or other clinical forms of atherosclerotic disease: LDL cholesterol goal < 100 mg/dL.

  Moderately High Risk: LDL cholesterol goal < 130 mg/dL; an optional goal < 100 mg/dL should be strongly considered for all moderately high-risk patients, particularly those with: advancing age; more than 2 risk factors; severe risk factors (e.g., continued cigarette smoking); elevated triglyceride ≥ 200 mg/dL plus non-HDL cholesterol ≥ 160 mg/dL; low HDL cholesterol < 40 mg/dL; the metabolic syndrome; and/or the presence of emerging risk factors (e.g., serum high-sensitivity CRP > 3 mg/L or coronary calcium > 75th percentile for a person's age and sex)

  Moderate Risk: LDL cholesterol goal < 130 mg/dL

  Lower Risk: LDL cholesterol goal < 160 mg/dL

Adapted from NCEP ATP III guideline (Circulation 2002;106:3145-3421) and ATP III update (Circulation 2004;110:227-239), and from AHA/ACC guideline update for secondary prevention (Circulation 2006;113:2363-2372).

Low HDL Cholesterol (Figure 3.4)

A. **Overview.** HDL is involved in reverse cholesterol transport from the peripheral tissues (including coronary arteries) to the liver. A depressed HDL cholesterol level, defined as < 40 mg/dL, is a powerful predictor of CHD risk, even more so than elevated total or LDL cholesterol levels. Causes of low HDL cholesterol include elevated triglycerides, obesity, physical inactivity, cigarette smoking, very high carbohydrate diets (> 60% of calories), type 2 diabetes, drugs (beta-blockers, anabolic steroids, progestational agents), and genetic factors. Nonpharmacologic interventions that increase HDL cholesterol include weight loss, exercise, and smoking cessation. Diets high in monounsaturated and omega-3 fatty acids can also increase HDL cholesterol without raising LDL cholesterol levels. Alcohol increases HDL cholesterol but is not recommended for that purpose.

B. Therapy. The primary goal of therapy for persons with low HDL cholesterol is to achieve the LDL cholesterol target (Table 2.3, p. 18). Weight reduction and intensive physical activity are also recommended if the metabolic syndrome is present. Once these goals are achieved, drug therapy to raise HDL cholesterol may be considered, particularly for high-risk individuals with CHD or CHD risk equivalents. For persons with one or more major risk factors, the presence of "emerging" risk factors (e.g., elevated homocysteine or C-reactive protein, high calcium score on EBCT imaging) can be used to identify higher-risk patients who may benefit from drug therapy, although no formal recommendation was made in ATP III. ATP III does not establish a goal for HDL cholesterol, but the American Heart Association recommends initiation of niacin or fibrate therapy in women with HDL cholesterol < 50 mg/dL (Circulation 2004;109:672-93). Also, the American Diabetes Association recommends an HDL cholesterol level > 40 mg/dL (noting that > 50 mg/dL has been advocated in women) and suggests the use of a fibrate, niacin, or combination therapy of statin + fibrate or statin + niacin to raise HDL cholesterol (Diabetes Care 2006;29:S4-42). Several forms of therapy can be used to raise HDL cholesterol levels:

1. **Therapeutic Lifestyle Changes.** Weight reduction, physical activity, and smoking cessation can increase HDL cholesterol by 5-20%, 5-30%, and 5%, respectively, and should be encouraged in all persons.

2. **Discontinuation of Drugs That Lower HDL Cholesterol.** Pharmacologic agents that decrease HDL cholesterol include androgens, progestins, beta-blockers, thiazide diuretics (variable effects), probucol, and nicotine.

3. **Niacin.** Niacin is the most effective agent for increasing HDL cholesterol, raising levels by 15-35% in a dose-dependent fashion. Although a mortality trial with niacin has not been performed in patients with low HDL cholesterol, niacin decreased the risk for MI by 27% at 5 years and all-cause mortality by 11% at 15 years in the Coronary Drug Project (p. 118).

4. **Statins.** Statins increase HDL cholesterol by 5-15% and are effective in low-HDL cholesterol patients if LDL cholesterol is even mildly elevated. In AFCAPS/TexCAPS, lovastatin decreased the risk for cardiovascular death or MI by 37% in healthy people without CHD who had total cholesterol 180-264 mg/dL (mean = 221 mg/dL) and HDL cholesterol ≤ 45 mg/dL in men or ≤ 47 mg/dL in women. Other trials demonstrating reduced CHD risk in persons with low HDL cholesterol include 4S, CARE, LIPID, WOSCOPS, LCAS, and Post-CABG (Chapter 11).

5. **Fibrates**. Fibrates increase HDL cholesterol by 10-35% and reduce cardiovascular risk in low-HDL cholesterol patients, as shown with gemfibrozil in the Veterans Affairs HDL Intervention Trial (VA-HIT) (p. 126). In this study of 2531 men with CHD, HDL cholesterol ≤ 40 mg/dL, and LDL cholesterol ≤ 140 mg/dL, gemfibrozil reduced the relative risk for nonfatal MI or coronary death by 22% compared to placebo. In contrast, benefit was not demonstrated for bezafibrate at 6.2 years in the Bezafibrate Infarction Prevention (BIP) study, except in patients with triglycerides ≥ 200 mg/dL at baseline (p. 116).

6. **Estrogens.** Estrogens raise HDL cholesterol by 10-15%. In the Postmenopausal Estrogen/Progestin Interventions (PEPI) trial, the greatest increase (9%) in HDL cholesterol occurred with unopposed estrogen. However, women in this treatment group with an intact uterus had increased risk for endometrial hyperplasia, which was not seen in the groups treated with estrogen plus progesterone. Estrogen also typically increases triglyceride level. Results from the Heart and Estrogen/progestin Replacement Study (HERS) and the Women's Health Initiative demonstrated a detrimental effect on cardiovascular prognosis with hormone replacement therapy in postmenopausal women (p. 111-112).

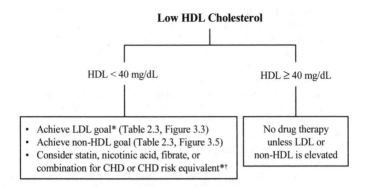

Figure 3.4. Treatment of Low HDL Cholesterol

See Table 2.7 (p. 21) for description of CHD/CHD risk equivalents
*   Statin is preferred drug therapy
†   Drug therapy can also be considered for individuals without CHD but with one
     or more risk factors plus significant asymptomatic atherosclerosis by coronary
     EBCT or carotid ultrasound
Adapted from: NCEP ATP III (Circulation 2002;106:3145-3421; Circulation
2004;110:227-239 [update])

Elevated Triglyceride (Figure 3.5)

A. Overview. Elevated triglyceride is an independent risk factor for CHD and
is associated with atherogenic VLDL remnant particles and small, dense
LDL particles. Elevated triglyceride is also associated with low HDL
cholesterol, insulin resistance, and hyperinsulinemia in patients with or
without overt type 2 diabetes (atherogenic dyslipidemia). ATP III defines
normal triglyceride as < 150 mg/dL, borderline-high triglyceride as 150-199
mg/dL, high triglyceride as 200-499 mg/dL, and very high triglyceride as ≥
500 mg/dL. Since atherogenic remnant lipoproteins are comprised of
partially degraded VLDL particles, elevated VLDL cholesterol can be used
as a marker for the presence of remnant lipoproteins and elevated CHD risk.
ATP III recognizes non-HDL cholesterol (LDL cholesterol + VLDL

cholesterol) as a secondary target of therapy in patients with high triglyceride (≥ 200 mg/dL) and sets the non-HDL cholesterol goal at 30 mg/dL higher than the LDL cholesterol goal (Table 2.3, p. 18); this is based on the assumptions that VLDL cholesterol levels < 30 mg/dL are normal and that higher levels are associated with the presence of atherogenic remnant lipoproteins and increased cardiovascular risk. Non-HDL cholesterol is determined by subtracting HDL cholesterol from total cholesterol. Causes of elevated serum triglyceride include lifestyle-related causes (obesity, physical inactivity, cigarette smoking, excess alcohol intake, high-carbohydrate diet), other secondary causes (diabetes mellitus, chronic renal failure, nephrotic syndrome, Cushing's disease, lipodystrophy, pregnancy, various drugs), and genetic causes. The potential benefits of lowering triglyceride levels on cardiovascular risk are not as well studied as those of lowering LDL cholesterol.

B. Therapy. For triglyceride levels of 150-199 mg/dL, emphasis is placed on therapeutic lifestyle changes and LDL cholesterol lowering. Drug therapy to reduce triglycerides is not recommended. For triglyceride levels of 200-499 mg/dL, primary therapy is directed at LDL cholesterol lowering, and non-HDL cholesterol is a secondary goal of therapy. In addition to weight reduction and increased physical activity, drug therapy may be considered in high-risk patients to achieve the non-HDL cholesterol goal. Pharmacologic approaches include intensification of LDL-lowering therapy, or the addition of nicotinic acid or fibrates when used with appropriate caution (Table 8.2, p. 82). For very high triglyceride levels (≥ 500 mg/dL), the primary goal of therapy is to prevent acute pancreatitis by rapidly lowering triglycerides to < 500 mg/dL with very low fat diets (≤ 15% of calories), weight reduction, increased physical activity, and the use of either fibrates or nicotinic acid. Once triglycerides are < 500 mg/dL, attention is directed toward achieving LDL cholesterol and non-HDL cholesterol targets.

1. **Therapeutic Lifestyle Changes.** Effective measures to lower triglyceride levels in compliant patients include weight loss, increased physical activity, smoking cessation, avoidance of excess alcohol use, and consumption of a Mediterranean diet (i.e., limiting consumption of sugars and processed starches; replacing saturated fats with monounsaturated fats).

2. **Statins.** Statins are modestly effective at lowering triglycerides (7-30%), especially if higher doses of the more potent agents (atorvastatin or rosuvastatin) are used. For patients with elevated triglyceride levels at baseline, greater (up to 45%) reductions may be obtained using high-dose atorvastatin or rosuvastatin. Some studies, like the Post Coronary Artery Bypass Graft (Post-CABG) trial (p. 142) and the Scandinavian Simvastatin Survival Study (4S) (p. 125), suggest that statin therapy markedly reduces the increased risk associated with hypertriglyceridemia, even when triglyceride levels are not completely normalized.

3. **Niacin.** Triglyceride levels can be reduced by 20-50% with niacin (3 gm/d). In the Coronary Drug Project, niacin (3 gm/d) reduced triglyceride by 26% and the risk for coronary death or nonfatal MI by 13% at 5 years (nonsignificant).

4. **Fibrates.** Triglyceride levels can be reduced by 20-50% with a fibrate. In VA-HIT, gemfibrozil (1200 mg/d) reduced the risk for CHD death or MI by 22% at 5 years (p = 0.006) (p. 126). Recommendations to reduce the risk for myopathy in patients taking statins and fibrates together are described in Table 8.2 (p. 82).

5. **Fish Oil.** Triglyceride levels can be reduced by 20-45% with eicosapentaenoic acid (EPA)/docosahexaenoic acid (DHA) (3-4 gm/d). In the Gruppo Italiano per lo Studio della Sopravvivenza nell'Infarto miocardico (GISSI) Prevention Study, low-dose highly concentrated fish oil supplement (~1 gm/d) significantly reduced sudden death by 45% and total mortality by 20% compared with placebo (p. 119).

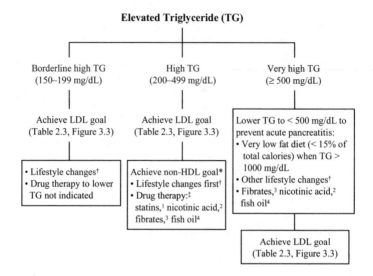

Figure 3.5. Treatment of Elevated Triglyceride

† Weight control, increased physical activity, smoking cessation, restriction of alcohol in some, avoidance of high-carbohydrate diets (> 60% of total calories), discontinuation of nonessential drugs that raise triglyceride

* See Table 2.3 (p. 18)

‡ May need high-dose statin or moderate-dose statin plus either nicotinic acid or fibrate

1. Statins lower triglycerides by 7-30% (20-50% or higher in patients with severely elevated triglyceride)

2. Nicotinic acid lowers triglycerides by 20-50%, but doses ≥ 2 gm/d can worsen hyperglycemia in persons with diabetes or insulin resistance

3. Fibrates lower triglycerides by 20-50% but can raise LDL cholesterol in patients with hypertriglyceridemia. Fibrates are the best choice when acute reductions in triglycerides are needed

4. EPA/DHA (3-4 gm/d) lowers triglycerides by 20-45% but can raise LDL cholesterol and may be a useful adjunct to statin therapy

---

Mixed Hyperlipidemia (Atherogenic Dyslipidemia)

A. **Overview.** Atherogenic dyslipidemia is common in patients with CHD and is characterized by elevated triglycerides ($\geq$ 150 mg/dL), depressed HDL cholesterol (< 40 mg/dL), and normal to moderately elevated LDL cholesterol. Atherogenic dyslipidemia may also be associated with other risk factors characteristic of the metabolic syndrome, including insulin resistance (although most patients do not have overt type 2 diabetes mellitus), hypertension, and abdominal obesity. Patients with atherogenic dyslipidemia often have rapid progression of CHD, as their LDL particles are small, dense, easily oxidized, and highly atherogenic, and their hemostatic function is prothrombogenic due to impaired fibrinolysis and activated platelets. Endothelial dysfunction is also typically present.

B. **Therapy.** Treatment consists of lifestyle changes (exercise, weight loss, smoking cessation) and drug therapy. Statins reduce small dense LDL particles and triglycerides and increase HDL cholesterol. However, statin monotherapy frequently does not normalize the entire lipid profile in these individuals, and more than one agent is often required. Niacin appears to be an excellent agent in combination with a statin for this subset of patients, as it will raise HDL cholesterol by 15-35% and lower LDL cholesterol by 10-25%, triglycerides by 20-50%, and lipoprotein(a) by 20-30%. Niacin also improves prothrombotic tendencies by reducing plasminogen activator inhibitor-1 (PAI-1) and fibrinogen levels. Both niacin and fibrates can shift small, dense LDL particles toward larger, more buoyant particles, which may be less atherogenic. Omega-3 fatty acids (3-4 gm) combined with a statin provide additional reduction in triglycerides and may further reduce non-HDL cholesterol.

Elevated Lipoprotein(a)

A. **Overview.** Lp(a) resembles LDL but contains the unique glycoprotein apo(a), which is highly homologous to plasminogen. Lp(a) is present in atherosclerotic lesions in proportion to plasma levels and has been speculated to provide a functional link between atherosclerosis and thrombosis, owing to its proatherogenic (intimal accumulation) and prothrombotic (interference with plasmin generation) nature. Lp(a) is an independent risk factor for atherosclerosis. The cutpoint for elevated Lp(a) varies with the assay; levels ≥ 75 nmol/L are considered elevated. Heredity is a strong determinant of Lp(a) levels, and patients with a positive family history of CHD and high levels of Lp(a) warrant aggressive risk factor reduction and lipid modification.

B. **Therapy.** Niacin and estrogen have been shown to lower Lp(a) levels, but statins and lifestyle modifications have no impact on Lp(a). Optimal pharmacotherapy for patients with high Lp(a) remains unknown. One approach is to lower LDL cholesterol aggressively (well below 100 mg/dL) with statins, which do not alter Lp(a) levels. Another approach is to reduce Lp(a) levels with niacin and/or estrogen. A post hoc analysis of HERS suggests that estrogen may have some benefit in women with high Lp(a) and CHD, but there are insufficient prospective data to recommend estrogen therapy to lower Lp(a).

Chapter 4

Dyslipidemia in Special Patient Populations (Table 4.1)

A. **Younger Adults (Men 20-35 Years; Women 20-45 Years).** Most younger adults are at low risk for CHD in the short term, but risk factor reduction is important to reduce long-term risk. Most young adults with LDL cholesterol ≥ 190 mg/dL are candidates for drug therapy, even if the 10-year risk for CHD is < 10%. If a genetic disorder is discovered (Appendix 1, p. 163), a family history and measurement of cholesterol levels in other family members should be obtained.

B. **Women (45-75 Years).** The management of dyslipidemia in women is similar to that in men. In HPS, which enrolled 15,454 men and 5082 women, simvastatin reduced major vascular events by 24% at 5 years, independent of gender (Lancet 2002;360:7-22). Recent AHA/ACC guidelines for cardiovascular disease prevention in women are in general consistent with ATP III and support the use of statin therapy in all women at high risk for CHD regardless of baseline LDL cholesterol levels, and include an HDL cholesterol goal > 50 mg/dL (J Am Coll Cardiol 2004;43:900-21). When estrogen replacement therapy is indicated for symptoms associated with menopause, topical preparations should be prescribed if appropriate, since oral preparations of estrogen can exacerbate hypertriglyceridemia. When needed for vasomotor symptoms, oral estrogen is best prescribed in low doses (e.g., 0.625 mg/d of conjugated estrogen or 1 mg/d of micronized estradiol). Adjunctive progestin is required for women without previous hysterectomy. Despite the favorable effects of estrogen replacement therapy on LDL cholesterol and HDL cholesterol, the Heart and Estrogen/progestin Replacement Study (HERS) and the Women's Health Initiative either failed to demonstrate a reduction in the CHD event rate or found that the number of events increased with hormone replacement therapy (JAMA 1998;280:605; JAMA 2002;288:366-8). The Women's Health Initiative also found no CHD benefit with estrogen alone in women who had undergone hysterectomy (JAMA 2004;291:1701-1712).Hormone replacement therapy should not be used for the treatment of dyslipidemia or for the prevention of cardiovascular disease. It may be prescribed for postmenopausal osteoporosis only if nonestrogen medications are considered inappropriate.

C. **Older Adults (Men ≥ 65 Years; Women ≥ 75 Years).** Advanced age by itself should not preclude diet and dyslipidemia drug therapy, especially in patients with established CHD or other forms of atherosclerosis. Pharmacologic treatment of dyslipidemia has been shown to provide morbidity and mortality benefits for older CHD patients and, unlike invasive CHD treatment options, does not carry significantly increased risk as a function of increased age. In HPS, simvastatin reduced major vascular events to a similar extent (~ 20-25% at 5 years) in patients aged < 60 , 65-70, and ≥ 70 years; for 1263 patients aged 75-80 years at enrollment (80-85 years at study end), simvastatin reduced event rate by one-third (23% vs. 32%, p = 0.0002). In the Prospective Study of Pravastatin in the Elderly at Risk (PROSPER), 5804 patients aged 70-82 years with a history of vascular disease or with cardiovascular risk factors were randomized to pravastatin 40 mg/d or placebo (Lancet 2002;360:1623-30). At 3.2 years, pravastatin reduced the risk for the composite primary endpoint of coronary death, nonfatal MI, or stroke by 15% (p = 0.014), driven by a 24% decrease in CHD death (p = 0.043). In addition, major coronary events (CHD death or nonfatal MI) were reduced by 19% (p = 0.006). Therapy with statins, niacin, and fibrates has been associated with a reduction in stroke. This may be of particular benefit to elderly patients, although PROSPER reported no effect on stroke with pravastatin vs. placebo. In the Cholesterol Treatment Trialists' Collaboration meta-analysis of 14 statin trials, incidence of first stroke was reduced by 17% with statin therapy, including a 22% reduction in ischemic stroke for each ~ 40-mg/dL reduction in LDL cholesterol (Lancet 2005;366:1267-78). In the Collaborative Atorvastatin Diabetes Study (CARDS), atorvastatin reduced stroke by 48% in patients with type 2 diabetes without high LDL cholesterol levels (Lancet 2004;364:685-696). In HPS, simvastatin reduced stroke early (within 2 years), with further divergence of stroke incidence during each subsequent year of treatment (Lancet 2004;363:757-67). In VA-HIT, gemfibrozil reduced stroke by 31% after adjustment for baseline variables (Circulation 2001;103:2828-33). In the Coronary Drug Project, niacin reduced the incidence of stroke or intermittent cerebral ischemic attack by 26% compared with placebo (JAMA 1975;231:360-81). Elderly patients with CHD or CHD risk equivalents should be treated similarly to younger persons at high risk, with the proviso that advanced age (esp. > 80 years), use of concomitant medications, and frailty may increase the risk for statin-associated myopathy (J Am Coll Cardiol 2002;40:576-572) (see Table 8.1, p. 81). Clinical judgment is important in determining the need for and intensity of treatment in elderly patients at intermediate risk for CHD.

D. Type 2 Diabetes. Diabetic dyslipidemia is characterized by elevated triglycerides ($\geq$ 150 mg/dL), depressed HDL cholesterol (< 40 mg/dL), and elevated small dense LDL particles that are easily oxidized and highly atherogenic. LDL cholesterol levels are normal to moderately elevated and generally are no different than levels in nondiabetic patients. Patients with diabetic dyslipidemia often have rapid progression of CHD, due to highly atherogenic LDL particles, prothrombogenic hemostatic function (impaired fibrinolysis, activated platelets), and endothelial dysfunction. It has been estimated that diabetic dyslipidemia confers a cardiovascular risk similar to an LDL cholesterol level of 150-220 mg/dL (Circulation 1997;95:1-4). Furthermore, the risk for cardiovascular events in diabetic patients without CHD is the same as the risk in nondiabetic patients with CHD, and about 80% of persons with diabetes eventually die of cardiovascular causes. Given the poor cardiovascular prognosis associated with diabetes, ATP III considers diabetes a CHD risk equivalent and recommends the same LDL cholesterol targets and drug initiation levels as for patients with CHD.

1. **Statin Trials in Type 2 Diabetes.** Statins are overwhelmingly the drug class of choice for improving dyslipidemia and cardiovascular prognosis in type 2 diabetes. In CARDS, 2838 patients with type 2 diabetes, no clinical cardiovascular disease (absence of coronary, cerebrovascular, or severe peripheral vascular disease), LDL cholesterol $\leq$ 160 mg/dL, and one risk factor (hypertension, retinopathy, micro- or macroalbuminuria, current smoking) were randomized to atorvastatin 10 mg/d or placebo. (LDL cholesterol was 119 mg/dL at baseline and 73 mg/dL on atorvastatin treatment.) At 3.9 years, atorvastatin reduced the first occurrence of any major vascular event (acute CHD events, coronary revascularization procedures, or stroke) by 37% (5.8% vs. 9.0% , p = 0.001). There was also a 27% reduction in all-cause mortality (borderline statistical significance). The absolute reduction in vascular events was 3.7%, and the number needed to treat for 4 years to prevent one major vascular event was only 27. It was estimated that 4 years of atorvastatin therapy in 1000 CARDS patients would prevent 37 first major cardiovascular events and 50 first or subsequent events.

Benefits were consistent regardless of baseline lipid levels, gender, or age. Atorvastatin was also extremely well tolerated: there were no cases of rhabdomyolysis and no differences in muscle or liver adverse effects compared to placebo (Lancet 2004;364:685-696). Further positive results were evident in the diabetes substudy of HPS, in which 5963 type 2 diabetic subjects (of 20,536 total patients in HPS) were randomized to simvastatin 40 mg/d or placebo. At 5 years, simvastatin reduced the first occurrence of any major vascular event (MI, coronary death, stroke, revascularization) by 22% (20.2% vs. 25.1% for placebo, p < 0.0001). There were also highly significant reductions among the 2912 diabetic subjects without occlusive arterial disease at entry (risk reduction 33%, p = 0.0003), and among 2426 diabetic subjects with pretreatment LDL cholesterol levels < 116 mg/dL (risk reduction 27%, p = 0.0007) (Lancet 2003;361:2005-16). It was estimated that 5 years of simvastatin therapy would prevent 80 major vascular events per 1000 diabetic patients.

2. **Fibrate Trials in Type 2 Diabetes.** In the Fenofibrate Intervention and Event Lowering in Diabetes (FIELD) study, 9795 patients with type 2 diabetes (including 2131 with previous cardiovascular disease), total cholesterol of 115-250 mg/dL, total cholesterol/HDL cholesterol ratio ≥ 4, and triglycerides of 90-445 mg/dL who were not on statin therapy at baseline were randomized to receive micronized fenofibrate 200 mg/d or placebo. At 1 year, LDL cholesterol was reduced by 12%, HDL cholesterol was increased by 4.5%, and triglycerides were reduced by 30% with fenofibrate compared with placebo. At 5 years, the primary endpoint of coronary events (CHD death or nonfatal MI) was not significantly different between treatment groups (hazard ratio 0.89, 95% CI 0.75-1.05; p = 0.16), but nonfatal MI was reduced by 24% (p = 0.01), coronary revascularization was reduced by 21% (p = 0.003), and total cardiovascular events were reduced by 11% (p = 0.035) (Lancet 2005;366:1849-61). There were no significant reductions in CHD mortality (1.19 [95% CI 0.90–1.57]) or total mortality (1.11 [0.95–1.29]). These results are difficult to apply to clinical practice, however, because FIELD patients were not on statin therapy, as would be expected in clinical practice, and during the trial 17% of placebo patients and 8% of fenofibrate patients began other lipid-lowering therapy, predominantly statins. Additional information is expected from the Action to Control Cardiovascular Risk in Diabetes (ACCORD) trial,

in which ~10,000 patients with type 2 diabetes will receive both a fibrate and a statin to examine the effects of combined triglyceride lowering, HDL cholesterol increase, and LDL cholesterol lowering on MI, stroke, and CHD death.

3. **Treatment of Dyslipidemia in Type 2 Diabetes**. Treatment of diabetic dyslipidemia consists of lifestyle changes (exercise, weight loss, smoking cessation), glycemic control (can raise HDL cholesterol and lower triglycerides), and antidyslipidemia drug therapy. The recent update to ATP III recommends use of a statin to reduce LDL cholesterol levels by *a minimum of 30-40%* in all diabetic patients at increased risk for cardiovascular disease, regardless of baseline LDL cholesterol levels. An LDL cholesterol target < 100 mg/dL is recommended, with an LDL target < 70 mg/dL for higher-risk diabetic patients with CHD or other clinical forms of atherosclerosis. Similar recommendations were espoused in guidelines from the American College of Physicians (ACP) (Ann Intern Med 2004;140:644-9). The role of statin therapy in lower-risk patients (e.g., younger patients with LDL cholesterol < 130 mg/dL and no other cardiovascular risk factors) awaits definition.

4. **Drug Therapy for Dyslipidemia in Type 2 Diabetes**
   a. **Statins.** Statins are overwhelmingly the drug class of choice for improving dyslipidemia and cardiovascular prognosis, but statin monotherapy may not completely normalize the lipid profile in all patients, and more than one lipid-lowering agent may be required.
   b. **Ezetimibe.** Ezetimibe is a newer agent that inhibits the absorption of cholesterol and phytosterols from the small intestine. When used as an adjunct to statin therapy, ezetimibe 10 mg/d can further reduce LDL cholesterol by approximately 20-25% and triglycerides by approximately 10% and further raise HDL cholesterol by approximately 3-5% (J Am Coll Cardiol 2002;40:2125-34; Circulation 2003;107:2409-15).
   c. **Niacin.** Niacin raises HDL cholesterol by 15-35% and lowers LDL cholesterol by 10-25%, triglycerides by 20-50%, and lipoprotein(a) by 20-30%. Niacin also improves prothrombotic tendencies by reducing plasminogen activator inhibitor-1 (PAI-1) and fibrinogen. Niacin (and fibrates) can shift small, dense LDL particles toward larger, more buoyant particles, which may be less atherogenic. However, niacin can impair glucose tolerance and raise HbA_{1c} levels in some diabetics, and there is an increased risk for

myopathy/rhabdomyolysis when niacin is used, particularly at higher doses, in conjunction with a statin. When niacin is used, lower doses are recommended (e.g., Niaspan ≤ 1.5 gm/d) and glucose monitoring is required.

d. **Omega-3 fatty acids.** Omega-3 fatty acids are also of value for diabetic dyslipidemia. Low doses (1-1.5 gm/d) have been shown to reduce cardiovascular mortality, primarily from a reduction in sudden death; higher doses (2-4 gm/d) can lower triglycerides by 20-50% and are safe, well-tolerated adjuncts to statin therapy.

e. **Fibrates.** Fibrates improve the lipid profile in diabetic dyslipidemia by lowering triglycerides by 20-50%, raising HDL cholesterol by 16-35%, and shifting small, dense LDL particles to larger, less atherogenic particles. However, the risk for myopathy and rhabdomyolysis is increased when fibrates are used in conjunction with statins, with the possible exception of fenofibrate (Drug Metab Dispos 2002;30:1280-7).

E. **Hypertensive Patients.** Two large-scale, randomized hypertension trials with lipid-lowering arms evaluated the role of statins in the prevention of cardiovascular disease. In the Anglo-Scandinavian Cardiac Outcomes Trial (ASCOT), 10,305 hypertensive patients aged 40-79 years with at least 3 other risk factors and total cholesterol ≤ 250 mg/dL were randomized to atorvastatin 10 mg/d or placebo. (Risk factors included male sex, age ≥ 55 years, smoking, type 2 diabetes, left ventricular hypertrophy (LVH), other specified abnormalities on ECG, peripheral artery disease, previous stroke or transient ischemic attack, microalbuminuria or proteinuria, ratio of total cholesterol to HDL cholesterol ≥ 6, and family history of premature CHD.) The trial was originally scheduled for 5 years but was halted early because of clear benefit with atorvastatin. At 3.3 years, atorvastatin reduced LDL cholesterol by about 40 mg/dL and the risk for fatal CHD and nonfatal MI (primary endpoint) by 36% (1.9% vs. 3.0%, p = 0.0005). Atorvastatin also reduced the relative risk for fatal/nonfatal stroke by 27% (p = 0.02), total cardiovascular events and procedures by 21% (p = 0.005), and total coronary events by 29% (p = 0.005). Benefits were evident at 1 year, and there was no difference in adverse effects between atorvastatin and placebo (Lancet 2003;361:1149-58). In contrast, LDL cholesterol lowering with pravastatin 40 mg/d did not reduce CHD among 10,355 moderately hypercholesterolemic, hypertensive patients at 4.8 years in the lipid-lowering arm of the Antihypertensive and Lipid-Lowering Treatment to Prevent Heart Attack Trial (ALLHAT) (JAMA 2002;288:2998-3007). The lack of benefit with pravastatin was thought to be due to substantial (30%) use of statins in the usual care group, leading to small differences in total cholesterol (9%) and LDL cholesterol (17%) between groups. Nevertheless, the 10% (albeit nonsignificant) reduction in CHD events associated with a net difference of 17 mg/dL in LDL cholesterol in ALLHAT is proportionally similar to the 35% reduction in CHD events associated with a net difference of 40 mg/dL in LDL cholesterol in ASCOT and does not detract from the findings of this trial. As described in Table 2.7 (p. 22), moderately high-risk patients, such as those in ASCOT and the majority of those in ALLHAT (14% of patients in ALLHAT had CHD and would therefore be considered high risk), should receive statin therapy to reduce LDL cholesterol levels at least to a target of < 130 mg/dL and most likely to a lower optional target of < 100 mg/dL (< 70 mg/dL if hypertension is accompanied by atherosclerotic vascular disease).

F. **Acute Coronary Syndromes (ACS).** Recent data indicate a role for in-hospital initiation of statins in patients with unstable angina or acute MI. In the Myocardial Ischemia Reduction with Aggressive Cholesterol Lowering (MIRACL) trial, 3086 patients with ACS were randomized to atorvastatin 80 mg or placebo 1-4 days after hospital admission. At 16 weeks, atorvastatin reduced the risk for a composite end-point event (death, nonfatal MI, resuscitated cardiac arrest, or recurrent unstable angina requiring hospitalization) by 16% (14.8% vs. 17.4%, p = 0.048) (JAMA 2001;285:1711-18). This was driven by a significant reduction in unstable angina, the only component for which there was a between-group difference. In PROVE IT, 4162 patients with ACS were randomized to in-hospital initiation of intensive LDL cholesterol lowering with atorvastatin 80 mg/d (median on-treatment LDL cholesterol 62 mg/dL) or standard LDL cholesterol lowering with pravastatin 40 mg/d (median on-treatment LDL cholesterol 95 mg/dL). At 2 years, atorvastatin reduced the primary endpoint (death, MI, unstable angina requiring hospitalization, revascularization after 30 days, or stroke) by 16% (22.4% vs. 26.3%, p = 0.005), based on significant decreases in revascularization and recurrent unstable angina (N Engl J Med 2004;350:1495-1504). Benefits were apparent as early as 30 days and were consistent over time. Benefits were also consistent across prespecified subgroups, including men and women, patients with unstable angina and acute MI, and patients with and without diabetes. When stratified according to LDL cholesterol and CRP levels, risk reduction for patients with CRP levels < 2.0 mg/ dL was nearly identical to patients with LDL levels < 70 mg/dL. Patients with low LDL cholesterol and low CRP levels had the greatest reduction in recurrent MI or coronary death. Although atorvastatin was more potent than pravastatin in reducing LDL cholesterol and CRP, event-free survival was similar, regardless of the drug, once target levels of cholesterol and CRP were achieved (N Engl J Med 2005;352:20-28). In the Z phase of the Aggrastat to Zocor (A to Z) trial, 4497 patients with ACS were randomized to early intensive statin therapy (simvastatin 40 mg/d x 1 month followed by 80 mg/d) or a delayed conservative approach (placebo x 4 months followed by simvastatin 20 mg/d). Patients were followed for 6-24 months. Early intensive statin therapy resulted in a favorable trend toward a reduction in the primary endpoint (cardiovascular death, MI, readmission for ACS, or stroke) (14.4% vs. 16.7%, p = 0.14). There was no difference in the primary endpoint at 4 months; however, between 4 months and the end of the study, early intensive statin therapy resulted in a significant 25% reduction in major cardiovascular events (6.8% vs. 9.3%, p = 0.02) (JAMA 2004;292:1307-16). C-reactive protein levels were reduced to a greater extent with atorvastatin in MIRACL (Circulation 2003;10:560-66) and PROVE IT than with simvastatin in A to Z (34-38% vs. 16.7%). In-hospital initiation of statin therapy has also been shown to improve patient compliance by linking statin therapy to hospitalization. In the Cardiac Hospitalization Atherosclerosis Management Program (CHAMP), in-hospital initiation of statins was associated with greater statin use at 1 year (91% vs. 10%) and a greater likelihood of having an LDL cholesterol level ≤ 100 mg/dL (58% vs. 6%). Despite these benefits, only 32% of patients with acute MI are discharged on lipid-lowering therapy (Circulation 2001;103:38-44). Based on these data, all patients with ACS should be started on statins in the hospital (within 10 days and after patient is stable) and continued on statins long term. LDL cholesterol measurement within 24 hours of hospitalization can help guide therapy.

G. **Percutaneous Coronary Intervention (PCI).** In the Lescol Intervention Prevention Study (LIPS), 1677 patients with successful first PCI were randomized to fluvastatin 40 mg twice daily or placebo, initiated at a median of 2 days after PCI. At 3.9 years, fluvastatin reduced the risk for cardiac death, nonfatal MI, or repeat interventional procedure (CABG, repeat PCI, PCI for new stenosis) by 22% (21.4% vs. 26.7%, p = 0.01). Benefits were independent of baseline LDL cholesterol level and were especially pronounced (37% risk reduction) in patients with diabetes or multivessel disease. Also noted was a 32% reduction in late revascularization procedures. In-hospital initiation of statin therapy also improves long-term compliance. In the Evaluation in PTCA to Improve Long-term Outcome With Abciximab GP IIb/IIIa Blockade (EPILOG) trial, patients undergoing PCI for stable or unstable angina who were started on lipid-lowering therapy before hospital discharge were almost 3 times as likely to be taking these medications at 6 months (Arch Intern Med 2003;163:2576-82). Fluvastatin has been approved by the FDA to reduce the risk associated with coronary revascularization procedures in patients with CHD, although updated guidelines recommend any statin at a dose providing a 30-40% reduction in LDL cholesterol.

H. **Renal Transplant Recipients and Chronic Kidney Disease.** Premature CHD is the leading cause of death in patients following renal transplantation (Lancet 2000;356:147-152). To assess the role of statins in this setting, 2102 patients with renal transplantation > 6 months and total cholesterol 155-232 mg/dL were randomized to fluvastatin 40 mg/d or placebo in the Assessment of Lescol in Renal Transplantation (ALERT) trial. At 5.1 years, fluvastatin lowered LDL cholesterol by 32% and reduced the relative risk for cardiac death or nonfatal MI by 35% (6.7% vs. 9.9%, p = 0.005). There was no difference in adverse effects between fluvastatin and placebo (Lancet 2003;361:2024-31). Patients with chronic kidney disease are considered to have risk status equivalent to that of patients with CHD in the AHA guidelines for cardiovascular disease prevention in women (Circulation 2004;109:672-93) and in the National Kidney Foundation clinical practice guidelines (Am J Kidney Dis 2002;39:S1, Am J Kidney Dis 2003;41 (suppl. 3):S1). However, the ATP III guidelines have not included chronic kidney disease or renal failure as a CHD risk equivalent. Among 4491 patients with CHD or at risk for CHD and with concomitant moderate chronic kidney disease (GFR 30-60 mL/min per 1.73 m^2) in the Pravastatin Pooling Project, which combined results from 3 randomized trials (CARE, LIPID, WOSCOPS) of pravastatin (40 mg/d) vs. placebo, pravastatin significantly reduced the primary outcome (MI, coronary death, or coronary revascularization) by 23% (95% CI 0.68-0.86) and appeared to reduce total mortality by 14% (p = 0.045) (Circulation 2004;110:1557-1563). In this study, moderate chronic kidney disease was independently associated with an increased risk for the primary outcome, and the absolute benefit of statins in moderate chronic kidney disease (absolute risk reduction of 6.3% in the primary endpoint) is similar to that seen in patients with diabetes. However, in Die Deutsche Diabetes Dialyse Studie (4D), in which 1255 diabetic patients receiving hemodialysis < 2 years and with LDL cholesterol of 80-189 mg/dL were randomized to atorvastatin 20 mg/d or placebo and followed up for a median of 4 years, the primary endpoint of cardiac death, nonfatal MI, and stroke was not significantly different between treatment groups (N Engl J Med 2005;353:238-48). Atorvastatin significantly reduced cardiac events by 18% (p = 0.03) but doubled the risk for fatal stroke (p = 0.03). The effects of statin therapy on clinical events in patients with chronic kidney disease is also being examined in ongoing trials. In A study to evaluate the Use of Rosuvastatin in subjects On Regular hemodialysis: an Assessment of survival and cardiovascular events (AURORA), more than 2700 patients receiving hemodialysis ≥ 3 months have been randomized to rosuvastatin 10 mg/d or placebo and will be followed up for about 4 years (Curr Control Trials Cardiovasc Med 2005;6:9). The Study of Heart and Renal Protection (SHARP) is studying the effects of combination therapy with simvastatin 20 mg/d and ezetimibe 10 mg/d vs. placebo in ~ 9000 patients with chronic kidney disease (receiving dialysis, or predialysis with creatinine ≥ 1.7 mg/dL in men and ≥ 1.5 mg/dL in women), with planned follow-up ≥ 4 years (www.sharpinfo.org; Kidney Int 2003;63:S207-10).

I. **Apparently Healthy People with Average LDL Cholesterol but Low HDL Cholesterol.** The Air Force/Texas Coronary Atherosclerosis Prevention Study (AFCAPS/TexCAPS) showed a 37% reduction in the risk for MI, unstable angina, or sudden cardiac death in healthy middle-aged men and women (without CHD) with average cholesterol levels treated with lovastatin for 5 years (p. 114). Data from AFCAPS/TexCAPS demonstrate that the use of statins is safe and effective in these patients. Importantly, only 17% of study participants would have qualified for drug therapy by the ATP II guidelines in effect at the time of the study. While the relative risk for an adverse cardiovascular event was reduced by more than one-third, the reduction in absolute risk was only 2.0%, meaning that 50 people would need to be treated for 5 years to prevent one event. Furthermore, all-cause mortality in AFCAPS/TexCAPS was not reduced. In patients at intermediate risk, additional tests for risk stratification may be useful, such as measurement of CRP or coronary EBCT scan.

Table 4.1. Management of Dyslipidemia in Special Populations

Patient Subgroup	Recommendations
Younger adults (men 20-35 years; women 20-45 yrs)	Short-term risk for CHD is low. Consider LDL-lowering therapy for LDL ≥ 190 mg/dL
Women 45-75 years	Treat the same as for dyslipidemia in men, with additional HDL goal of > 50 mg/dL
Older adults (men ≥ 65 years; women ≥ 75 years)	Elderly patients with CHD or CHD risk equivalents should be treated the same as younger persons at high risk, although advanced age, polypharmacy, and frailty can increase the risk for statin-associated myopathy. Clinical judgment is important in determining the need for and intensity of drug therapy in patients at intermediate risk for CHD
Type 2 diabetes	Diabetic dyslipidemia is associated with rapid progression of CHD. Treat the same as patients with CHD. Consider an LDL target < 70 mg/dL for patients with CHD or other clinical forms of atherosclerosis
Hypertension	Patients with hypertension plus other risk factors conferring a 10-year risk for CHD of 10-20% should be treated to a minimum LDL target < 130 mg/dL and probably to an LDL target < 100 mg/dL
Acute coronary syndromes	Initiate statin therapy in the hospital to achieve an LDL target < 70 mg/dL
Percutaneous coronary intervention (PCI)	Initiate statin therapy prior to hospital discharge after PCI to an LDL target < 100 mg/dL. Consider LDL target < 70 mg/dL
Renal transplant recipients	Consider statin therapy to reduce CHD events. Monitor for statin-cyclosporine interaction

Chapter 5

Therapeutic Lifestyle Changes: Diet Modification

Diet modification, weight control, and increased physical activity are important therapeutic lifestyle changes (TLC) for all patients with dyslipidemia. For patients who require drug therapy, the drug should be added to, not substituted for, diet therapy and other lifestyle modifications.

Therapeutic Lifestyle Changes (TLC) Diet

By limiting total fat, saturated fat, and dietary cholesterol in patients consuming a typical Western diet, initiation of the TLC Diet (Tables 5.1, 5.2), as recommended by ATP III, has been estimated to lower LDL cholesterol levels by 10-20% (individual response is highly variable). A registered dietitian can be helpful in improving compliance. Other dietary measures to lower LDL cholesterol and reduce risk for CHD are described in Table 5.3.

Table 5.1. Therapeutic Lifestyle Changes (TLC) Diet

Food Composition	Recommendation
Total fat *Saturated fat** *Polyunsaturated fat* *Monounsaturated fat*	25-35% of total calories < 7% of total calories Up to 10% of total calories Up to 20% of total calories
Carbohydrates	50-60% of total calories†
Fiber	20-30 gm/d
Protein	~ 15% of total calories
Cholesterol	< 200 mg/d
Total calories	Sufficient to achieve/maintain desirable body weight

* Trans fats also raise LDL cholesterol and should be kept to a minimum
† More than half as complex carbohydrates from whole grains, fruits, vegetables
From: NCEP ATP III (Circulation 2002;106:3145-3421)

Table 5.2. Components of the TLC Diet: Recommendations from ATP III

Component	Evidence Statement*	Recommendations
Total fat	Unsaturated fats do not raise LDL cholesterol when substituted for carbohydrates in the diet (A2, B2).	It is not necessary to restrict total fat intake for the purpose of reducing LDL cholesterol, provided saturated fats are reduced to goal levels.
Saturated fats	High intakes of saturated fats raise LDL cholesterol and are associated with high population rates of CHD (C2). Reduction in intake of saturated fats reduces CHD risk (A1, B1).	A therapeutic diet to maximize LDL lowering should contain < 7% of total calories as saturated fats.
Trans fats	Trans fats raise LDL cholesterol (A2). Prospective studies support an association between higher intakes of trans fatty acids and CHD incidence (C2).	Intakes of trans fats should be kept low. Liquid vegetable oil, soft margarine, and trans fat-free margarine are encouraged instead of butter, stick margarine, and shortening.
Polyunsaturated fats	Linoleic acid, a polyunsaturated fat, reduces LDL cholesterol levels when substituted for saturated fats (A1, B1). Polyunsaturated fats can cause a small reduction in HDL cholesterol compared to monounsaturated fats (B2). Clinical trials indicate that substitution of polyunsaturated fats for saturated fats reduces risk for CHD (A2, B2).	Polyunsaturated fats can replace saturated fat. Most polyunsaturated fats should be derived from liquid vegetable oils, semi-liquid margarines, and margarines low in trans fats. Intake can range up to 10% of total calories.

* *Type of Evidence:* A: Major randomized controlled trials (RCTs); B: Smaller RCTs and meta-analyses of other clinical trials; C: Observational and metabolic studies; D: Clinical experience. *Strength of Evidence:* 1: Very strong; 2: Moderately strong; 3: Strong trend. *From:* NCEP ATP III. Circulation 2002;106:3145-3421.

Table 5.2. Components of the TLC Diet: Recommendations from ATP III (cont'd)

Component	Evidence Statement*	Recommendations
Mono-unsaturated fats	Monounsaturated fats lower LDL cholesterol relative to saturated fatty acids (A2, B2) but do not lower HDL cholesterol or raise triglycerides (A2, B2). Diets rich in monounsaturated fats provided by plant sources and rich in fruits, vegetables, and whole grains and low in saturated fats decrease CHD risk (C1).	Monounsaturated fats are one form of unsaturated fatty acid that can replace saturated fats. Intake can be up to 20% of total calories. Most monounsaturated fats should be derived from vegetable sources, including plant oils and nuts.
Cholesterol	High intakes of dietary cholesterol raise LDL cholesterol (A2, B1) and the risk for CHD. Reducing intakes from high to low decreases LDL cholesterol (A2, B1).	Less than 200 mg per day of cholesterol should be consumed in the TLC Diet to maximize LDL cholesterol lowering.
Carbohydrates	When carbohydrate is substituted for saturated fats, LDL cholesterol levels fall (A2, B2). However, very high intakes of carbohydrate (>60 percent of total calories) are accompanied by a reduction in HDL cholesterol and a rise in triglyceride (B1, C1).	Daily intake should be limited to 60% of total calories in persons with the metabolic syndrome. Lower intakes (e.g., 50% of calories) should be considered for persons who have elevated triglycerides or low HDL cholesterol. Most carbohydrates should come from grain products (esp. whole grains), vegetables, fruits, fat-free/low-fat dairy.

* *Type of Evidence:* A: Major randomized controlled trials (RCTs); B: Smaller RCTs and meta-analyses of other clinical trials; C: Observational and metabolic studies; D: Clinical experience. *Strength of Evidence:* 1: Very strong; 2: Moderately strong; 3: Strong trend. *From:* NCEP ATP III. Circulation 2002;106:3145-3421.

Table 5.2. Components of the TLC Diet: Recommendations from ATP III (cont'd)

Component	Evidence Statement*	Recommendations
Protein	Dietary protein in general has little effect on LDL cholesterol or other lipoprotein fractions. However, substituting soy protein for animal protein has been reported to lower LDL cholesterol (A2, B2).	Protein intake should constitute ~ 15% of total calories. Plant sources of protein include legumes, dry beans, nuts, and to a lesser extent, grain products and vegetables, which are low in saturated fats/cholesterol. Animal sources of protein lower in saturated fat/cholesterol include fat-free/low-fat dairy, egg whites, fish, skinless poultry, lean meats.

* *Type of Evidence:* A: Major randomized controlled trials (RCTs); B: Smaller RCTs and meta-analyses of other clinical trials; C: Observational and metabolic studies; D: Clinical experience. *Strength of Evidence:* 1: Very strong; 2: Moderately strong; 3: Strong trend. *From:* NCEP ATP III. Circulation 2002;106:3145-3421.

Table 5.3. Dietary Options for LDL Lowering and Cardiovascular Risk Reduction: Recommendations from ATP III

Measure	Evidence Statement*	Comments
Increasing viscous fiber in the diet	5-10 gm/d of viscous fiber reduces LDL cholesterol levels by ~ 5% (A2, B1).	The use of dietary sources of viscous fiber is a therapeutic option to enhance LDL lowering.
Plant stanols/sterols	Intakes of 2-3 gm/d of plant stanol/sterol esters reduce LDL cholesterol by 6-15% (A2, B1).	Plant stanol/sterol esters are a therapeutic option to enhance LDL lowering.

**Table 5.3. Dietary Options for LDL Lowering and Cardiovascular
Risk Reduction: Recommendations from ATP III**

Measure	Evidence Statement*	Comments
Soy protein	High intakes of soy protein can cause small reductions in LDL cholesterol levels, especially when it replaces animal food products (A2, B2).	Food sources containing soy protein are acceptable as replacements for animal food products containing animal fats.
n-3 (omega-3) polyunsaturated fatty acids	Higher intakes of n-3 fatty acids may reduce risk for coronary events/mortality (A2, C2).	Higher dietary intakes of n-3 fatty acids in the form of fatty fish or vegetable oils are an option for reducing CHD risk.
Folic acid and vitamins B_6 and B_{12}	There are no randomized trials to show whether lowering homocysteine levels through dietary intake or vitamin supplements will reduce CHD risk.	ATP III endorses the Institute of Medicine RDA for dietary folate (400 mcg/d).
Antioxidants	Clinical trials have failed to show that antioxidant supplements reduce CHD risk (A2).	The Institute of Medicine's RDAs for dietary antioxidants are recommended (vitamin C: 75 mg and 90 mg/d for women and men; vitamin E: 15 mg/d).

* *Type of Evidence:* A: Major randomized controlled trials (RCTs); B: Smaller RCTs and meta-analyses of other clinical trials; C: Observational and metabolic studies; D: Clinical experience. *Strength of Evidence:* 1: Very strong; 2: Moderately strong; 3: Strong trend. *From:* NCEP ATP III. Circulation 2002;106:3145-3421.

Table 5.3. Dietary Options for LDL Lowering and Cardiovascular Risk Reduction: Recommendations from ATP III

Measure	Evidence Statement*	Comments
Moderate alcohol intake	Moderate alcohol intake in middle-aged/older adults may reduce CHD risk (C2). High intakes of alcohol produce multiple adverse effects (C1).	Alcohol should be limited to 2 drinks per day for men and 1 drink per day for women. A drink is defined as 5 oz. wine, 12 oz. beer, or 1.5 oz. 80-proof whiskey.
Dietary sodium, potassium, and calcium	Lower salt intake lowers blood pressure or prevents its rise.	ATP III supports JNC 7 recommendation of ≤ 2.4 gm/d sodium or 6 gm/d sodium chloride intake and adequate intakes of dietary potassium, calcium, and magnesium.
Herbal or botanical dietary supplements	Trial data are not available to support the use of herbal and botanical supplements in the prevention or treatment of heart disease.	ATP III does not recommend use of herbal or botanical dietary supplements to reduce CHD risk. Patients should be asked whether such products are being used because of potential drug interactions.
High-protein, high-total fat, and high-saturated fat weight loss regimens	These diets have not been shown in controlled trials to produce long-term weight reduction, and their nutrient composition does not appear to be conducive to long-term health.	These regimens are not recommended for weight reduction in clinical practice.

* *Type of Evidence:* A: Major randomized controlled trials (RCTs); B: Smaller RCTs and meta-analyses of other clinical trials; C: Observational and metabolic studies; D: Clinical experience. *Strength of Evidence:* 1: Very strong; 2: Moderately strong; 3: Strong trend. *From:* NCEP ATP III. Circulation 2002;106:3145-3421.

Mediterranean-Style Diet

A. **Lyon Heart Study**. Increasing evidence suggests that a Mediterranean-style diet emphasizing consumption of monounsaturated and omega-3 fatty acids can play an important role in the prevention of cardiovascular disease. The Lyon Heart Study randomized 605 post-MI patients to a Mediterranean diet providing increased levels of alpha-linolenic acid (from olive oil and canola oil) or usual dietary instruction. Patients in the Mediterranean diet group were instructed to consume more fish, bread, and root and green vegetables; eat less meat; have fruit at least once daily; and use canola-based margarine and olive oil as a fat source. At 27 months, patients on the Mediterranean diet showed a 70% reduction in all-cause mortality (p = 0.03). The rate of cardiovascular death and nonfatal MI was 1.32 per 100 patient-years in the treated group compared to 5.55 per 100 patient-years in the control group (p = 0.001) (Lancet 1994;343:1454-9). Risk reduction correlated with increased omega-3 intake in the treatment group. Benefits were maintained at 4 years (Circulation 1999;99:779-85).

B. **Other Studies.** Further evidence for the cardioprotective benefits of omega-3 fatty acids (eicosapentaenoic acid [EPA] and docosahexaenoic acid [DHA]) from fish or fish oil supplements come from the GISSI Prevention study and Diet and Reinfarction Trial (DART). The GISSI Prevention study randomized 11,324 Italian men and women (who presumably were eating a Mediterranean diet) with MI within the preceding 3 months to omega-3 fatty acid capsules (850-882 mg/d), vitamin E (300 mg/d), both, or neither. After 3.5 years, the omega-3 fatty acid group had a significant 20% reduction in all-cause mortality and 45% reduction in sudden cardiac death (Lancet 1999;354:447-55). In DART, 2033 men with prior MI were randomized to receive different types of dietary advice to prevent another MI. After 2 years, the group told to increase their omega-3 fatty acid intake by eating oily fish (e.g., salmon, herring, mackerel) at least twice weekly had a 29% reduction in overall mortality (p < 0.05) (Lancet 1989;2:757-61). Results from the Nurses' Health Study, which examined the risk for CHD in 84,688 previously healthy women, found that higher consumption of fish and omega-3 fatty acids reduced the risk for cardiac death by up to 45% at 16 years (JAMA 2002;287:1815-1821). Furthermore, there was an inverse relationship between fish/omega-3 fatty acid intake and thrombotic stroke. Compared to women who ate fish < 1 time/month, relative risk reductions for women who ate fish 1-3 times/month, 1 time/week, 2-4 times/week, and ≥ 5 times/week were 0.93, 0.78, 0.73, and 0.48, respectively (JAMA 2001;285:304-312). Fish consumption 1-3 times per week also reduced ischemic stroke in men in the Health Professional Follow-up Study (JAMA 2002;288:3130-6). Fish oil supplements incorporate into atherosclerotic plaque to enhance plaque stability (Lancet 2003;361:477-85). These studies suggest that the type of fat, not only the amount, can affect cardiovascular health.

C. Recommendations. Diet modification should be recommended as part of a comprehensive program to reduce cardiovascular risk. Suggested diets are the TLC Diet recommended in the ATP III guidelines or a Mediterranean-style diet. Tables 5.4 and 5.5 describe basic components of a Mediterranean diet and how to incorporate these steps into everyday living.

Table 5.4. Basic Components of a Mediterranean Diet

Component	Benefits
Omega-3–rich[1] fish 1-2 times per week or omega-3 supplements[2]	Reduces all-cause mortality and sudden cardiac death post-MI; lowers triglycerides (high doses) and blood pressure; improves insulin resistance; boosts the immune system; may help prevent cancer, arthritis, depression, Alzheimer's disease.
Monounsaturated cooking oils (olive, flaxseed, or canola)	Does not increase LDL cholesterol or decrease HDL cholesterol (unlike high intake of saturated fat or refined carbohydrate). "Metabolically neutral" calorie source for people with insulin resistance. Particularly effective when substituted for high-glycemic load carbohydrates.
Fresh fruit and vegetables (5-10 servings per day); use wide variety	High concentrations of vitamins, minerals, fiber, and phytochemicals[3] help prevent heart disease, stroke, and many types of cancer (colon, stomach, prostate). Minimize high-glycemic load fruit (e.g., bananas) and potatoes.
Vegetable protein from nuts and beans 1-2 times per week	Lowers LDL cholesterol; improves digestion; may reduce CHD and certain cancers. Nuts are an excellent source of protein, monounsaturated fat, fiber, and minerals. Beans contain high-quality protein, fiber, potassium, and folic acid.[4]

Table 5.4. Basic Components of a Mediterranean Diet

Component	Benefits
Limit saturated fats to < 10-20 grams per day	Saturated fats increase LDL cholesterol, which promotes atherosclerosis and increases the risk for CHD and stroke. Saturated fats are also linked to certain cancers.
Avoid trans fats	Trans fats are manufactured from vegetable oils and are used to enhance the taste and extend the shelf-life of fast foods, French fries, packaged snacks, commercial baked goods, and most margarines. Trans fats may be more atherogenic than saturated fats. Effective January 2006, food manufacturers are required to list trans fats on food labels. Instruct patients to avoid foods with trans fats.
Increase dietary fiber to 20-30 grams per day	Lowers LDL cholesterol; improves insulin resistance; reduces the risk for heart disease and diabetes; protects against colon cancer, and possibly breast cancer, irritable bowel syndrome, diverticulitis and hemorrhoids; prevents constipation.
At least one source of high-quality protein with every meal	Produces satiety that lasts longer than high carbohydrate meals (reduces hunger and cravings); maintains muscle mass and bone strength. Lack of protein increases the risk for breast cancer, diabetes, and osteoporosis.

Adapted from *The Omega Diet*, by A. Simopoulos, MD

1. The typical American diet consists of an unhealthy ratio (> 15:1) of omega-6:omega-3 essential fatty acids, favoring excessive production of proinflammatory, prothrombotic, and vasoconstrictive mediators of the arachidonic acid cascade (e.g., leukotrienes, thromboxane). Increasing consumption of omega-3 essential fatty acids helps regulate inflammation, thrombogenicity, arrhythmogenicity, and vascular tone.

2. Omega-3 fatty acid supplements may be considered for patients with documented CHD, especially if risk factors for sudden death are present (LV dysfunction, LVH, ventricular dysrhythmias).

3. Phytochemicals are naturally occurring chemicals found in plants—many of them plant pigments—that act as free radical scavengers and protease inhibitors, among other functions. Examples include lycopene, beta-carotene, indoles, thiocyanates, lutein, resveratrol, ellagic acid, genistein, and allium.

4. Folic acid lowers levels of homocysteine, a by-product of methionine metabolism associated with atherosclerosis.

Table 5.5. How to Incorporate a Mediterranean Diet into Daily Living

Step	Choose	Go Easy On	Avoid
Eat omega-3–rich food 1-2 times per week	Salmon, trout, herring, water-packed tuna, sardines, mackerel, flaxseed, spinach, purslane, fish oil supplements	Raw shellfish (due to danger of infection risk, including hepatitis A and B)	Deep-fried fish, fish sticks, fish from seriously contaminated water
Switch vegetable oils	Extra virgin cold pressed olive oil or canola oil (check the label), flaxseed oil, mayonnaise made from olive oil or canola oil	High-oleic safflower, sunflower, or soybean oil	Corn oil, safflower oil, sunflower oil, palm oil, peanut oil, other oils, mayonnaise not made from olive oil or canola oil
Load up on fresh fruit and vegetables	Fresh fruit: 3-5 daily. Fresh vegetables: 4-6 daily. Use a wide variety	Fruit juice (no more than 1-2 cups/d), dried fruit, canned fruit, bananas, potatoes	Vegetables or fruit prepared in heavy cream sauces or butter
Add nuts and beans 1-2 times per week	Soybeans, kidney beans, lentils, navy beans, split peas, other beans, nuts of all kinds (especially almonds, Brazil nuts, pecans, walnuts, other tree nuts)	Heavily salted nuts	Stale or rancid nuts
Limit saturated fats to 10-20 grams per day; eat at least one source of high-quality protein with every meal	Fish, lean fresh meat with fat trimmed off, chicken and turkey without skin, nonfat or lowfat dairy products (skim milk, yogurt, low-fat cottage cheese), dark chocolate, egg whites or egg substitute, omega-3–enriched eggs	Processed lowfat meats (bologna, salami, other luncheon meats), 2% milk, "lite" cream cheese, part-skim mozzarella cheese, milk chocolate, egg yolks (3-4 per week)	Prime-grade fatty cuts of meat, goose, duck, organ meats (liver, kidneys), sausages, bacon, full-fat processed meats, hot dogs, whole milk, cream, full-fat cheeses, cream cheese, sour cream, ice cream

Table 5.5. How to Incorporate a Mediterranean Diet into Daily Living

Step	Choose	Go Easy On	Avoid
Avoid trans fats	Stanol-enriched margarine (Benecol, Take Control), natural peanut butter, almond butter	Commercial peanut butter, water crackers and other crackers that contain no fat, bagels	Fast food, French fries and other deep-fried food, chips and other packaged snacks, most commercial baked goods, most margarines
Add more fiber; aim for 20-30 grams per day	Whole-grain breads and cereals, oats, brown rice, whole grain pasta, potatoes with skin (baked, boiled, steamed), whole-grain bagels	Pasta, white rice, mashed instant potatoes, plain bagels, dinner rolls, egg noodles	Sweetened cereals, white bread, crackers, table sugar, honey, syrup, candy, all highly processed foods, especially those made with white flour and sugar
Drink at least 64 ounces of water per day	Drink 8 glasses of pure, nonchlorinated water per day. Additional drinks: skim milk (up to 4 glasses); pure fruit juice (up to 2 glasses); tea, especially green tea (up to 4 cups); a smoothie made with plain nonfat yogurt and fresh fruit	Coffee (regular or decaf), 1% or 2% milk, artificially sweetened fruit juice (the tip-off is "corn syrup" in the label), sports drinks, soft drinks, alcohol (no more than 1 drink daily for women, 2 drinks daily for men)	Sugared soft drinks, milkshakes, excess alcohol

Chapter 6

Other Therapeutic Lifestyle Changes

Physical Activity

A. **Overview.** Physical inactivity increases the risk for heart disease and stroke
   as much as cigarette smoking, yet more than 70% of adults get little or no
   exercise. All patients should be encouraged to obtain 30-45 minutes of
   aerobic activity on most days of the week. Observational studies suggest that
   regular exercise that increases heart rate to 60-80% of maximal peak heart
   rate for 30 minutes on all or most days of the week may reduce the risk for
   MI and stroke by 50% and the risk for death post-MI by 25%. It also
   improves insulin resistance and type 2 diabetes (lowers HbA_{1c} by 10-20%);
   raises HDL cholesterol levels by up to 30%; prevents/improves
   hypertension, diabetes, obesity, anxiety, and depression; helps smokers quit;
   and improves functional capacity in patients with congestive heart failure
   or claudication from peripheral artery disease. Noncardiac benefits include
   a lower risk for cancer (colon, prostate, breast) and salutary effects on
   osteoporosis, arthritis, constipation, mood, insomnia, and postmenopausal
   symptoms.

B. **Amount of Exercise.** To promote health, psychological well-being, and
   healthy body weight, the recent USDA recommendations for the general
   population include engaging in at least 30 minutes of moderate-intensity
   physical activity most days of the week and reducing sedentary activities
   (U.S. Department of Health and Human Services and U.S. Department of
   Agriculture. *Dietary Guidelines for Americans.* 6th ed. Washington, DC:
   U.S. Government Printing Office, 2005). Traditionally, exercise programs
   have focused exclusively on aerobic activities such as walking, running,
   cycling, and swimming. Recent data suggest that a strength (weight) training
   program is an important supplement to aerobic exercise, increasing muscle
   mass (which increases metabolic rate), improving insulin sensitivity, and
   helping maintain bone and muscular strength to prevent injuries and
   disability. Importantly, recent studies indicate that physical activity does

not need to be performed in a traditional structured exercise program to provide health benefits, and that a lifestyle-based exercise program incorporating physical activity into daily living is effective at improving risk factors, weight, and long-term cardiovascular prognosis (JAMA 1999;281:327-34). This can be accomplished by encouraging patients to use the stairs, walking whenever possible, gardening, playing actively with children, etc. Examples of moderate physical activity from the Surgeon General's Report on Physical Activity and Health (JAMA 1996;276:522) include:

- Washing and waxing a car, or washing windows or floors for 45 minutes
- Gardening, dancing fast (social), or raking for 30 minutes
- Walking 1¾ miles in 35 minutes (20 min/mile)
- Pushing a stroller 1½ miles or bicycling 5 miles in 30 minutes
- Stairwalking, shoveling snow, or jumping rope for 15 minutes

Exercise should not be exhausting, but it does need to be invigorating and should increase heart rate. Individuals are exercising at the right level of intensity if they can talk without gasping for breath but do not have enough breath to sing (e.g., brisk walking at a pace of 3-4 miles per hour, like walking to catch a bus). For motivated patients able and willing to take their pulse, a reasonable goal is to exercise at 60-80% of maximal heart rate (220 – age [yrs]). Additionally, exercise does not need to be done all at one time during the day to receive health benefits. The important factor is to accumulate at least 30 minutes of moderate physical activity all or most days of the week (which can be split in three 10-minute blocks). Health benefits may plateau at 3500 kcal per week, the equivalent of moderately intense jogging or bicycling for 1 hour per day.

C. Stress Testing. Patients with cardiovascular or respiratory disease and sedentary patients with multiple CHD risk factors interested in participating in a vigorous exercise program should be considered for stress testing.

Weight Control

A. Overview. An estimated 1.1 billion adults worldwide are overweight or obese (Lancet 2005;366:1197-209), including 65% of U.S. adults (130 million) (JAMA 2002;288:1723-7), a number that has tripled over the last 2 decades. Overweight and obesity increase the risk for all-cause mortality, and they increase morbidity from hypertension, dyslipidemia, type 2 diabetes, CHD, stroke, gallbladder disease, osteoarthritis, sleep apnea, respiratory problems, and cancer (endometrial, breast, prostate, colon). In 2000, poor diet and physical inactivity (major lifestyle factors leading to obesity) were the underlying cause for 365,000 deaths (15.2%) in the US, compared to 435,000 deaths (18.1%) due to smoking (JAMA 2004;291:1238-45; correction JAMA 2005;293:298). Obesity has been shown to reduce life expectancy by 7 years at the age of 40 (An Intern Med 2003;138:24-32), and overweight adults are more likely to have overweight children. Weight control improves blood pressure, triglycerides, LDL and HDL cholesterol, blood glucose, and hemoglobin A_{1c} levels in type 2 diabetics. The following information summarizes key recommendations from the NHLBI Clinical Guidelines for the Identification, Evaluation, and Treatment of Overweight and Obesity in Adults (Obesity Res 1998;6:51S-209S; Executive Summary, Arch Intern Med 1998;158:1855-67). The American Heart Association has also issued scientific statements on obesity and its effect on cardiovascular disease (Circulation 2004;110:2952-67; Circulation 2006;113:898-918).

B. **Classification of Obesity.** All patients should be stratified by body mass index (BMI) to assess overweight/obesity and by waist circumference to assess abdominal fat content, which identifies increased risk for CHD independent of BMI and is a criterion for diagnosis of the metabolic syndrome (Table 6.1).

C. **Evaluation of Obesity.** Patient medications should be reviewed to see if adjustments or substitutions can be made for drugs associated with weight gain, including antidepressants, glucocorticoids, phenothiazines, lithium, cyproheptadine, sulfonylureas, and insulin. It is also important to examine the patient for features suggestive of Cushing's syndrome (truncal obesity, moon facies, ecchymosis, muscle atrophy, edema, striae, acne, hirsutism, osteoporosis, glucose intolerance, hypokalemia) or hypothyroidism (weakness, fatigue, cold intolerance, constipation, dry skin, bradycardia, hyporeflexia). Patients with suspected sleep apnea (cessation of breathing during sleep, snoring, restless sleep, excessive daytime sleepiness ± headaches, memory impairment) should be referred to a specialist.

Table 6.1. Classification of Overweight and Obesity

Category	BMI*	Waist Circumference†	Risk for Type 2 Diabetes, Hypertension, CHD
Underweight	< 18.5	N or ↑	N
Normal	18.5 - 24.9	N or ↑	N or ↑
Overweight	25.0 - 29.9	N ↑	Increased High
Obesity, class I	30.0 - 34.9	N ↑	High Very high
II	35.0 - 39.9	N or ↑	Very high
III	≥ 40.0	N or ↑	Extremely high

BMI = body mass index, CHD = coronary heart disease, N = not elevated

* Body mass index = weight in kilograms divided by height in meters squared (kg/m^2). Estimated BMI using nonmetric measurements = (weight in pounds x 703) divided by height in inches squared

† Increased waist circumference: men > 102 cm (> 40 inches); women > 88 cm (> 35 inches). Increased waist circumference can be a marker for increased risk even in persons of normal weight

Adapted from: NHLBI Guidelines on Overweight and Obesity (Obesity Res 1998;6:51S-209S)

D. Treatment of Obesity. The treatment of overweight/obesity requires a combination of dietary restriction, increased physical activity, and behavior modification; patients requiring additional measures may benefit from drug therapy and weight loss surgery (refractory cases). Total caloric intake and energy expenditure (physical activity) should be adjusted to achieve and maintain a desirable body weight (BMI 21-25 kg/m^2) and waist circumference (<102 cm in men, <88 cm in women). A reasonable initial goal is to reduce body weight by 10% over 6 months, which typically requires calorie deficits of 300-500 kcal/d in patients with BMIs of 27-35 kg/m^2 (0.5-1 lb/week) and 500-1000 kcal/d (1-2 lb/week) in patients with BMIs ≥ 35 kg/m^2. Further weight loss can be considered once this goal is achieved. Calorie deficits are best accomplished through a combination of dietary restriction and increased physical activity.

1. **Dietary Restriction.** Calorie deficits of 500-1000 kcal/d usually require a diet providing 1000-1200 kcal/d for women and 1200-1500 kcal/d for men. Low-carbohydrate and other "fad" diets may facilitate early weight loss, but these diets are difficult to maintain, frequently unhealthy, and often result in diminished self-esteem as weight is inevitably regained. The best approach to diet is to eat smaller portions of a well-rounded (TLC or Mediterranean-style) diet (Chapter 5).

2. **Increased Physical Activity.** Increased physical activity is an essential component of an effective weight loss program, leading to calorie deficits and improvements in cardiovascular risk factors, mood, and self-esteem. Walking is an excellent option for obese patients, initially at 10 minutes per day 3 times weekly, and building to 30-45 minutes per day on most or all days of the week. Ordinary household tasks can also lead to substantial calorie deficits. Examples of calories burned in 1 hour for a 130-pound woman and a 180-pound man include cleaning windows (208/288), gardening (416/576), mowing the lawn (351/486), painting the house (273/378), washing the car (195/270), and dancing (208/288). A stress test should be considered prior to initiating an exercise program in individuals with known cardiovascular or pulmonary disease, and for sedentary males > 40 years or females > 50 years with 2 or more cardiovascular risk factors (hypertension, dyslipidemia, diabetes mellitus, smoking, family history).

3. **Behavior Therapy.** It is essential to communicate encouragement, support, and understanding in order to optimize compliance. Other useful behavior modification techniques include self-monitoring (food consumption and exercise), stress management (coping strategies, relaxation techniques, drug therapy), problem solving (coping with urges and cravings), contingency management (rewarding achieved goals), cognitive restructuring (changing unrealistic goals and improving self-image), and social support (positive reinforcement).

4. **Drug Therapy.** Pharmacotherapy can be a useful adjunct to dietary restriction, increased physical activity, and behavior modification, but is unlikely to be effective as monotherapy. Antiobesity drugs approved by the FDA include sibutramine (mixed neurotransmitter reuptake inhibitor) and orlistat (lipase inhibitor; inhibits dietary fat absorption by 30%). These drugs are especially useful for patients with BMI ≥ 30 kg/m^2 or ≥ 27 kg/m^2 in the presence of other risk factors (hypertension, dyslipidemia, type 2 diabetes, CHD, sleep apnea). Rimonabant, a

cannaboid receptor 1 (CB1) antagonist, has shown great promise as a treatment for obesity and smoking, the two top preventable causes of death in the US. In the Rimonabant in Obesity (RIO)-Lipids Study, 1036 overweight or obese subjects were randomized to rimonabant (20 mg or 5 mg) or placebo for 1 year. Compared to placebo, rimonabant 20 mg significantly improved several risk factors, including weight (–15 lb), waist circumference (–7.1 cm), HDL cholesterol (+19%), triglycerides (–13%), LDL particle size, and CRP (–0.9 mg/L); 33% of patients taking rimonabant 20 mg lost $\geq$ 10% of their body weight (N Engl J Med 2005;353:2121-34). Similar results were obtained in RIO-Europe, in which 1508 overweight or obese subjects were also randomized to rimonabant 20 mg, rimonabant 5 mg, or placebo; 27% of subjects randomized to rimonabant 20 mg lost $\geq$ 10% of their body weight at 1 year compared to 7.3% of the placebo group. Rimonabant 20 mg also significantly improved waist circumference, HDL cholesterol, triglycerides, non-HDL cholesterol, insulin resistance, and the prevalence of the metabolic syndrome (Lancet 2005;365:1389-97). In RIO-North America, 3040 patients were randomized to rimonabant 20 mg, rimonabant 5 mg, or placebo. Among patients who completed the study, rimonabant was shown to reduce body weight and weight circumference at 1 year, and reduction in waist circumference was maintained at 2 years. In addition, in patients receiving rimonabant 20 mg/d, HDL cholesterol was increased by 24.5%, triglycerides were reduced by 10%, and prevalence of the metabolic syndrome was reduced from 34.8% to 22.5% at 2 years (American Heart Association Scientific Sessions 2004, New Orleans, LA). In RIO-Diabetes, 1047 obese or overweight patients with type 2 diabetes were randomized to the same 3 treatments. For the primary endpoint, body weight decreased by 12 lb from baseline with rimonabant 20 mg; significant improvements were also observed for waist circumference (–5.2 cm), hemoglobin A_{1C} (–0.6%), HDL cholesterol (+15%), and triglycerides (–9%). The hemoglobin A_{1C} target of < 7% recommended by the American Diabetes Association was achieved at 1 year by 53% of patients on rimonabant 20 mg, compared with 27% of patients on placebo (American Diabetes Association Scientific Sessions 2005, San Diego, CA). Favorable results were also obtained for rimonabant as drug therapy for smoking cessation (p. 69). Rimonabant also improved all seven dimensions of a 31-item quality-of-life questionnaire, including physical function, self-esteem, sexual life, public distress, work, sleep, and food cravings (European Society of Cardiology Congress 2004, Munich, Germany). Potential adverse effects of rimonabant include depression.

5. **Weight Loss Surgery.** Gastrointestinal surgery (gastric restriction or bypass) should be reserved for motivated patients with extreme obesity (BMI $\geq$ 40 kg/m^2 or $\geq$ 35 kg/m^2 with comorbid conditions) despite nonsurgical intervention. Lifelong medical monitoring and nutritional supplementation with minerals and vitamins lost through malabsorption are required.

Smoking Cessation

A. **Overview.** Tobacco use is one of the most important risk factors for CHD and is the most preventable cause of death in the U.S. Each year, an estimated 440,000 deaths are attributable to tobacco use (MMWR 2002;51:300-3), more than alcohol abuse, automobile accidents, AIDS, homicide, suicide, heroin, and cocaine combined. Compared to age-matched nonsmokers, persons who smoke 1 pack of cigarettes per day are 14 times more likely to die from cancer of the lung, throat, or mouth; 4 times more likely to die from cancer of the esophagus; twice as likely to suffer an MI or stroke; and twice as likely to die from heart disease or cancer of the bladder. At any age, the risk for death is doubled in smokers compared with nonsmoking age-matched controls. Fifty-year follow-up data on the 34,439 male subjects enrolled into a prospective study of British doctors found that smokers died approximately 10 years before nonsmokers, and that smokers were almost 3 times as likely to die in middle age (35-69 years) as nonsmokers (43% vs. 15%). Compared to persistent smoking, smoking cessation at ages 30, 40, 50, and 60 added 10, 9, 6, and 3 years of life expectancy, respectively (BMJ 2004;328:1519-28). Despite these statistics, few physicians routinely ask patients about cigarette smoking or offer counseling about smoking cessation. For physicians, there is virtually nothing more effective at improving a patient's long-term prognosis than convincing and helping him or her to stop smoking. If a physician discusses this topic even briefly with the smoker and makes a strong statement about the medical necessity of discontinuing this habit, a person's chances of permanent cessation of smoking is increased. The use of bupropion hydrochloride (Zyban) and nicotine replacement therapy (NRT) also increase the chances of successful smoking cessation. Varenicline (Champix), a new oral nicotine-receptor blocker (also a partial agonist), was shown in one study to be significantly more effective at helping maintain abstinence compared to bupropion (presented at AHA meeting, November, 2005, Dallas, TX). As described in the section on weight control, rimonabant, a cannaboid receptor 1 (CB1) antagonist, has shown great promise as treatment for overweight/obesity (p. 61) as well as for smoking. In the Studies with Rimonabant and Tobacco Use (STRATUS)-US, 787 smokers who had failed to quit on an average of 4 prior occasions were randomized to receive rimonabant 20 mg, rimonabant 5 mg, or placebo x 10 weeks. Subjects taking rimonabant were nearly twice as likely to quit smoking (28% vs. 16%, $p = 0.004$), and they demonstrated a 77% reduction in postcessation weight gain compared with the placebo group (American College of Cardiology Scientific Session 2004, New Orleans, LA). However, rimonabant is not as yet approved for smoking cessation.

B. **Guidelines.** The U.S. Public Health Service issued a clinical practice guideline for treating tobacco use and dependence (JAMA 2000;283:3244-54), recognizing that more than 70% of smokers visit a health care setting each year and that most smokers want to quit completely. The report concluded that *every* patient should be asked about cigarette smoking at *every* visit, and that all smokers should be strongly encouraged to stop and should be offered NRT and/or bupropion hydrochloride. The following strategies were recommended to help patients who are willing to quit smoking:

- **Step 1: Systematically identify all tobacco users at every visit.** Place tobacco-use status stickers on all patient charts.

- **Step 2: Strongly urge all tobacco users to quit.**   Advice should be clear, strong, and personalized: "I think it is important for you to quit smoking now, and I can help you." "As your clinician, I need you to know that quitting smoking is the most important thing you can do to protect your health now and in the future. The clinic staff and I will help you." Tie tobacco use to the patient's current health/illness, its social and economic costs, and its impact on children and others in the household.

- **Step 3: Determine willingness to make a quit attempt.** If the patient is willing to make a quit attempt, assist the patient in quitting or refer the patient to a quit-smoking program. If the patient is unwilling to make a quit attempt, provide a motivational intervention.

- **Step 4: Aid the patient in quitting** (Tables 6.2, 6.3).

- **Step 5: Schedule follow-up contact.** Follow-up contact should occur soon after the quit date, preferably during the first week. A second follow-up contact is recommended within the first month. Schedule further follow-up contacts as indicated. Congratulate success during follow-up contact. If tobacco use has occurred, review the circumstances and elicit a recommitment to total abstinence. Remind the patient that a lapse can be used as a learning experience. Identify problems already encountered and anticipate challenges in the immediate future. Assess pharmacotherapy use and problems, and consider use or referral to more intensive treatment.

For patients who continue to smoke, it is important to recognize interactions between cardiovascular drug therapy and cigarette smoking. These include increased metabolism/elimination of anticoagulants and beta-blockers, possibly requiring higher doses, and decreased diuretic effect due to increased secretion of vasopressin.

Table 6.2. Strategies to Assist Patients Willing to Quit Smoking

Step	Strategies for Implementation
Help the patient with a quit plan	• Set a quit date, ideally within 2 weeks. • Tell family, friends, and coworkers about quitting; request understanding and support. • Anticipate withdrawal symptoms and discuss ways to resist urges and cravings (clean the house; take a 5-minute walk; do stretching exercises; put a toothpick, cinnamon gum, or lemon drop in your mouth; take several slow deep breaths; brush teeth; call a nonsmoking friend and talk). • Remove tobacco products from your environment. Throw out ashtrays. Clean clothes, car, carpets. • Learn as much about how to quit smoking as possible. Useful sources for reading materials include: – American Heart Association, 7272 Greenville Avenue, Dallas, TX 75231, (800) 242-8721; www.americanheart.org – American Cancer Society, 1599 Clifton Road, NE, Atlanta, GA 30329, (800) 227-2345; www.cancer.org – American Lung Association, 1740 Broadway, 14th floor, New York, NY 10019, (800) 586-4872; www.lungusa.org – National Cancer Institute, Bethesda, MD 20894, (202) 4-CANCER (422-6237); www.nci.nih.gov – *For pregnant women:* American College of Obstetricians and Gynecologists, 409 12th Street, SW, Washington, DC 20024, (202) 638-5577; www.acog.org
Provide practical counseling	• Total abstinence is essential. "Not even a single puff after the quit date." • Identify what helped and hurt in previous quit attempts. • Discuss challenges/triggers and how to overcome them. • Since alcohol can cause relapse, the patient should consider limiting/abstaining from alcohol while quitting. • Patients should encourage housemates to quit with them or not to smoke in their presence. • Provide a supportive clinical environment while encouraging the patient during the quit attempt: "My office staff and I are available to assist you."

Table 6.2. Strategies to Assist Patients Willing to Quit Smoking

Step	Strategies for Implementation
Recommend approved drug therapy	• Recommend the use of first-line drug therapy (Table 6.4) to all smokers trying to quit, except in special circumstances (e.g., medical contraindications, those smoking fewer than 10 cigarettes/day, pregnant/breastfeeding women, adolescent smokers). If drug therapy is used with lighter smokers (10-15 cigarettes/day), consider reducing the dose of NRT; no dosage adjustment is necessary for sustained-release bupropion hydrochloride.
	• Some studies suggest that bupropion may be more effective than NRT for achieving permanent cessation of tobacco use, and that some synergism between the two approaches may exist. There are insufficient data to rank-order these medications, so initial therapy must be guided by factors such as clinician familiarity with the medications, contraindications for selected patients, patient preference, previous patient experience with a specific therapy (positive or negative), and patient characteristics (e.g., history of depression, concerns about weight gain). Sustained-release bupropion hydrochloride and NRT, in particular nicotine gum, have been shown to delay but not prevent weight gain. Sustained-release bupropion hydrochloride and nortriptyline hydrochloride are particularly well suited for patients with a history of depression.
	• There is evidence that combining the nicotine patch with either nicotine gum or nicotine nasal spray increases long-term abstinence rates over those produced by a single form of NRT, based on a meta-analysis.
	• The nicotine patch in particular is safe in patients with cardiovascular disease. However, the safety of NRT products has not been established for the immediate post-MI period or in patients with severe or unstable angina.
	• Long-term therapy may be helpful for smokers who report persistent withdrawal symptoms. A minority of individuals who successfully quit smoking use NRT medications (gum, nasal spray, inhaler) long term. The long-term use of these medications does not present a known health risk, and the FDA has approved the use of sustained-release bupropion hydrochloride for long-term maintenance.
	• Clonidine and nortriptyline (Table 6.4) may be considered when first-line medications are contraindicated or not helpful.

Adapted from: The U.S. Public Health Service Clinical Practice Guidelines for Treating Tobacco Use and Dependence (JAMA 2000;283:3244-54)

Table 6.3. Drug Therapy for Smoking Cessation*

Therapy	Precautions	Adverse Effects	Dosage and Duration
First-line *Bupropion HCl (Zyban)†*	Contraindicated if history of seizures, eating disorder, MAO inhibitor within 14 days	Insomnia, dry mouth, seizures	150 mg every morning for 3 days, then 150 mg twice daily. Begin treatment 1-2 weeks prior to quit date. Treat for 7-12 weeks. Maintenance therapy may be needed for up to 6 months
Nicotine gum (Nicorette)	Concurrent cigarette smoking is contraindicated due to the risk for nicotine overdose	Mouth soreness, dyspepsia	For < 25 cigarettes/d: 2-mg gum. For ≥ 25 cigarettes/d: 4-mg gum. Weeks 1-6: 1 piece every 1-2 hours (at least 9 pieces/d); weeks 7-9: 1 piece every 2-4 hours; weeks 10-12: 1 piece every 4-8 hours
Nicotine inhaler (Nicotrol inhaler)		Irritation of mouth and throat, coughing, rhinitis	6-16 cartridges/d x 12 weeks followed by a 6- to12-week weaning period, if needed. Best effect achieved through continuous puffing (20 minutes)
Nicotine nasal spray (Nicotrol NS)		Nasal irritation	8-40 doses/d for 3 months. Each dose consists of 2 sprays (1 per nostril) and delivers 1 mg of nicotine to the nasal mucosa
Nicotine patch (Nicoderm CQ; Nicotrol)		Local skin reaction, insomnia	*Nicoderm CQ:* 21 mg/24 h (6 weeks), then 14 mg/24 h (2 weeks), then 7 mg/24 h (2 weeks). Light smokers (≤ 10 cigarettes/d) should start with 14-mg dose. *Nicotrol patch:* 15 mg/24 h (6 weeks)
Second-line *Clonidine*	Rebound hypertension	Dry mouth, drowsiness, dizziness, sedation	0.15-0.75 mg/d for 3-10 weeks
Nortriptyline	Risk for arrhythmias	Sedation, dry mouth	75-100 mg/d for 12 weeks

* See package inserts for additional information. First-line therapies have been approved for smoking cessation by the FDA; second-line therapies have not. Adapted from: The U.S. Public Health Service Clinical Practice Guidelines for Treating Tobacco Use and Dependence (JAMA 2000;283:3224-54).

† Varenicline (Champix), a new oral nicotine-receptor blocker (also a partial agonist), was shown in one study to be significantly more effective at helping maintain abstinence compared to bupropion (AHA meeting, November, 2005, Dallas, TX).

Chapter 7

Overview of Drug Therapy for Dyslipidemia

Drug therapy plays a critical role in the management of dyslipidemia—improving lipid profile, slowing the progression of atherosclerosis, stabilizing rupture-prone plaques, reducing the risk for arterial thrombosis, and improving cardiovascular prognosis. For patients who require drug therapy, the drug should be added to, not substituted for, diet therapy and other lifestyle modification. Table 7.1 lists effective lipid-modifying drug therapy, Chapter 8 provides clinical information about the various drug classes used for dyslipidemia, and Chapter 12 describes dosing and administration guidelines for individual drugs.

Table 7.1. Effective Lipid-Modifying Drug Therapy

Drug (usual starting dose/max)	Effect on Lipids	Comments
HMG-CoA Reductase Inhibitors (Statins)		
Atorvastatin (10/80 mg/d) Fluvastatin (40/80 mg/d) Lovastatin (20/80 mg/d) Pravastatin (20/80 mg/d) Rosuvastatin (5/40 mg/d) Simvastatin (20/80 mg/d)	LDL: ↓ 18-55% HDL: ↑ 5-15% TG: ↓ 7-30%	*Major use:* Overwhelmingly the drug class of choice for elevated LDL levels. Highly effective for lowering LDL and preventing cardiovascular and cerebrovascular events. *Absolute CI:* active or chronic liver disease, pregnancy, lactation. *Relative CI:* concomitant use of cyclosporine, macrolide antibiotics, various antifungal drugs, cytochrome P-450 inhibitors; previous intolerance to statins due to myalgias, elevated liver transaminases, other side effects. *Adverse effects:* myopathy, ↑ liver transaminases. Fibrates and nicotinic acid should be used with caution in combination with statins.

Table 7.1. Effective Lipid-Modifying Drug Therapy

Drug (usual starting dose/max)	Effect on Lipids	Comments
Cholesterol Absorption Inhibitor		
Ezetimibe (10 mg/d)	LDL: ↓ 18-20% HDL: ↑ 1-5% TG: ↓ 5-11%	*Major use:* Safe and effective adjunct to statins when further LDL lowering is required. Not recommended in moderate or severe hepatic insufficiency. Effectiveness reduced when given within 2-4 hours of bile acid sequestrant. *CI:* combination with statin in patients with active liver disease or unexplained persistent transaminase elevations. *Adverse effects:* GI complaints.
Nicotinic Acid (Niacin)		
Immediate-release form (50 mg/4.5 gm/d) Sustained-release form (500 mg/2 gm/d) Extended-release form (500 mg/2 gm/d)	LDL: ↓ 5-25% HDL: ↑ 15-35% TG: ↓ 20-50%	*Major use:* Useful in nearly all dyslipidemias. Uniquely effective in atherogenic dyslipidemia. Also useful for elevated Lp(a) levels and as adjunctive therapy for mixed dyslipidemia. *Absolute CI:* chronic liver disease, significant or unexplained hepatic dysfunction, severe gout, active peptic ulcer disease, arterial bleeding. *Relative CI:* hyperuricemia, high doses (> 3 gm/d) in type 2 diabetes. Caution in active liver or peptic ulcer disease, hyperuricemia, gout, and in patients who consume substantial quantities of alcohol or have past history of liver disease. *Adverse effects:* flushing, hyperglycemia, hyperuricemia/gout, upper GI distress, hepatotoxicity (especially sustained-release form).

Table 7.1. Effective Lipid-Modifying Drug Therapy (cont'd)

Drug (usual dose)	Effect on Lipids	Comments
Bile Acid Sequestrants		
Colesevelam (3.8/4.4 gm/d) Cholestyramine ([4-16]/24 gm/d) Colestipol ([5-20]/30 gm/d)	LDL: ↓ 15-30% HDL: ↑ 3-5% TG: usually not affected; may ↑	*Major use:* Moderate hypercholesterolemia, younger patients with elevated LDL cholesterol, and women with elevated LDL cholesterol who are considering pregnancy (sequestrants are not absorbed out of the GI tract and lack systemic toxicity). Also useful as adjunctive therapy with statins. *Absolute CI:* familial dysbetalipoproteinemia, triglyceride > 400 mg/dL. *Relative CI:* triglyceride > 200 mg/dL. *Adverse effects:* GI complaints common, decreased absorption of several drugs.
Fibric Acid Derivatives (Fibrates)		
Gemfibrozil (600 mg bid) Fenofibrate (160 mg/d) Clofibrate (1000 mg bid)	LDL: ↓ 5-20% (may ↑ LDL with ↑ baseline TG) HDL: ↑ 10-35% TG: ↓ 20-50%	*Major uses:* Hypertriglyceridemia, atherogenic dyslipidemia (especially in type 2 diabetes). *Absolute CI:* severe hepatic or renal dysfunction, primary biliary cirrhosis, gallbladder disease. *Relative CI:* combined therapy with statins (occasional occurrence of severe myopathy or rhabdomyolysis; less with fenofibrate). Use with caution when combining with coumarin anticoagulants or cyclosporine. *Adverse effects:* dyspepsia, upper GI complaints, cholesterol gallstones, myopathy.

Table 7.1. Effective Lipid-Modifying Drug Therapy (cont'd)

Drug (usual dose)	Effect on Lipids	Comments
Omega-3 Fatty Acids (Fish Oil)		
Omega-3 acid ethyl esters (4 gm/d)	TG: ↓ 45% non-HDL-C: ↓ 14% LDL: ↑ 44% HDL: ↑ 9%	*Major use:* Hypertriglyceridemia (TG ≥500 mg/dL). *CI:* Use with caution in patients with known hypersensitivity or allergy to fish, and in women who are pregnant or breastfeeding. *Adverse effects:* eructation, dyspepsia, taste perversion.

↑ = increases, ↓ = decreases, CI = contraindication, HDL = HDL cholesterol, LDL = LDL cholesterol, Lp(a) = lipoprotein(a), TG = triglyceride

Chapter 8

Drug Classes Used To Treat Dyslipidemia

Statins

A. **Introduction**. 3-hydroxy-3-methylglutaryl coenzyme A (HMG-CoA) reductase inhibitors, more commonly known as "statins," play an extremely important role in the prevention and treatment of atherosclerotic vascular disease. Lovastatin was the first drug of this class to be approved and became available in 1987. Since then pravastatin, simvastatin, fluvastatin, atorvastatin, and rosuvastatin have been added to the list of available statins marketed in the U.S. Cerivastatin was withdrawn by the manufacturer due to reports of fatal rhabdomyolysis.

B. **Mechanism of Action.** Statins competitively inhibit HMG-CoA reductase, blocking the conversion of HMG-CoA to mevalonate, an early critical step in hepatic cholesterol biosynthesis. By decreasing intracellular cholesterol production in the liver, statins increase hepatic LDL receptor activity and facilitate LDL clearance from the circulation. Putative mechanisms by which statins may promote plaque stability include increasing endothelial nitric oxide synthesis, decreasing extracellular and macrophage lipid deposits, decreasing neointimal inflammation, maintaining fibrous cap integrity (by reducing metalloproteinase-9 secretion into the matrix by macrophages), and restoring antithrombotic and vasodilatory properties to dysfunctional endothelium.

C. **Effects on Lipids.** Statins lower LDL cholesterol by 18-55%, raise HDL cholesterol by 5-15%, and lower triglycerides by 7-30% (Table 7.1, p. 74).

D. **Clinical Trials (Chapter 11).** Numerous large-scale, randomized trials have shown that compared to placebo, statins reduce nonfatal MI or coronary death by 24-37%, stroke by 20-30%, revascularization procedures by 20-40%, and all-cause mortality by 22-30%. Benefits are greatest for higher-risk populations (e.g., documented CHD plus high baseline LDL cholesterol), but significant reductions in cardiovascular events have also been demonstrated in primary prevention patients with "normal" or only mildly elevated LDL cholesterol levels. Dramatic results from recent, large-scale, randomized trials prompted updates to ATP III and AHA/ACC guidelines recommending expanded and more intensive use of statin therapy (Circulation 2004;110:227-239, Circulation 2006;113:2363-72) (Chapters 1-4). Statins have also been shown to reduce progression of atherosclerotic lesions in multiple angiographic trials and to induce regression if very low levels of LDL cholesterol are achieved with concomitant increases in HDL cholesterol.

E. Administration. Peak activity of HMG-CoA reductase occurs around midnight, so lipid-lowering efficacy is slightly better when the drugs are administered in the evening. (Because of atorvastatin's and rosuvastatin's long half-lives, lipid reductions with these agents are independent of administration time.) Since maximal lipid effects are apparent by 2-4 weeks, a lipid profile should be obtained after 4-6 weeks of statin therapy; if LDL cholesterol levels remain elevated, the dose should be adjusted and a repeat profile should be obtained 4-6 weeks later (Figure 3.2, p. 29).

F. Adverse Effects and Monitoring. Statins are very well tolerated, with infrequent and reversible adverse events. In large placebo-controlled studies, the frequency of adverse effects was similar to placebo (2-3%). Albeit rare, rhabdomyolysis, acute renal failure, and death have been reported with statins, usually in association with concomitant use of fibrates, antifungal agents (azole derivatives), cyclosporine, or macrolide antibiotics (e.g., erythromycin). Table 8.1 lists factors associated with increased risk for statin-associated myopathy. Table 8.2 provides administration guidelines to minimize the risk for myopathy when statins and fibrates are used in combination. The ACC, AHA, and NHLBI have issued a joint clinical advisory on the use and safety of statins, emphasizing the favorable benefit/risk ratio for most patients while outlining appropriate precautions to reduce adverse events (J Am Coll Cardiol 2002;40:567-72). A meta-analysis of 14 statin trials, including data on a total of more than 90,000 patients, indicated that each ~ 40-mg/dL reduction in LDL cholesterol with statin therapy was associated with reductions of 12% in all-cause mortality, 19% in coronary mortality, 23% in MI or coronary death, 24% in coronary revascularization, 17% in fatal or nonfatal stroke, and 21% for any major vascular event, with no significant increase in rhabdomyolysis, nonvascular mortality, or cancer (Lancet 2005;366:1267-78).

1. **Elevated Liver Transaminases.** Dose-dependent elevations in hepatic transaminases occur in 0.5-2.0% of persons receiving statins. It is unclear whether this represents true hepatotoxicity and whether statins cause liver failure. Nevertheless, alanine aminotransferase (ALT) and aspartate aminotransferase (AST) levels should be obtained initially, at 12 weeks of therapy, and annually thereafter. Patients with hepatic disease or excessive alcohol use and those receiving hepatotoxic medical therapy should have liver enzymes monitored more frequently (every 3-4 months or with any unusual symptoms). Minor elevations in transaminase levels (< 3 times upper limit of normal [ULN]) should be rechecked in 2-6 weeks. These elevations are usually transient and do not warrant discontinuation of therapy. If transaminase levels are > 3 times ULN, the test should be repeated; if they remain > 3 times ULN, statin therapy should be discontinued and transaminase levels rechecked at 14 days, at which time they should be normal or near-normal. Once levels have normalized, statin therapy can usually be reinitiated at a reduced dosage or with a different statin without incident.

2. **Muscle Toxicity.** Muscle toxicity is even less common than hepatotoxicity in patients receiving statin therapy. However, rare cases of rhabdomyolysis, myoglobinuria, and acute renal failure or death have occurred. In these cases, elevations in creatine kinase (CK), the best indicator of statin-associated myopathy, are typically 10-40 times normal. This catastrophic complication is usually associated with concomitant use of fibrates, antifungal agents (azole derivatives), cyclosporine, or macrolide antibiotics (e.g., erythromycin). Patients at risk for serious muscle toxicity frequently have comorbidities at baseline, with immunosuppression, infection, long-standing diabetes, or renal failure; such patients should be closely monitored if a statin is started. High-dose statins and statin-fibrate combinations are best withheld during hospitalization for major surgery. Serious myopathy is frequently associated with muscle pain, tenderness, and weakness of the muscles; patients should be instructed to report these symptoms as well as brown urine (myoglobinuria) to their physician immediately. If myopathy is suspected, CK should be measured and if ≥ 10 times ULN, the statin should be immediately discontinued. Because CK elevations are noted in up to 30% of patients on placebo, routine measurement may lead to unwarranted interruptions of therapy and is not recommended in asymptomatic patients receiving statins. It is important that patients

receive appropriate information on the signs and symptoms of myopathy. However, it is also important to reassure patients that the incidence of statin-associated myopathy with the 6 approved statins is low, i.e., ≤ 1/1000 patients (0.1%). Factors associated with increased risk for statin-associated myopathy are shown in Table 8.1; administration guidelines to minimize the risk for muscle toxicity when statins and fibrates are used in combination are shown in Table 8.2; and management of statin-associated myopathy is described in Table 8.3. Although concern has been raised about potentially greater risk for muscle toxicity with more potent statins, careful review by the FDA concluded that risk was no greater with rosuvastatin than with the other available statins (www.fda.gov/cder/drug/infopage/rosuvastatin/crestor_CP.pdf).

3. **Others.** Headache, gastrointestinal (cramps, diarrhea, flatulence, constipation, dyspepsia), myalgias, arthralgias, rash, proteinuria, and pruritus may occur during statin therapy.

Table 8.1. Increased Risk States for Statin-Associated Myopathy

- Advanced age (especially > 80 years; women more than men)
- Small body frame and frailty
- Multisystem disease (e.g., chronic renal insufficiency, esp. due to diabetes)
- Perioperative periods
- Multiple medications or specific concomitant medications or consumption (check specific statin package insert for warnings): fibrates (esp. gemfibrozil, but other fibrates too), nicotinic acid (rarely), cyclosporine, azole antifungals, itraconazole and ketoconazole, macrolide antibiotics, erythromycin and clarithromycin, HIV protease inhibitors, nefazodone (antidepressant), verapamil, amiodarone, large quantities of grapefruit juice (usually > 1 quart/day), alcohol abuse (independently predisposes to myopathy)

From: ACC/AHA/NHLBI Clinical Advisory (J Am Coll Cardiol 2002;40:567-72).

Table 8.2. Administration Guidelines for Combination Therapy with Statins and Fibrates

DO:
- Document the need for combination therapy such as failure to respond to monotherapy in a high-risk patient
- Instruct patients to stop both drugs if they develop severe muscle soreness, pain, or weakness
- Instruct patients to stop the medication (at least one) if they become acutely ill, dehydrated, require antibiotics, or are admitted to the hospital for any cause
- Check baseline renal function, liver function, and creatine kinase
- In patients on full-dose fibrate, begin with a low dose of statin
- In patients on a moderate statin dose, begin with a low dose of fibrate (fenofibrate 54 mg/d, gemfibrozil 300 mg BID)

DO NOT:
- Do not use in patients with impaired liver function
- Do not use in patients with impaired renal function (creatinine ≥ 2.0 mg/dL)
- Do not use in patients receiving cyclosporine or tacrolimus
- Do not use in patients on chronic erythromycin or antifungal (azole) therapy
- Do not use in patients > 70 years of age (relative contraindication)
- Do not use high dose of statins (80 mg/d atorvastatin, simvastatin or lovastatin, or 40 mg/d rosuvastatin) in combination with fibrates. For gemfibrozil, limit doses of rosuvastatin to ≤ 10 mg/d and simvastatin to 10 mg/d (per package inserts)

Table 8.3. Monitoring and Management of Statin-Associated Myopathy

Presentation	Recommendation
Baseline	Evaluate muscle symptoms and CK prior to therapy; evaluate muscle symptoms at 6-12 weeks and at each follow-up visit.
Asymptomatic* *CK 3-10 times ULN*	Can usually continue statin monotherapy. Monitor symptoms and CK closely until concern is allayed or symptoms occur.
CK > 10 times ULN	Discontinue statin, then rechallenge, lower the dose, or switch to another statin. If on combination therapy (statin plus niacin or a fibrate), discontinue both agents and wait until CK levels return to normal before reinitiating only one drug at a lower dose. Monitor CK and symptoms closely. If CK remains normal for 3 months and no symptoms occur, consider adding fenofibrate to low-dose statin; continue periodic CK monitoring.
Muscle soreness, tenderness, pain	Discontinue statin. Obtain CK level and compare with baseline. Rule out hypothyroidism (obtain TSH) and common causes (exercise, strenuous work).
CK normal	Rechallenge with statin. If symptoms persist, try changing statin or reducing dose.
CK 3-10 times ULN	If no symptoms of weakness, rechallenge with statin and repeat CK within 1 week. If CK is still significantly elevated (3-10 times ULN with symptoms), reduce statin dose or temporarily discontinue until symptoms abate and CK returns to normal.
CK > 10 times ULN	Do not resume statin (or statin plus niacin or fibrate if patient is on combination therapy). Repeat CK within 3-7 days to document improvement; encourage PO fluids. If symptoms and CK return to normal, rechallenge with a statin at a lower dose. If symptoms and CK remain normal after 3 months, consider cautiously adding fenofibrate (if needed).
CK > 10,000 IU	Stop statin; check electrolytes, BUN, creatinine; encourage PO fluids; and inquire as to color of urine and urine output. Repeat CK, electrolytes, BUN, and creatinine in 24 hours for more severe rhabdomyolysis. If renal insufficiency with increased potassium, then hospitalize and administer IV fluids.

BUN = blood urea nitrogen, CK = creatine kinase, TSH = thyroid-stimulating hormone, ULN = upper limit of normal. * Test CK levels periodically if patient is taking other medications that may increase the risk for myopathy (Table 8.1, p. 81). Adapted from: ACC/AHA/NHLBI Clinical Advisory (J Am Coll Cardiol 2002;40:567-72).

Cholesterol Absorption Inhibitor

A. **Introduction.** Ezetimibe is in a new class of lipid-lowering agents that selectively inhibits the intestinal absorption of cholesterol and is used primarily as an adjunct to statin therapy for patients requiring further reductions in LDL cholesterol.

B. **Mechanism of Action.** Ezetimibe reduces blood cholesterol by inhibiting the absorption of cholesterol and phytosterols such as sitosterol from the small intestine. Intestinal cholesterol is derived primarily from cholesterol secreted in the bile and from dietary cholesterol. By inhibiting cholesterol absorption, ezetimibe reduces the delivery of intestinal cholesterol to the liver, which causes a reduction of hepatic cholesterol stores and an increase in cholesterol clearance from the blood. This mechanism is complementary to that of statins.

C. **Effect on Lipids.** Ezetimibe lowers LDL cholesterol by 18-20% and triglyceride by 5-14% and raises HDL cholesterol by 1-5%. Cholesterol lowering effects are observed when ezetimibe is given as monotherapy or as an adjunct to statins. When added to ongoing statin therapy, ezetimibe provided additional reductions of 17% in total cholesterol, 25% in LDL cholesterol, and 14% in triglycerides and an additional 3% increase in HDL cholesterol compared with statin-treated baseline (respective additional changes with statin plus placebo were –2%, –4%, –3%, and +1%) (Am J Cardiol 2002;90:1084-91). Near-maximal effects occur within 2 weeks and are maintained during chronic therapy. When added to statins, ezetimibe also lowers CRP levels by approximately an additional 10% (Circulation 2003;107:2409-15).

D. **Dosage and Administration.** Ezetimibe is given at a dose of 10 mg/d with or without food and can be administered with a statin for incremental effect. No dosage adjustment is necessary in patients with renal insufficiency or mild hepatic insufficiency. Ezetimibe should not be administered at same time as bile acid sequestrants because of decreased availability of ezetimibe with coadministration.

E. **Side Effects.** Ezetimibe is well tolerated with few adverse effects. When given as monotherapy, the incidence of elevated liver transaminases, myopathy, or rhabdomyolysis does not differ from placebo. When initiated concurrently with a statin, elevated transaminase (3 times ULN) occurred in 1.3% of patients receiving ezetimibe plus statin and 0.4% of those receiving statin alone. These elevations were generally asymptomatic, did not lead to cholestasis, and returned to baseline after discontinuation of therapy.

Niacin

A. **Introduction.** Nicotinic acid (niacin) has been utilized for dyslipidemia for 40 years. Niacin is available without a prescription, and generic niacin is quite inexpensive. Because niacin is almost always associated with subjective side effects when first initiated, only 50-65% of patients will tolerate high-dose immediate-release niacin therapy long term. Nonetheless, niacin is a very effective agent for treatment of dyslipidemia, especially in patients with multiple lipid abnormalities, particularly depressed HDL cholesterol with elevated triglycerides. Tolerability is improved with sustained-release and extended-release (e.g., Niaspan) formulations used in lower doses (1000-2000 mg).

B. **Mechanism of Action.** Niacin decreases the production and release of very low density lipoprotein (VLDL). Niacin also decreases the release of free fatty acids from adipose tissue into the circulation.

C. **Effects on Lipids.** When administered at a dosage of 1.5-4.5 gm/d, niacin decreases LDL cholesterol by 5-25%, increases HDL cholesterol by 15-35%, and decreases triglyceride by 20-50%. Niacin is one of the few lipid-regulating agents that also reduces lipoprotein(a).

D. **Clinical Trials (Chapter 11).** The Coronary Drug Project conducted in the 1970s showed a 27% reduction in MI at 5 years and an 11% decrease in all-cause mortality at 15 years in patients with prior MI treated with niacin (JAMA 1975;231:360-81). The Stockholm Ischaemic Heart Disease Study, Familial Atherosclerosis Treatment Study (FATS), Cholesterol Lowering Atherosclerosis Study (CLAS), and HDL Atherosclerosis Treatment Study (HATS) used niacin in combination therapy and showed reductions in cardiovascular events and reduced progression of atherosclerosis. The ongoing Atherothrombosis Intervention in Metabolic Syndrome with Low

HDL-C/High Triglyceride and Impact on Global Health Outcomes (AIM-HIGH) study will examine the effect of combination therapy with extended-release niacin and simvastatin on cardiovascular events in patients with documented cardiovascular disease and atherogenic dyslipidemia (HDL cholesterol < 40 mg/dL in men or <50 mg/dL in women and triglycerides >150 mg/dL but < 400 mg/dL).

E. **Dosage and Administration.** The typical starting dosage for immediate-release (crystalline) niacin is 250 mg once or twice daily, with gradual titration over 1-3 weeks up to 2-3 gm daily, often using a schedule of 1 gm two or three times daily (with meals to decrease side effects). A once-daily, extended-release formulation (Niaspan) produces less flushing and similar lipid efficacy compared to immediate-release niacin. Niaspan is started at 500 mg at bedtime, after a low-fat snack, and titrated up to 1000 to 2000 mg every evening at bedtime over 4-6 weeks. Patients should be warned prior to starting therapy about the intense cutaneous flushing associated with niacin. The flushing is a prostaglandin-mediated phenomenon that generally becomes less bothersome with time. However, flushing will return if the dose is increased or if the patient has been off niacin for more than 24 hours. Aspirin (81-325 mg) taken 30 minutes to 6 hours prior to niacin will partially prevent the cutaneous flushing; however, the risks for gastrointestinal bleeding associated with the use of multiple doses of aspirin per day may outweigh the benefits of this approach. For many patients with severe mixed dyslipidemia characterized by elevated LDL cholesterol levels and elevated triglyceride/low HDL cholesterol, combination niacin and statin therapy is the most effective way to normalize all lipid parameters, including elevated proportions of small dense LDL particles. Combination therapy with low-dose (1-2 gm/d) niacin plus a statin is better tolerated than high-dose niacin and can raise HDL cholesterol by 30% and lower LDL cholesterol and triglyceride by 30-40%. Combining niacin with a statin may increase the risk for myopathy; this combination should be avoided in patients with significant underlying hepatic or renal disease and in patients receiving concomitant medication that increases toxicity, such as cyclosporine, erythromycin, or itraconazole. Patients should be taught to recognize the symptoms of myopathy and to discontinue the medication if they become acutely ill or hospitalized.

F. **Adverse Effects.** Although niacin is arguably the most effective drug for improving the entire lipid profile, it may be difficult for patients to tolerate because of cutaneous flushing, gastrointestinal upset, and the multiple-dose regimen required for optimal results. Because Niaspan is associated with less cutaneous flushing and can be taken once daily, it appears to be a safe and effective option for patients intolerant to regular niacin because of flushing.

1. **Metabolic.** Niacin can cause mild worsening of glucose intolerance, although recent studies show only a 3- to 5-mg/dL rise in mean fasting glucose levels and no change in glycosylated hemoglobin levels in nondiabetic patients receiving ≤ 2 gm daily. Type 2 diabetic patients may experience a 25% increase in serum glucose levels, which may be controlled by altering the doses of diabetic medications. However, in the Assessment of Diabetes Control and Evaluation of the Efficacy of Niaspan Trial (ADVENT), conducted in patients with stable type 2 diabetes, hemoglobin A_{1C} change at 16 weeks in placebo patients (–0.02%) was not significantly different from that in patients receiving extended-release niacin 1000 mg/d (+0.07%) and only borderline significant (p = 0.048) in patients receiving extended-release niacin 1500 mg/d (+0.29%) (Ann Intern Med 2002;162:1568-76). Individual response will vary, and marked increases in glucose can be seen in some patients, particularly in persons with underlying insulin resistance or those receiving high-dose (≥ 3000 mg) niacin. Niacin can also raise uric acid levels and precipitate gout.

2. **Gastrointestinal.** Elevated hepatic enzymes are seen in approximately 1-2% of patients and occasionally can progress to irreversible chronic liver disease and rarely to fulminant hepatic failure. Hepatic dysfunction occurs more often in patients on high-dose sustained-release niacin. Niacin can also cause nausea, diarrhea, dyspepsia, abdominal cramping, activation of peptic ulcers and peptic ulceration, and jaundice.

3. **Cardiovascular.** Niacin can cause atrial fibrillation and other cardiac arrhythmias, orthostasis, and hypotension.

4. **Skin.** Niacin can cause minor cosmetic skin changes (acanthosis nigricans), characterized by increased pigmentation in the axillary, groin, and back regions. This disappears when therapy is discontinued.

5. **Other.** Other side effects include toxic amblyopia, cystoid macular edema, and migraine.

Fibric Acid Derivatives

A. **Introduction.** Fibrates are effective agents for reducing elevated triglyceride levels. They also effectively raise HDL cholesterol levels, and in a secondary prevention trial (VA-HIT), gemfibrozil reduced the risk for nonfatal MI or coronary death in patients with CHD and low HDL cholesterol. Fibrates are generally well tolerated and side effects are mild, although the risk for myopathy and rhabdomyolysis is increased when fibrates are used in conjunction with statins. The fibrates most commonly used in clinical practice are gemfibrozil and fenofibrate.

B. **Mechanism of Action.** Fibrates lower triglyceride levels by increasing lipoprotein lipase activity, which hydrolyzes triglycerides from VLDL. Other effects include reduced hepatic cholesterol synthesis and increased cholesterol excretion in bile. The increase in HDL cholesterol concentration seen with fibrates is mediated by peroxisome proliferator-activated receptor (PPAR) α through transcriptional induction of apo A-I, apo A-II, and lipoprotein lipase synthesis and decreased hepatic transcription of apo C-III.

C. **Effect on Lipids.** When administered according to dosing guidelines, fibrates typically reduce serum triglycerides by 20-50% and raise HDL cholesterol by 10-35%. LDL cholesterol usually falls by 5-20%, but LDL cholesterol levels may increase in patients with severe hypertriglyceridemia. Fenofibrate may lower LDL cholesterol levels more effectively than gemfibrozil. Fibrates have been shown to improve LDL particle size, and the increase in LDL cholesterol may reflect the shift of small, dense LDL to a larger, less atherogenic species.

D. **Clinical Trials (Chapter 11).** In the Coronary Drug Project, 1103 men with previous MI (of 8341 total patients) were assigned to clofibrate. At 5 years, there was no difference in mortality between clofibrate and placebo, and the risk for developing cholelithiasis and cholecystitis requiring surgery was twice as great for patients in the clofibrate group (JAMA 1975;231:360-81). In the World Health Organization (WHO) Cooperative Trial, 15,745 men without CHD were randomized to clofibrate or placebo. At 5 years, a 25% increase in mortality was seen in the clofibrate group, due in large part to an increase in deaths caused by malignancies and diseases of the liver, gallbladder and intestines (Lancet 1984;2:600-4). In the

Helsinki Heart Study, 4081 hypercholesterolemic middle-aged males without CHD were randomized to gemfibrozil or placebo. Gemfibrozil was associated with a 34% reduction in cardiac events without any significant reduction in total mortality. Gallbladder surgery was required in 0.9% of patients in the gemfibrozil group compared with 0.5% for the placebo group (not statistically significant) (N Engl J Med 1987;317:1237-45). In VA-HIT, 2531 males with CHD, HDL cholesterol ≤ 40 mg/dL, and LDL cholesterol ≤ 140 mg/dL were randomized to gemfibrozil (1200 mg/d) or placebo. At 5 years, gemfibrozil decreased the risk for nonfatal MI or death from coronary causes by 22% (p = 0.006) without a significant reduction in total mortality. At 1 year, gemfibrozil increased mean HDL cholesterol concentrations by 6% and reduced mean triglyceride levels by 31% compared with placebo; LDL cholesterol was not significantly different from placebo (N Engl J Med 1999;341:410-8). Fenofibrate was studied in diabetic patients in the angiographic Diabetes Atherosclerosis Intervention Study (DAIS) and the FIELD study. In DAIS, 418 men and women with type 2 diabetes and angiographic evidence of CHD were randomized to fenofibrate 200 mg/d or placebo. At 3-year follow-up the primary endpoint of mean segment diameter was not significantly different between treatment groups, but changes in percent diameter stenosis and minimum lumen diameter both indicated significantly less lesion progression with fenofibrate. Fenofibrate also significantly improved LDL cholesterol, HDL cholesterol, and triglyceride levels compared with placebo (Lancet 2001;357:905-10). In FIELD, 9795 men and women with type 2 diabetes (2131 of whom also had previous cardiovascular disease) were randomized to receive micronized fenofibrate 200 mg/d or placebo. At 5-year follow-up the primary endpoint of coronary events (CHD death or nonfatal MI) was not significantly different between treatment groups, although nonfatal MI was reduced by 24% (p = 0.01) and total cardiovascular events were reduced by 11% (p = 0.035). There were no significant reductions in CHD mortality (1.19 [95% CI 0.90–1.57]) or total mortality (1.11 [0.95–1.29]). Compared with placebo, LDL cholesterol was reduced by 12%, HDL cholesterol was increased by 4.5%, and triglycerides were reduced by 30% with fenofibrate at 1 year (Lancet 2005;366:1849-61).

E. **Dosage and Administration.** Gemfibrozil is given as 1200 mg/d in 2 divided doses 30 minutes before morning and evening meals. The usual dose for fenofibrate is 145 mg once daily; lower doses (one 48-mg capsule) should be initiated in patients with renal insufficiency and may be preferred for some patients in combination therapy with statins.

F. **Precautions and Side Effects.** Fibrates are metabolized in the liver and excreted in the urine and should be used with extreme caution, if at all, in patients with severe hepatic or renal insufficiency, including primary biliary cirrhosis. Preexisting gallbladder disease is also considered a contraindication to fibrate therapy due to the increased risk for cholelithiasis and cholecystitis. Side effects are usually mild and well tolerated. Gastrointestinal disturbances (dyspepsia, nausea, vomiting, constipation, diarrhea) and skin rash are among the most common side effects. An unusual flu-like syndrome has also been reported. Increased lithogenicity of bile has been reported with clofibrate therapy but has not been clearly demonstrated with other fibrates.

1. **Elevated Transaminases.** Fibrates may occasionally cause an elevation in liver transaminases, which usually returns to normal upon discontinuation of drug therapy. Periodic LFTs are recommended. If elevations are persistent, fibrates should be discontinued.

2. **Hematologic Disturbances.** Mild decreases in hemoglobin, hematocrit, and white blood cell counts may occur but usually stabilize during long-term fibrate administration. Periodic complete blood counts are recommended during the first 12 months of therapy.

3. **Myositis/Myopathy.** Myositis, myopathy, and rhabdomyolysis can occur during fibrate therapy, and this risk increases with concomitant statin therapy. (Fenofibrate appears to have less of a drug interaction with statins than gemfibrozil and therefore may have less risk for myopathy [Arch Intern Med 2003;163:2394-5].) Rhabdomyolysis causing acute renal failure is more common in patients with pre-existing renal insufficiency, and the risk for myositis, myopathy, and rhabdomyolysis is increased when fibrates are used in conjunction with statins. Administration guidelines to minimize this risk are described in Table 8.2 (p. 82). Patients should be instructed to report muscle pain, tenderness, weakness, or brown urine promptly, especially if accompanied by malaise or fever. Fibrates should be discontinued if myopathy is diagnosed or markedly elevated CK levels ($\geq$ 10 times normal) are detected.

G. **Drug Interactions**

1. **Oral Anticoagulants.** Fibrates displace warfarin from its albumin-

binding site, potentiating the effect of oral anticoagulants and increasing the risk for bleeding. It may be necessary to decrease the warfarin dose by as much as 30%; prothrombin times should be followed to optimize warfarin dosing and prevent bleeding complications.

2.   **Statins.** The risk for myositis, myopathy, and rhabdomyolysis is increased when fibrates are used in conjunction with statins (Table 8.2, p. 82). Fenofibrate appears to have less of a drug interaction with statins than gemfibrozil and therefore may have less risk for myopathy (Arch Intern Med 2003;163:2394-5). Combination therapy with a fibrate and a statin should be used with caution and only in patients for whom the lipid benefit is likely to outweigh the increased risk for adverse effects.

3.   **Bile Acid Sequestrants.** Cholestyramine and colestipol can bind fibrates and impair their absorption. To minimize this risk, fibrates should be given 1 hour before or 4-6 hours after bile acid sequestrants.

Bile Acid Sequestrants

A. **Introduction.** Bile acid sequestrants are anion exchange resins used primarily as adjuncts to statin therapy for patients requiring further reductions in LDL cholesterol. Traditionally, compliance has been problematic because of the frequent occurrence of constipation with the first-generation bile acid sequestrants cholestyramine and colestipol. Colesevelam is a newer bile acid sequestrant that is well tolerated and is an option as monotherapy for isolated mild or moderate LDL cholesterol elevation or as an adjunct to statin or niacin therapy for more severe mixed dyslipidemias.

B. **Mechanism of Action.** During normal digestion, bile acids—produced in the liver from cholesterol—are secreted into the intestine, where they bind to, emulsify, and facilitate the absorption of fat present in food. Normally, about 97% of endogenously produced bile acids are reabsorbed from the intestine and returned to the liver via the portal (enterohepatic) circulation; only 3% of bile acids are typically excreted in the stool. Nonabsorbable resins work by binding bile acids in the intestine and increasing their excretion in the stool. In response to partial removal of bile acids from the enterohepatic circulation, the liver increases the conversion of cholesterol to bile acids; the resultant decrease in intrahepatic cholesterol stimulates

LDL-receptor activity, which increases the rate of clearance of LDL cholesterol from the plasma. The LDL-lowering effect of bile acid sequestrants when used in conjunction with statins is additive.

C. **Effects on Lipids.** When administered according to dosing guidelines, bile acid sequestrants typically reduce LDL cholesterol by 15-30%. HDL cholesterol may increase slightly (3-5%) and plasma triglycerides are usually not affected but may increase. LDL-lowering effects may occur as early as 4-7 days, and maximum effects are usually evident within 1 month.

D. **Clinical Trials (Chapter 11).** The Lipid Research Clinics Coronary Primary Prevention Trial provided the first clinical trial evidence that lipid-lowering therapy could reduce CHD events. Among 3806 asymptomatic men with hypercholesterolemia (mean baseline LDL cholesterol 216 mg/dL), cholestyramine prescribed at 24 gm/d (mean dose actually taken ~14 gm/d) decreased LDL cholesterol by 12% compared with placebo and decreased nonfatal MI and CHD death by 19% at mean 7.4-year follow-up (JAMA 1984;251:351-64). Angiographic trials demonstrating benefit on atherosclerotic lesion progression with bile acid sequestrants include the NHLBI Type II Coronary Intervention study (cholestyramine), and CLAS and FATS (colestipol in combination with niacin or lovastatin).

E. **Dosage and Administration**
   1. **Cholestyramine** is given at a starting dose of 4-8 gm/d (1-2 packets or scoops) and increased gradually as tolerated up to 12-24 gm/d in 2-3 divided doses before or during meals.
   2. **Colestipol** is given at a starting dose of 5-10 gm/d (1-2 packets or scoops) and increased gradually as tolerated up to 15-30 gm/d in 2-3 divided doses before or during meals. Long-term compliance with high-dose cholestyramine (>12 gm/day) or colestipol (>15 gm/day) is poor because of gastrointestinal side effects.
   3. **Colesevelam** is given at a starting dose of 3750 mg/d in 2 divided doses or once daily with meals and can be increased up to 4375 mg/d.
   4. **Administration.** Since cholestyramine and colestipol can bind to many drugs, other medications should be taken 1 hour before or 4 hours after these bile acid sequestrants. Preparations should be taken with water or juice to mitigate gastrointestinal irritation or obstruction. Colesevelam does not impair absorption of coadministered drugs and therefore can be given simultaneously with other drugs.

F. Side Effects

1. **Gastrointestinal.** Constipation, which can be severe, is the most common side effect, occurring in up to 30% of patients treated with colestipol or cholestyramine, but to a lesser extent with colesevelam. To minimize constipation, recommendations include initiating drug therapy at a low dose (e.g., colestipol 2 gm 1-2 times per day); gradually titrating the dose upward; increasing fluid and dietary fiber intake (e.g., glass of prune juice or 3 tbs. of psyllium-husk fiber); and recommending the use of stool softeners (not as useful as other measures). Other gastrointestinal side effects include abdominal discomfort, flatulence, hemorrhoids, fecal impaction, and anal irritation/fissures. Compliance is often limited by gastrointestinal side effects. Resins are better tolerated in lower doses, as when used with other hypolipidemic agents. Colesevelam is better tolerated than other resins, with fewer adverse gastrointestinal effects.

2. **Elevated Transaminases.** Mild increases in liver enzymes may occur. The risk and severity of this adverse effect may be aggravated by concomitant use of statins.

3. **Metabolic Disturbances.** Resins may increase serum triglycerides by 5-10% (possibly greater in patients with hypertriglyceridemia) and induce hyperchloremic metabolic acidosis in children and patients with renal failure (cholestyramine).

4. **Drug Interactions.** Cholestyramine and colestipol bind to and inhibit the intestinal absorption of many drugs, including warfarin, digoxin, thiazide diuretics, beta-blockers, penicillin G, tetracycline, phenobarbital, and thyroxine; these and other medications should be taken 1 hour before or 4 hours after bile acid sequestrants. Resins also bind to fat-soluble vitamins (usually not problematic) and may lower serum folate levels; supplemental multivitamins containing folic acid should be considered. Colesevelam does not appear to affect the bioavailability of coadministered drugs and can be given at the same time as other drugs.

Omega-3 Fatty Acids

A. **Introduction.** Omega-3 fatty acids—DHA and EPA—are useful in high dosages in the treatment of hypertriglyceridemia.

B. **Mechanism of Action.** High doses of omega-3 fatty acids reduce VLDL production, possibly because DHA and EPA are not effectively metabolized by the enzymes involved in triglyceride synthesis. DHA and EPA also inhibit esterification of other fatty acids and increased peroxisomal β-oxidation in the liver.

C. **Effects on Lipids.** Triglyceride levels typically decrease by 20-45%. HDL cholesterol response is variable, but on average modest (5-10%) increases occur, although less than seen with fibrates or niacin. LDL cholesterol decreases in normolipidemic individuals but often increases in hypertriglyceridemic patients; however, this increase is thought to reflect a shift in LDL particle size to a larger, less atherogenic species.

D. **Clinical Trials (Chapter 11).** In the GISSI Prevention Study, low-dose fish oil (approximately 1 gm/d) reduced the risk for sudden death by 45% and decreased total mortality by 20% (Lancet 1999;354:447-55). Fish oil was combined with statin therapy in the Japan EPA Lipid Intervention Study (JELIS). At 4.5 years, patients randomized to receive highly purified EPA capsules in addition to statin had a significant 19% reduction in relative risk for a major coronary event (sudden cardiac death, fatal or nonfatal MI, unstable angina, and revascularization) compared with statin plus placebo (American Heart Association Scientific Sessions 2005, Dallas, Texas).

E. **Dosage and Administration.** Fish oil is available in a prescription formulation containing at least 900 mg of ethyl esters of omega-3 fatty acids (~375 mg DHA and ~465 mg EPA) in a single capsule. The daily dosage is 4 gm/d (4 capsules), which can be divided into 2 doses. Health food supplements contain varying amounts of DHA and EPA and require daily doses of 6-12 capsules. Compliance with supplements is improved by initiating therapy with 2 capsules 2-3 times daily with meals and then increasing the dose. Patients should be provided information on how to identify higher potency fish oil formulations based on content of DHA/EPA versus total oil, as ≥ 3 gm of combined DHA/EPA is required for significant triglyceride reduction. Omega-3 fatty acids can be used as monotherapy, or combined with a fibrate or niacin, to treat severe hypertriglyceridemia (≥ 500 mg/dL). Omega-3 fatty acids have been used successfully in combination with statins in patients with mixed dyslipidemia (J Intern Med 1998;243:163-70; Eur J Clin Invest 2002;32:429-36), but omega-3 fatty acids do not have an indication for that purpose.

F. Side Effects. Because of their antithrombotic effect, omega-3 fatty acids were thought to potentially increase the risk for bleeding, but this has not been demonstrated in clinical trials. In GISSI, the most common side effects were gastrointestinal disturbances and nausea. Complaints about taste and odor vary with the formulation. Omega-3 fatty acids should be used with caution in patients with known sensitivity or allergy to fish.

Combination Therapy

A. Introduction. On the basis of clinical trial evidence, the ATP III guidelines and update recommend increasingly aggressive LDL cholesterol goals for more patients. The ATP III update recommends that drug therapy be of sufficient intensity to reduce LDL cholesterol levels by at least 30-40%, and in very high risk patients, LDL cholesterol reductions of at least 50% are frequently required to achieve the optimal goal of < 70 mg/dL. With the availability of more potent statins, high-dose statin monotherapy can provide substantial LDL cholesterol reductions, but for many patients, the combination of a statin with another LDL-lowering agent with a complementary mechanism of action may be required to achieve target levels. In addition, the ATP III guidelines' establishment of the metabolic syndrome and, in patients with high triglycerides, non-HDL cholesterol as secondary targets of therapy provides for increased emphasis on treatment of mixed dyslipidemia, which may require combining agents that predominantly affect different lipid fractions.

B. Intensification of LDL Cholesterol Lowering. Statins are the drug of choice for most patients and can reduce LDL cholesterol by up to 55%. For patients who require greater reductions in LDL cholesterol or who cannot tolerate high-dose statin monotherapy, the addition of ezetimibe, niacin, or a bile acid sequestrant can provide further LDL cholesterol reduction. The combination of ezetimibe and simvastatin is also available in a single formulation (ezetimibe 10 mg plus simvastatin 10, 20, 40, or 80 mg), which reduces LDL cholesterol by 45-60%. In patients who cannot tolerate or do not respond to statin therapy and who do not achieve recommended LDL cholesterol target on monotherapy with either niacin or a bile acid sequestrant, combination therapy with both these agents may provide additional LDL cholesterol lowering.

C. Intensification of Triglyceride Lowering. The ATP III guidelines also lowered the cutpoints for triglyceride, to focus more attention on moderate hypertriglyceridemia. For patients whose triglyceride level remains elevated on monotherapy, omega-3 fatty acids may be added to fibrate or niacin for further triglyceride reductions, and fibrate plus niacin may also provide greater efficacy.

D. Mixed Dyslipidemia. All lipid-regulating agents affect multiple components of the lipid profile, but patients with elevations in both LDL cholesterol and triglycerides may need combination therapy with agents that specifically target each of these lipid fractions. The combination of statin plus niacin is useful in mixed dyslipidemia, and statin plus fibrate may be used with appropriate monitoring in selected patients for whom the potential benefit outweighs the potential risk for adverse effects. The combination of statin plus fish oil has been reported to reduce both triglycerides and LDL cholesterol in patients with mixed dyslipidemia, but fish oil does not have an indication for that purpose.

E. Side Effects. Combining lipid-regulating agents can provide greater lipid effects but may also increase risk for adverse effects. As noted above, the combinations of statin plus fibrate and statin plus niacin may increase risk for myopathy, and the combination of fibrate plus first-generation bile acid sequestrant (cholestyramine or colestipol) may decrease bioavailability of the fibrate.

Chapter 9
Dyslipidemia Pitfalls

Pitfall: Failure to screen for and treat dyslipidemia
Dyslipidemia is the most prevalent and important modifiable risk factor for atherosclerosis, affecting one in two U.S. adults. All adults should be screened for total and HDL cholesterol for risk stratification and to optimize therapy. Proper treatment reduces the risk for MI and stroke by 25-50%, cardiovascular and all-cause mortality by 20-40%, and revascularization procedures by 22-30%. It has been estimated that for each 1% decrease in LDL cholesterol or 1% increase in HDL cholesterol, the risk for cardiovascular events falls by 2% and 3%, respectively. Angiographic trials of statin therapy have consistently demonstrated slowed progression and increased regression of atherosclerotic lesions and a reduction in new lesion development. Despite the marked benefits of lipid therapy, dyslipidemia is grossly undertreated: 70% of high-risk patients without CHD and 80% of patients with CHD do not meet the LDL cholesterol targets established by ATP III.

Pitfall: Failure to identify dyslipidemias and other risk factors in patients with CHD and normal total cholesterol levels
The vast majority of patients with atherosclerotic vascular disease have some form of dyslipidemia, even though 35-40% of all patients with CHD have "normal" (< 200 mg/dL) total cholesterol levels. It is important to identify other modifiable risk factors in these high-risk patients, including low HDL cholesterol and elevated levels of triglycerides, lipoprotein(a), small dense LDL particles, homocysteine, CRP, and fibrinogen.

Pitfall: Not searching for secondary causes of dyslipidemia or screening family members of high-risk patients
Clinical evaluation of dyslipidemia should include a history, physical examination, and basic laboratory tests that screen for the presence of secondary causes of dyslipidemia before initiating lipid therapy. These include high-fat or high-carbohydrate diets, medications that raise LDL cholesterol and lower HDL cholesterol (e.g., progestins, anabolic steroids, corticosteroids), alcohol abuse, and medical disorders such as diabetes mellitus, hypothyroidism, chronic renal failure, nephrotic syndrome, and obstructive liver disease. If severe

hypercholesterolemia is present (total cholesterol > 300 mg/dL), family members should be screened. If a genetic dyslipidemia is discovered, a family history and cholesterol measurement are needed in other family members.

Pitfall: Failure to initiate drug therapy concurrently with therapeutic lifestyle changes in higher-risk groups

Therapeutic lifestyle changes (diet modification, exercise, weight control, smoking cessation) are considered first-line therapy for all patients with dyslipidemia. In most patients, this will improve lipid levels only modestly (< 10% total cholesterol lowering). Therefore, drug therapy should be initiated concurrently with nonpharmacologic measures in higher-risk groups, including: patients with an LDL cholesterol ≥ 70 mg/dL plus either CHD or other clinical forms of atherosclerotic disease; patients with an LDL cholesterol ≥ 100 mg/dL plus either diabetes mellitus or ≥ 2 risk factors conferring a 10-year CHD risk ≥ 20% but without CHD or other atherosclerotic disease; patients with an LDL cholesterol ≥ 100-130 mg/dL with multiple risk factors conferring a 10-year CHD risk of 10-20%; and patients with very high LDL cholesterol levels (≥ 220 mg/dL) at lower risk.

Pitfall: Inadequate dosing of statins

Most physicians initiate statin therapy at a low dose and fail to titrate upward to a dose needed to achieve LDL cholesterol targets recommended by ATP III. When indicated, statins should be dosed to reduce LDL cholesterol levels by *at least* 30-40% (Table 2.5, p. 19), and ≥50% reductions are usually needed to achieve LDL cholesterol of <70 mg/dL (Table 2.6, p. 20). Use of minimal drug therapy to produce a small reduction in LDL cholesterol to barely attain LDL cholesterol goal is not recommended. To achieve the full benefit of therapy, the dose of statins (and other hypolipidemic agents) should be titrated upward every 4-6 weeks as necessary to achieve LDL cholesterol targets. Once in target range, lipid levels should be rechecked every 6-12 months.

Pitfall: Inadequate use of combination therapy in higher-risk patients who have not achieved LDL cholesterol target

Multiple surveys have shown that the majority of higher-risk patients do not achieve the ATP III LDL cholesterol target of < 100 mg/dL. Although initiation of statin therapy at a higher dose will improve achievement of target LDL cholesterol levels, many patients will require upward titration and/or use of combination therapy. Furthermore, combination therapy will be required in many patients at very high risk in order to achieve the new lower LDL cholesterol target < 70 mg/dL recommended in the ATP III update (Circulation 2004;110:227-239). Physicians routinely use combination therapy to control hypertension, but combination therapy has been used less frequently for dyslipidemia. Addition of ezetimibe, a bile acid sequestrant, or niacin to statin therapy provides further reductions in LDL cholesterol, as these agents alter lipid metabolism by different mechanisms than statins.

Pitfall: Lack of patient follow-up after starting lipid therapy
Approximately 50% of patients discontinue lipid therapy during the first year without consulting a physician. Surprisingly, this high rate of noncompliance is largely independent of whether patients are paying for the medications themselves or their insurance is subsidizing the cost. Since hypercholesterolemia is an asymptomatic chronic disease that often does not cause problems for years after diagnosis, many patients lose interest and motivation in maintaining their medication. Patients started on lipid therapy should be given a definite plan for follow-up by enrollment into a formal risk factor modification clinic, where periodic follow-up visits are scheduled with face-to-face feedback. This program can usually be accomplished without a physician visit, especially if a registered nurse experienced in treating dyslipidemia is involved. At each visit, the appointment for the next visit should be scheduled, and patients should be reminded by phone call, mail, or e-mail to keep the return appointment.

Pitfall: Failure to educate patients about the benefits of lipid therapy beyond cholesterol modification
It has now been well established that the most dangerous atherosclerotic plaques are not necessarily the most severe, and that most acute coronary syndromes are caused by lesions < 70% stenotic prior to ulceration and thrombosis. Nonobstructive plaques with extensive inflammation, lipid-rich cores, and thin fibrous caps are particularly prone to ulceration and rupture. Moderate reductions in LDL cholesterol slow the progression of CHD in most patients, and lesion regression is more frequent with intensive LDL cholesterol lowering. Nevertheless, most of the beneficial effect of lipid therapy is due to plaque stabilization, not change in stenosis severity. Plaque stabilization, particularly with statins, can be accomplished in weeks to months of aggressive therapy, and may be related to resorption of extracellular and macrophage lipid deposits, reduction in neointimal inflammation, and maintenance of fibrous cap integrity. Effective treatment transforms the inflamed friable plaque into a stable fibrotic

plaque that is less prone to ulceration, rupture, and thrombosis. In addition, lipid therapy improves endothelial dysfunction caused by dyslipidemia, resulting in vasodilatory, antithrombotic, and anti-inflammatory effects. Efforts to educate patients about the plaque-stabilizing effects of statins may improve compliance.

Pitfall: Failure to initiate statin therapy during hospitalization for acute coronary syndromes

Recent data indicate a role for in-hospital initiation of statins in patients with unstable angina or acute MI. In MIRACL, 3086 patients with acute coronary syndromes were randomized to atorvastatin 80 mg or placebo 1-4 days after admission. At 16 weeks, atorvastatin reduced the risk for death, MI, resuscitated cardiac arrest, or unstable angina by 16% (14.8% vs. 17.4%, p = 0.048) (JAMA 2001;285:1711-18). In PROVE IT, 4162 patients with acute coronary syndromes were randomized to in-hospital initiation of intensive LDL cholesterol lowering with atorvastatin 80 mg/d (median on-treatment LDL cholesterol 62 mg/dL) or standard LDL cholesterol lowering with pravastatin 40 mg/d (median on-treatment LDL cholesterol 95 mg/dL). At 2 years, atorvastatin reduced the primary endpoint of death, MI, unstable angina requiring hospitalization, revascularization after 30 days, and stroke by 16% (22.4% vs. 26.3%, p = 0.005) (N Engl J Med 2004;350:1495-504). In-hospital initiation of statin therapy has also been shown to improve patient compliance by linking statin therapy to hospitalization. In CHAMP, in-hospital initiation of statins was associated with greater statin use at 1 year (91% vs. 10%) and a greater likelihood of having an LDL cholesterol level ≤ 100 mg/dL (58% vs. 6%). Despite these benefits, only 32% of patients with acute MI are discharged on lipid-lowering therapy according to the National Registry of Myocardial Infarction (NRMI) (Circulation 2001;103:38-44). Based on PROVE IT, all patients with acute coronary syndromes should be started on statin therapy while in the hospital (within 10 days and after patient is stable) to reduce LDL cholesterol to < 70 mg/dL, and continued on statins long term.

Pitfall: Undertreatment of dyslipidemia in diabetics

The risk for cardiovascular events in diabetics without CHD is the same as the risk for cardiovascular events in nondiabetics with CHD, and about 80% of diabetics eventually die of cardiovascular causes. ATP III upgraded diabetes from a major risk factor to a CHD "risk equivalent," recommending the same LDL cholesterol targets and drug initiation levels for diabetics as for individuals with CHD (Circulation 2002;106:3145-421). Treatment of diabetic dyslipidemia consists of lifestyle changes (exercise, weight loss, smoking cessation), glycemic control (can raise HDL and lower triglycerides), and antidyslipidemia drug therapy. The ATP III update recommends use of a statin to reduce LDL cholesterol levels by *a minimum of 30-40%* in all diabetic patients at increased risk for cardiovascular disease, regardless of baseline LDL cholesterol levels. A minimum LDL cholesterol target < 100 mg/dL is recommended, with a target < 70 mg/dL considered reasonable for diabetic patients with CHD or other clinical forms of atherosclerosis (AHA/ACC guideline update - Circulation 2006;113:2363-2372). The role of statin therapy in lower-risk patients with type 2 diabetes (e.g., younger patients with LDL cholesterol < 130 mg/dL and no other cardiovascular risk factors) awaits definition. In addition to LDL cholesterol lowering, treatment should include aggressive management of elevated triglycerides and low HDL cholesterol, which are common in diabetic subjects. The American Diabetes Association recommends lipid targets of LDL cholesterol < 100 mg/dL, triglycerides < 150 mg/dL, and HDL cholesterol > 40 mg/dL (> 50 mg/dL suggested in women) in patients with diabetes, to be achieved by lifestyle modification and, as needed, pharmacological therapy (Diabetes Care 2006;29:S4-42).

Pitfall: Undertreatment of dyslipidemia in the elderly
Advanced age by itself should not preclude diet and drug therapy when dyslipidemia is present, especially in patients with established CHD or other manifestations of atherosclerosis. Drug treatment is associated with morbidity and mortality benefits in older patients with CHD, and unlike angioplasty or coronary bypass surgery, does not carry increased risk as a function of increased age. Elderly patients with atherosclerotic vascular disease or multiple risk factors should be treated with lipid-lowering therapy. Statins, niacin, and fibrates have been shown to reduce the risk for stroke, which may be of particular benefit to elderly patients. Patients > 80 years of age with dyslipidemia but without existing atherosclerotic vascular disease should be treated less aggressively with drug therapy.

Pitfall: Cessation of statin/lipid therapy because of minor elevations of CK or hepatic transaminases or complaint of myalgia
Rhabdomyolysis or severe hepatic disease is very rarely seen with lipid-lowering monotherapy. Since CK elevations occur frequently (~30%) even in patients receiving placebo, therapy should not be discontinued for mild (< 3 times normal) CK elevations. In addition, symptoms of muscle soreness are commonly

seen in patients on placebo, occurring in approximately 30% of placebo patients in the Heart Protection Study (Lancet 2002;360:7). It is important that patients receive appropriate information on the signs and symptoms of myopathy. However, it is also important to reassure patients that the incidence of statin-associated myopathy with the 6 approved statins is low, i.e., ≤ 1/1000 patients (0.1%). Similarly, hepatic transaminases elevations < 3 times normal do not warrant drug discontinuation. For patients receiving monotherapy with statins, niacin, or fibrates, routine CK monitoring in asymptomatic patients is usually unnecessary. When combination therapy is used, it is reasonable to measure CK, ALT, and AST at baseline and every 6 months, or if the patient complains of diffuse myalgias or weakness. Liver function testing can be performed infrequently (every 6-12 months) after the first 6 months of therapy in patients who have been on a stable dose of a statin. When patients complain of myalgia, CK should be measured and physical examination performed to verify that weakness is not present. If symptoms are persistent, options include changing statins, reducing the dose of statin and adding ezetimibe or bile acid sequestrant, or adding coenzyme Q10. Although there are no large randomized placebo-controlled trials to show that the addition of coenzyme Q10 reduces symptoms, many lipidologists report anecdotal benefits from their patients.

Pitfall: Failure to measure and treat HDL cholesterol

While LDL cholesterol is the primary therapeutic target in ATP III, a depressed HDL cholesterol level (< 40 mg/dL) is a powerful predictor of cardiovascular risk, more so than elevated total or LDL cholesterol. Many patients with CHD have low HDL cholesterol with average or only mildly elevated total and LDL cholesterol. The primary goal of therapy for patients with low HDL cholesterol is LDL cholesterol reduction. Once the LDL cholesterol target is achieved, low HDL should be treated with TLC. In patients with CHD or CHD risk equivalent, niacin or a fibrate can be considered to raise HDL cholesterol levels. Treatment of low HDL cholesterol includes control of underlying causes such as diabetes, elevated triglycerides, obesity, and physical inactivity. Pharmacologic agents that decrease HDL cholesterol include androgens, progestins, beta-blockers, thiazide diuretics (variable effects), probucol, and nicotine. Lifestyle changes that can increase HDL cholesterol include weight loss, exercise, and smoking cessation. Diets that are high in monounsaturated or omega-3 fatty acids can also increase HDL cholesterol without raising LDL cholesterol. Alcohol can increase HDL cholesterol but is not recommended for that purpose. With respect to drug therapy, niacin is the most effective agent, raising HDL cholesterol by 15-35% in a dose-dependent fashion. Fibrates increase HDL cholesterol by 10-25% and were shown to reduce cardiovascular risk in patients with low HDL cholesterol in VA-HIT (p. 126), although the clinical benefit of gemfibrozil was only partly explained by the change in HDL cholesterol. Statins are effective for patients with low HDL cholesterol and LDL cholesterol above ATP III target; on average, statins increase HDL cholesterol by 5-15%. Estrogen raises HDL cholesterol by 10-15%, but estrogen also typically increases triglyceride, and data from HERS (JAMA 1998;280:605), the Estrogen Replacement and Atherosclerosis (ERA) trial (N Engl J Med 2000;343:522), and the Women's Health Initiative (JAMA 2002;288:321-33; JAMA 2004;291:1701-12) failed to show cardiovascular benefit, or increased cardiovascular risk, with hormone replacement therapy in postmenopausal women.

Pitfall: Failure to measure and treat triglyceride
Severe hypertriglyceridemia increases the risk for CHD and pancreatitis. Some patients have triglycerides that "cannot be controlled" because secondary factors have not been addressed, including excessive alcohol consumption, drug use (e.g., oral estrogen, antiretroviral protease inhibitors), or poorly controlled diabetes, and it may be difficult to control triglycerides in some diabetic patients until hyperglycemia is controlled. Treatment consists of lifestyle modification—weight loss and exercise are particularly beneficial in patients with severely elevated triglycerides—and drug therapy. The most effective drugs for severely elevated triglycerides are fibrates and nicotinic acid. Omega-3 fatty acids can be added to either niacin or fibrates, and some patients may require therapy with all three agents. Metformin and PPAR-γ agonists (e.g., rosiglitazone, pioglitazone) are especially beneficial in patients with diabetes and hypertriglyceridemia. The ATP III guidelines define normal triglyceride levels as < 150 mg/dL (Circulation 2002;106:3145-3421). Although LDL cholesterol reduction is the primary goal of lipid therapy, a secondary goal in patients with triglycerides $\geq$ 200 mg/dL is to lower non-HDL cholesterol (i.e., total cholesterol minus HDL cholesterol) to a target 30 mg/dL above the LDL cholesterol target. Individuals requiring drug therapy to achieve non-HDL goal can be managed by intensification of an LDL-lowering drug or by the addition of niacin, a fibrate, or fish oil.

Chapter 10
Other Measures to Prevent Atherothrombosis

In addition to therapeutic lifestyle changes and control of dyslipidemia, hypertension, and diabetes mellitus, the risk for atherothrombotic events may be reduced by therapies that improve endothelial function and reduce thrombosis.

Evidence-Based Therapy

A. **Antiplatelet Therapy**
   1. **Aspirin.** Aspirin has been consistently shown to prevent MI and stroke in patients at risk for atherosclerotic vascular disease. Although aspirin does not prevent atherosclerosis, it does inhibit platelet function and decreases the likelihood that an occlusive thrombus will form at the site of an inflamed, ulcerated atherosclerotic plaque. The optimal aspirin dose is 81-325 mg daily; doses in excess of 325 mg per day are associated with increased risk for gastrointestinal bleeding in a dose-dependent fashion. Enteric-coated or buffered forms of aspirin are no less likely to cause gastrointestinal bleeding than soluble aspirin. Low-dose aspirin (75-162 mg) should be considered for patients receiving ACE inhibitors and for those with a history of serious bleeding, especially from the gastrointestinal tract. All patients with CHD should be on aspirin therapy for secondary prevention unless a very strong contraindication exists (e.g., anaphylaxis). In a recent sex-specific meta-analysis of randomized controlled trials of aspirin for primary prevention, aspirin therapy was associated with a significant 17% reduction in ischemic stroke among 51,342 women and a significant 32% reduction in MI among 44,114 men. Aspirin did not reduce the risk of MI or cardiovascular mortality in women, or stroke or cardiovascular mortality in men. Bleeding risk was significantly increased to a similar degree among women and men (JAMA 2006;295:306-13). The AHA recommends low-dose aspirin (75-160 mg/d) for primary prevention in patients at higher CHD risk, especially those with 10-year risk ≥ 10% (Circulation 1997;96:2751-3; Circulation 2002;106:388-91). The U.S. Preventive Services Task Force report on the use of aspirin for primary

prevention of CHD concluded that the benefit/risk ratio is most favorable in patients with a 5-year CHD risk ≥ 3% (Ann Intern Med 2002;136:157-160).

2. **Clopidogrel.** Clopidogrel interferes with ADP-mediated platelet activation and is somewhat more effective at platelet inhibition than aspirin. In the Clopidogrel versus Aspirin in Patients at Risk of Ischemic Events (CAPRIE) trial, a secondary prevention study involving 19,185 patients with prior MI, prior stroke, or peripheral artery disease, clopidogrel improved event-free survival at 1.6 years compared to aspirin (p. 117; Lancet 1996;348:1329-39). In the Clopidogrel in Unstable angina to prevent Recurrent Events (CURE) trial, the combination of aspirin plus clopidogrel was superior to aspirin alone at preventing major vascular events in patients with non-ST-elevation acute coronary syndrome with or without PCI (Lancet 2001;358:527-33). In the Clopidogrel for the Reduction of Events During Observation (CREDO) trial, the addition of clopidogrel to aspirin for 1 year (vs. 4 weeks) reduced major cardiovascular events in patients undergoing elective percutaneous coronary intervention (JAMA 2002;288:2411-20). In the Clopidogrel as Adjunctive Reperfusion Therapy (CLARITY)-TIMI 28 trial, the addition of clopidogrel to aspirin and fibrinolytic therapy in patients with ST-elevation MI < 12 hours improved the patency rate of the infarct-related artery and reduced ischemic complications (N Engl J Med 2005;352:1179-89). In the Clopidogrel and Metoprolol in Myocardial Infarction Trial (COMMIT), clopidogrel reduced major cardiovascular events, including mortality, in patients with acute MI (ST-segment change or left bundle branch block). In contrast to studies of acute coronary syndromes or percutaneous coronary intervention, in the Clopidogrel for High Atherothrombotic Risk and Ischemic Stabilization and Management (CHARISMA) trial, the addition of clopidogrel to aspirin in stable patients with vascular disease or multiple risk factors did not reduce the primary endpoint of MI, stroke, or cardiovascular death at 28 months (N Engl J Med 2006;354;1706-17). The safety profile of clopidogrel is similar to that of low-dose aspirin, with rare incidence of thrombotic thrombocytopenic purpura (N Engl J Med 2000;342:1773-7). Clopidogrel is indicated for use in aspirin-intolerant patients and in patients at very high risk for cardiovascular or cerebrovascular events. Some analyses have suggested that coadministration of atorvastatin

inhibits the antiplatelet effects of clopidogrel, but a prospective study designed to examine this potential interaction did not find a significant difference in platelet measures (Ann Intern Med 2004;164:2051-7).

2. **Ticlopidine.** Ticlopidine is an antiplatelet agent with a structure and mechanism of action similar to those of clopidogrel. This agent has been shown to be more effective than aspirin at preventing recurrent ischemic stroke in high-risk patients. However, occasional life-threatening neutropenia and thrombotic thrombocytopenic purpura have limited its use. Clopidogrel is generally used instead of ticlopidine.

B. **Low-Dose Omega-3 Fatty Acids.** In the GISSI Prevention Study of 11,324 patients with prior MI, 1 gm/d (850 mg of DHA and EPA) of fish oil, a dose too low to affect lipid levels, reduced total mortality by 20% at 3.5 years, due in large part to a 45% reduction in sudden cardiac death (Lancet 1999;354:447-55). Similar clinical benefits were seen in DART, in which men with prior MI who were instructed to eat fatty fish at least twice weekly had a 29% reduction in total mortality (Lancet 1989;2:757-61). Consumption of fish and omega-3 fatty acids has also been shown to reduce the risk for CHD in otherwise healthy persons and is an important component of the Mediterranean-style diet (pp. 58-61).

C. **ACE Inhibitors.** Angiotensin-converting enzyme (ACE) inhibitors block the conversion of angiotensin I to angiotensin II and inhibit the breakdown of bradykinin, resulting in physiologic benefits that confer unique cardioprotective and renoprotective properties to this class of drugs. ACE inhibitors have been shown to improve prognosis in a wide variety of cardiovascular disorders, including hypertension, heart failure, asymptomatic LV dysfunction, MI, post-coronary revascularization procedures, and proteinuric nephropathy. Compelling data from the Heart Outcomes Prevention Evaluation (HOPE) and the EUropean trial On reduction of cardiac events with Perindopril in stable coronary Artery disease (EUROPA) demonstrate an important role for ACE inhibitors in the prevention of atherosclerotic vascular disease. Based on the Prevention of Events with Angiotensin Converting Enzyme Inhibitors (PEACE) trial, use of ACE inhibitors in very low risk patients is less compelling.

1. **HOPE** (N Engl J Med 2000;342:145-53). In HOPE, 9297 patients aged ≥ 55 years with either atherosclerotic arterial disease (prior MI, prior stroke, or peripheral artery disease) or diabetes plus one additional risk

factor (hypertension, elevated total cholesterol, depressed HDL cholesterol, smoking, or microalbuminuria) received ramipril (10 mg/d) or placebo. At a mean follow-up of 5 years, ramipril reduced the primary composite endpoint of MI, stroke, or death from cardiovascular disease by 22% (14.0% vs. 17.8%, p < 0.001). In addition, death from cardiovascular causes was reduced by 26% (6.1% vs. 8.1%), and all-cause mortality was reduced by 16% (10.4% vs. 12.2%). Significant risk reduction was also noted for MI (20%), stroke (32%), cardiac arrest (38%), revascularization procedures (15%), and new-onset diabetes mellitus (34%). The beneficial effects of ramipril were observed in patients with and without diabetes, hypertension, or cardiovascular disease and were independent of the effects of concomitant cardiovascular medications (aspirin, beta-blockers, lipid-lowering agents, other blood pressure drugs). Ramipril is approved to reduce the risk for MI, stroke, and death from cardiovascular causes in patients 55 years or older who are at high risk for developing a major cardiovascular event because of a history of coronary artery disease, stroke, peripheral artery disease, or diabetes that is accompanied by at least one other cardiovascular risk factor (hypertension, elevated total cholesterol levels, low HDL levels, cigarette smoking, or documented microalbuminuria). Ramipril can be used in addition to other needed treatment, including antihypertensive, antiplatelet, and lipid-lowering therapy. The recommended starting dose is 2.5 mg once daily for 1 week, followed by 5 mg once daily for the next 3 weeks, then increased as tolerated to a maintenance dose of 10 mg once a day (which may be given in 2 divided doses for hypertensive or recent post-MI patients).

2. **EUROPA** (Lancet 2003;362:782-8). EUROPA was undertaken to evaluate the role of ACE inhibitors on cardiovascular risk in low-risk patients aged ≥ 18 years without clinical heart failure and with stable CHD (prior MI > 3 months before screening, coronary revascularization > 6 months before screening, ≥ 70% coronary artery stenosis on angiography, or men with a history of chest pain and a positive stress test). Of the 12,218 men and women randomized to perindopril 8 mg/day (4 mg/day in patients > 70 years) or placebo, 12% had diabetes (vs. 38% in HOPE), 27% had hypertension (vs. 47% in HOPE), 81% had no angina (vs. 20% in HOPE), and 17% had mild angina. At a mean follow-up of 4.2 years, perindopril reduced the primary composite endpoint of cardiovascular death, MI, or cardiac arrest by 20% (8.0%

vs. 9.9%, p < 0.0003). The beneficial effects of perindopril were observed in all age groups (≤ 55 years, 56-65 years, > 65 years), and in patients with and without diabetes, hypertension, or prior MI. Benefits were independent of the effects of concomitant cardiovascular medications (aspirin, beta-blockers, lipid-lowering agents, other blood pressure drugs).

3. **PEACE.** In this trial, lower-risk patients (compared to HOPE and EUROPA) with stable coronary artery disease and normal/near normal left ventricular function being treated with aggressive coronary revascularization and risk factor modification derived no benefit from the addition of trandolapril at 4.8 years (N Engl J Med 2004;351:2058-68). Average baseline EF was 58%, creatinine and cholesterol levels were normal, BP was 133/78 mmHg, and the annualized death rate was only 1.6%, similar to age/sex-matched general population.

4. **Potential Mechanisms for Improved Cardiovascular Prognosis with ACE Inhibitors.** ACE inhibitors have been shown to lower blood pressure, improve endothelial dysfunction, and reduce LVH and arterial wall mass, all of which have been associated with improved cardiovascular prognosis. ACE inhibitors improve endothelial dysfunction by blocking the production of angiotensin II and preventing the breakdown of bradykinin, shifting the balance in favor of vasodilation, fibrinolysis, and reduced platelet aggregation. They are also among the most effective antihypertensive agents for the prevention and regression of LVH (JAMA 1996;275:1507-13), both by lowering blood pressure and blocking the formation of angiotensin II/aldosterone, which stimulates myocyte hypertrophy and extracellular matrix (collagen) formation. One longitudinal study showed that ACE inhibition reduced LV mass by 40% over 3 years (Am J Hypertens 1998;11:631-9). Hypertension and insulin resistance promote smooth muscle cell hypertrophy/hyperplasia and fibrous tissue deposition within arterial walls, resulting in arterial wall stiffness and endothelial dysfunction. ACE inhibition facilitates reversal of these processes and normalization of arterial wall structure and function.

5. **Recommendations.** ACE inhibitors improve cardiovascular prognosis in higher-risk patients and are generally safe, well tolerated, and affordable. Patients with atherosclerotic vascular disease, diabetes, or insulin resistance should be considered for ACE inhibitor therapy. For patients who are intolerant of ACE inhibitors, an angiotensin receptor

blocker (ARB) may be used as an alternative. For very low risk patients with stable coronary artery disease (similar to patients in PEACE, i.e., normal EF, BP, and lipids undergoing aggressive treatment of CHD and risk factors), the evidence for ACE inhibitors is less compelling.

Other Therapies Used to Prevent Atherothrombosis

A. **Folic Acid.** Homocysteine is an amino acid by-product of protein metabolism. An elevated fasting homocysteine level is an independent risk factor for cardiovascular events and cardiovascular mortality, particularly in patients already diagnosed with CHD. Although the mechanism of action is not clearly understood, homocysteine appears capable of damaging endothelium and promoting a prothrombogenic environment. All adults should be encouraged to take at least 400 mcg of folic acid daily by diet and/or supplementation, which will lower homocysteine levels. Foods that are rich in folate include broccoli, spinach, other green leafy vegetables, citrus fruits, asparagus, and beans. Currently there are no consensus panel recommendations on criteria for measurement of homocysteine. In our practices, we measure homocysteine in patients with premature or severe atherosclerosis. Folic acid supplementation as well as supplementation with vitamins B_6 and B_{12} has been shown to decrease homocysteine levels by approximately 15-30%. If elevated homocysteine levels are present, folic acid (800-1600 mcg per day), vitamin B_{12} (250 mcg per day), and vitamin B_6 (20-25 mg per day) should be prescribed. However, the first randomized trials of folic acid and vitamins B_6 and B_{12} to reduce homocysteine showed no difference in cardiovascular events in stroke or CHD patients (JAMA 2004;291:565-75; N Engl J Med 2006;354:354;1567-1577), and a randomized trial in patients with elevated homocysteine (> 3 mM) showed no effect on measures of endothelial function, coagulation, fibrinolysis, or inflammation despite a 24% reduction in homocysteine (Thromb Haemost 2005;94:96-100).

B. **Alcohol.** Most observational studies show that people who consume 2-14 drinks per week (e.g., 1 drink per day or every other day) have lower rates of cardiovascular events and all-cause mortality compared to nondrinkers. One drink is defined as 12 ounces of beer, 5.5 ounces of wine, or 1.5 ounces of 80-proof distilled liquor (spirits). However, blood pressure and triglycerides rise proportionately with alcohol intake of more than 3 drinks per day; at this level of alcohol consumption, the reduction in cardiovascular mortality is offset by the increased risk of cancer, strokes, and accidents. Optimal intake of alcohol is not more than 2 drinks daily for men or 1 drink daily for women. Although moderate alcohol consumption (up to 1 oz ethanol per day) has been associated with a lower risk of CHD, it is not recommended as a therapeutic agent because of possible deleterious effects, such as hypertriglyceridemia and hypertension, and because of the risk for abuse with larger intakes. In addition, there are no prospective randomized trials to confirm the benefit of alcohol on cardiovascular event reduction as reported in observational epidemiological studies.

C. **Antioxidants.** Since oxidation of LDL is required for LDL to accumulate into evolving atherosclerotic plaque and to stimulate neointimal inflammation, attention has focused on the use of antioxidant vitamins for primary and secondary prevention of atherosclerosis.

1. **Vitamin E.** Vitamin E is an antioxidant vitamin that gets incorporated into lipoprotein particles and prevents the oxidation of LDL, an integral step in atherogenesis. In the Cambridge Heart Antioxidant Study (CHAOS), vitamin E decreased the risk for MI in patients with documented coronary disease (Lancet 1996;347:781-6). However, in the much larger GISSI Prevention Study, HOPE, and Heart Protection Study, vitamin E produced no benefit on cardiovascular endpoints. At present, there is no evidence to recommend the use of vitamin E to reduce CHD events.

2. **Vitamin C.** Vitamin C (250-500 mg daily) is another antioxidant that may be used in conjunction with vitamin E. However, no benefit was observed in the Heart Protection Study with vitamin C combined with vitamin E and beta-carotene (Lancet 2002;360:23-33). Therefore, antioxidant therapy cannot be considered an evidence-based approach.

3. **Beta-carotene.** No cardiovascular benefit has been shown with beta-carotene in the Linxian Cancer Prevention Trial; the Alpha-Tocopherol, Beta-Carotene Cancer Prevention Study; or the Physicians' Health Study. In addition, no benefit was observed in the Heart Protection Study with beta-carotene in combination with vitamins A and C. Therefore, beta-carotene therapy cannot be considered an evidence-based approach.

D. Hormone Replacement Therapy

1. **Estrogen.** Estrogen has many potentially beneficial effects on the cardiovascular system, including antioxidant effects and improvements in lipid profile and endothelial function. In observational epidemiologic studies, hormone replacement therapy has been associated with decreased risk for MI and cardiovascular death in women with established CHD or risk factors for CHD. However, no benefit on nonfatal MI or CHD death was demonstrated in HERS, which randomized 2763 women (average age 67 years) with CHD to combination conjugated estrogen (0.625 mg/d) and medroxyprogesterone (2.5 mg/d) vs. placebo (JAMA 1998;280:605). In addition, more cardiovascular events occurred in the first year in women receiving hormone therapy than those receiving placebo, but fewer events occurred in the hormone group in years 4 and 5. Hormone therapy was also associated with an increased risk for thromboembolic events and gallbladder disease. In HERS II, in which 2321 HERS patients were followed up for an additional 2.7 years, the benefit reported in the latter years of HERS did not persist; relative hazards for CHD events were similar between treatment groups. Estrogen also provided no angiographic benefit in the ERA trial, which randomized 309 women with angiographic CHD to estrogen alone, estrogen plus medroxyprogesterone acetate, or placebo. The primary endpoint, per-patient mean minimum lumen diameter of 10 coronary segments at mean 3.2-year follow-up, was not significantly different among treatment groups (N Engl J Med 2000;343:522–9). In the Women's Health Initiative, 16,608 healthy postmenopausal women aged 50-79 years with an intact uterus were randomized to either conjugated equine estrogens (0.625 mg/d) plus medroxyprogesterone acetate (2.5 mg/d) or placebo. After a mean of 5.2 years of follow-up, absolute excess risks per 10,000 person-years attributable to hormone replacement therapy included 7 more CHD events, 8 more strokes, 8 more pulmonary embolisms, and 8 more invasive breast cancers; absolute risk reductions per 10,000 person-years were 6 fewer colorectal cancers and 5 fewer hip fractures (JAMA 2002;288:321-33). In addition, estrogen alone also showed no benefit in the Women's Health Initiative (JAMA 2004;291:1701-12). These results, combined with the results from HERS, indicate that hormone replacement therapy should not be initiated or continued for primary or secondary prevention of CHD.

2. **Selective Estrogen Receptor Modulators (SERMs).** Agents such as raloxifene appear to provide many of the benefits of estrogen without the increased risk for cancer. In the Multiple Outcomes of Raloxifene Evaluation (MORE), 7705 osteoporotic postmenopausal women were randomized to raloxifene 60 mg/d or 120 mg/d or placebo for 4 years. Cardiovascular events were no different between groups in the overall cohort, but in the subset of 1035 women with increased cardiovascular risk at baseline, cardiovascular events occurred in 12.9% in the placebo group and 7.8% in the raloxifene group (RR = 0.60) (JAMA 2002;287:847-57). Recommendations on the use of SERMs for the prevention of cardiovascular disease await the results of ongoing trials, such as Raloxifene Use for The Heart (RUTH), which is evaluating cardiovascular events as a predefined outcome in 10,000 postmenopausal high-risk women (Am J Cardiol 2001;88:392-5).

Chapter 11

Dyslipidemia and Cardiovascular Risk Reduction Trials

Table 11.1. Clinical Event Trials

Trial	Design	Results
A to Z: Aggrastat to Zocor (JAMA 2004;292:1307)	4497 patients with ACS were randomized to early intensive statin therapy (simvastatin 40 mg/d x 1 month followed by 80 mg/d) or a delayed conservative approach (placebo x 4 months followed by simvastatin 40 mg/d). Follow-up: 6-24 months.	Early intensive statin therapy resulted in a favorable trend toward a reduction in the primary endpoint (cardiovascular death, MI, readmission for ACS, or stroke) (14.4% vs. 16.7%, p = 0.14). There was no difference in the primary endpoint at 4 months; however, between 4 months and the end of the study, early intensive statin therapy resulted in a significant 25% reduction in major cardiovascular events (6.8% vs. 9.3%)

Dyslipidemia Essentials

Table 11.1. Clinical Event Trials

Trial	Design	Results
AFCAPS/ TexCAPS: Air Force/Texas Coronary Atherosclerosis Prevention Study (JAMA 1998;279:1615)	6605 men and women with no history of coronary disease, total cholesterol 180–264 mg/dL, and HDL ≤ 45 mg/dL for men or ≤ 47 mg/dL for women were randomized to lovastatin (20-40 mg/dL) or placebo. Many had average lipid levels, and only 17% of trial participants would have qualified for drug therapy according to ATP II guidelines. Mean cholesterol 221 mg/dL, mean LDL 150 mg/dL, mean HDL 36 mg/dL. Mean follow-up: 5.2 years.	Incidence of primary endpoint–first acute major coronary event (fatal and nonfatal MI, unstable angina, or sudden cardiac death)–was reduced by 37% with lovastatin. Revascularization procedures (CABG, PTCA) were reduced by 33%.
ALERT: Assessment of Lescol in Renal Transplantation (Lancet 2003;361:2024)	2102 patients with renal transplantation > 6 months, stable graft function, and total cholesterol 155-348 mg/dL (4.0-9.0 mmol/L) were randomized to fluvastatin 40 mg daily vs. placebo. Mean duration of follow-up: 5.1 years.	Fluvastatin lowered LDL cholesterol levels by 32% and reduced the relative risk of cardiac death or nonfatal MI by 35% (p = 0.005). The primary endpoint of first major adverse cardiac event (cardiac death, nonfatal MI, coronary revascularization) was not significantly different between treatment groups.

Table 11.1. Clinical Event Trials

Trial	Design	Results
ALLHAT-LLT: Antihypertensive and Lipid-Lowering Treatment to Prevent Heart Attack Trial (JAMA 2002;288:2998)	10,355 men and women aged ≥ 55 years with stage 1 or 2 hypertension, ≥ 1 additional CHD risk factor, and LDL 120-189 mg/dL (100-129 mg/dL in patients with CHD) were randomized to pravastatin 40 mg/d or usual care. Mean follow-up: 4.8 years.	Pravastatin did not significantly reduce all-cause mortality (primary endpoint) or CHD events (relative risk 0.91, p = 0.16). Lack of benefit attributed to substantial (30%) use of statins in the placebo group, resulting in a modest 17% differential in total cholesterol between pravastatin and usual care groups.
ALLIANCE: Aggressive Lipid Lowering Initiation Abates New Cardiac Events (J Am Coll Cardiol 2004;44:1772)	2442 patients with CHD and LDL 110-200 mg/dL on therapy (130-250 on no therapy; mean baseline LDL 147 mg/dL) were randomized to aggressive lipid lowering (atorvastatin up to 80 mg/d to lower LDL < 80 mg/dL; median dose 40.5 mg/d; 45% of patients on 80 mg/d) or usual care. Primary endpoint: time to cardiac death, nonfatal MI, resuscitated cardiac arrest, cardiac revascularization, unstable angina requiring hospitalization. Median follow-up: 4.5 years.	Aggressive lipid lowering reduced the primary endpoint by 17% (p = 0.02) and nonfatal MI by 47%, (p = 0.0002). There were no cases of myopathy or rhabdomyolysis. On-treatment LDL: aggressive therapy 95 mg/dL; usual care 111 mg/dL.

Table 11.1. Clinical Event Trials

Trial	Design	Results
ASCOT-LLA: Anglo-Scandinavian Cardiac Outcomes Trial - Lipid Lowering Arm (Lancet 2003;361:1149)	10,305 men and women aged 40-79 years with hypertension, ≥ 3 other risk factors, and normal or slightly elevated total cholesterol (≤ 250 mg/dL) were randomized to atorvastatin 10 mg/d or placebo. Primary endpoint: CHD death or nonfatal MI.	Atorvastatin arm of trial was prematurely stopped at 3.3 years due to a significant 36% reduction in the primary endpoint. Benefits were apparent within the first year. Atorvastatin also reduced fatal or nonfatal stroke by 27%, total cardiovascular events by 21%, and total coronary events by 29%. At 1 year, atorvastatin reduced total and LDL cholesterol by 24% and 35%, respectively.
BIP: Bezafibrate Infarction Prevention study (Circulation 2000;102:21; Circulation 2004;109:2197)	3122 men and women aged 45–74 years with prior MI and/or stable angina with ischemia were randomized to bezafibrate 400 mg/d or placebo. Lipid criteria: total cholesterol 180–250 mg/dL (mean 212 mg/dL), LDL ≤ 180 mg/dL (≤ 160 mg/dL in patients aged <50 years; mean 148 mg/dL), HDL ≤ 45 mg/dL (mean 35 mg/dL). Mean follow-up: 6.2 years.	No difference in nonfatal or fatal MI or sudden death (primary endpoint) between groups. Post hoc analysis of the subgroup of patients with baseline TG ≥ 200 mg/dL indicated a significant 39.5% reduction in the primary endpoint. At 6 years, among 303 nondiabetic CHD patients with impaired fasting glucose, bezafibrate reduced onset of type 2 diabetes ($p = 0.04$) and delayed conversion by ~ 10 months ($p = 0.004$).

Table 11.1. Clinical Event Trials

Trial	Design	Results
CAPRIE: Clopidogrel vs. Aspirin in Patients at Risk of Ischemic Events (Lancet 1996;348:1329)	19,185 men and women with atherosclerotic vascular disease (MI within 35 days or ischemic stroke within 6 months before randomization, or established peripheral arterial disease) were randomized to clopidogrel (75 mg/d) or aspirin (325 mg/d). Mean follow-up: 1.9 years.	Clopidogrel reduced the combined endpoint of new ischemic stroke, new MI, or other vascular death by 8.7% relative to aspirin (p = 0.043). Benefit was greatest in patients with peripheral artery disease.
CARDS: Collaborative Atorvastatin Diabetes Study (Lancet 2004;364:685)	2838 type 2 diabetic patients with LDL ≤ 160 mg/dL, no clinical history of heart disease, and at least 1 other risk factor (retinopathy, albuminuria, current smoking, hypertension) were randomized to atorvastatin 10 mg/d or placebo. Median follow-up: 3.9 years.	Atorvastatin reduced the first occurrence of any major vascular event (acute CHD events, coronary revascularization, stroke) by 37% (5.8% vs. 9.0%, p = 0.001). There was a 27% reduction in all-cause mortality (borderline significance). No excess of adverse events occurred in the atorvastatin group.
CARE: Cholesterol and Recurrent Events (N Engl J Med 1996;335:1001)	4159 MI survivors were randomized to pravastatin 40 mg/d or placebo. Entry criteria included total cholesterol <240 mg/dL (mean 209 mg/dL) and LDL 115–174 mg/dL (mean 139 mg/dL). Median follow-up: 5.0 years.	Pravastatin reduced coronary death and recurrent MI (primary endpoint) by 24%, coronary bypass surgery by 26%, coronary angioplasty by 23%, and stroke by 31%.

Table 11.1. Clinical Event Trials

Trial	Design	Results
CDP: Coronary Drug Project (JAMA 1975;231:360, J Am Coll Cardiol 1986;8:1245) [15-year follow-up]; Am J Cardiol 2005;95:254 [benefits by glycemic status])	Enrolled 8341 men with previous MI. Followed up at least 5 years. Agents used were estrogen, dextrothyroxine, clofibrate, and niacin. Estrogen and dextrothyroxine treatment halted because of adverse effects. Niacin was used in 1119 patients, clofibrate in 1103, and placebo in 2789.	At 5 years, total mortality (primary endpoint) and combined nonfatal MI or CHD death were not different from placebo in either the clofibrate or the niacin groups. However, at 15-year follow-up (9 years after the trial ended), all-cause mortality was significantly reduced by 11% in the niacin group. Benefits were evident regardless of glycemic status.
DART: Diet and Reinfarction Trial (Lancet 1989;2:757)	2033 men with prior MI were randomized to receive or not receive advice on 3 dietary factors: fat, fatty fish, and/or fiber. Follow-up: 2 years.	All-cause mortality was reduced by 29% in men advised to eat fatty fish at least twice weekly; no significant difference in mortality was seen for the other diet interventions.
EUROPA: European Trial on Outcome of Cardiac Events with Perindopril in Stable Coronary Artery Disease (Lancet 2003;362:782)	12,218 low-risk men and women aged $\geq$ 18 years without clinical heart failure and with stable coronary heart disease were randomized to perindopril 8 mg/d (after tolerating 4 mg/d) x 2 weeks or placebo. Follow-up: 4.2 years.	Perindopril reduced the primary endpoint of cardiovascular death, MI, or cardiac arrest by 20% (8.0% vs. 9.9%, p < 0.0003). Beneficial effects were observed in all age groups and in patients with and without diabetes, hypertension, or prior MI.

Table 11.1. Clinical Event Trials

Trial	Design	Results
FIELD: Fenofibrate Intervention and Event Lowering in Diabetes (Lancet 2005;366:1849)	9795 men and women aged 50-75 years with type 2 diabetes (including 2131 with previous cardiovascular disease), total cholesterol 115-250 mg/dL, total cholesterol/HDL cholesterol ratio ≥ 4, and TG 90-445 mg/dL who were not on statin therapy were randomized to receive micronized fenofibrate 200 mg/d or placebo. Follow-up: 5 years.	The primary endpoint of coronary events (CHD death or nonfatal MI) was not significantly different between treatment groups (hazard ratio 0.89, 95% CI 0.75–1.05; p = 0.16). However, nonfatal MI was reduced by24% (p = 0.01), and total cardiovascular events were reduced by 11% (p = 0.035).
GISSI: Gruppo Italiano per lo Studio della Sopravvivenza nell'Infarto Miocardico (Lancet 1999;354:447)	11,324 men and women with prior MI were randomized to fish oil ~1 gm/d, vitamin E 300 mg/d, both, or placebo for 3.5 years. Baseline LDL was 138 mg/dL.	Fish oil alone or in combination reduced all-cause mortality by 20%, sudden death by 45%, and cardiovascular death by 30%. Vitamin E produced no benefit on these endpoints.
Helsinki Heart Study (N Engl J Med 1987;317:1237, Circulation 1992;85:37)	4081 middle-aged (40-55 years) hypercholesterolemic (non-HDL ≥ 200 mg/dL) men without CHD were randomized to gemfibrozil 1200 mg/d or placebo and followed up for 5 years. Mean LDL 189 mg/dL.	Cardiac events (fatal and nonfatal MI and cardiac death; primary endpoint) were reduced by 34% in the gemfibrozil group. There was no difference in all-cause mortality between groups. Post hoc analysis indicated that the greatest benefit occurred in the subgroup with TG > 204 mg/dL and LDL/HDL ratio > 5.

Table 11.1. Clinical Event Trials

Trial	Design	Results
HOPE: Heart Outcomes Prevention Evaluation (N Engl J Med 2000;342:145 [ramipril]; N Engl J Med 2000;342:154 [vitamin E])	9297 men and women aged ≥ 55 years with either atherosclerotic vascular disease or diabetes plus 1 other cardiovascular risk factor but without LV dysfunction or heart failure were randomized to ramipril 10 mg/d, vitamin E 400 IU, both, or placebo and followed up for a mean of 5 years.	The primary endpoint–composite of MI, stroke, or death from cardiovascular causes–was reduced by 22% with ramipril (14.0% vs. 17.8%, $p < 0.001$). Ramipril also reduced death from cardiovascular causes by 26% and all-cause mortality by 16%. Vitamin E had no benefit on events.
HPS: Heart Protection Study (Lancet 2002;360:7 [simvastatin]; Lancet 2002;360:23 [antioxidant vitamins]; Lancet 2003;361:2005 [diabetes]; Lancet 2004;363:757 [stroke])	20,536 men and women with coronary disease, peripheral artery disease, cerebrovascular disease, or diabetes and with total cholesterol > 135 mg/dL were randomized to simvastatin 40 mg/d or placebo, and to antioxidant vitamins (600 mg vitamin E, 250 mg vitamin C, and 20 mg beta-carotene) or placebo. Mean total cholesterol 228 mg/dL, mean LDL 131 mg/dL, mean HDL 41 mg/dL. Included 3424 patients with baseline LDL < 100 mg/dL. Follow-up: 5 years.	Simvastatin resulted in a significant 12% reduction in all-cause mortality due largely to an 18% reduction in coronary death. Simvastatin also reduced MI by 38%, stroke by 25%, revascularization procedures by 24%. Proportional reductions were similar in all subgroups, including those without CHD and those with LDL < 100 mg/dL at baseline. Simvastatin reduced the risk of a first major vascular event by 22% in 5963 diabetics, *(cont'd next page)*

Table 11.1. Clinical Event Trials

Trial	Design	Results
HPS: Heart Protection Study *(cont'd)*	See previous page	including a 33% reduction in 2912 diabetics without arterial occlusive disease at baseline and a 27% reduction in 2426 diabetics with baseline LDL < 116 mg/dL. Simvastatin was safe and well tolerated. No benefits were observed with antioxidant vitamins.
IDEAL: Incremental Decrease in Endpoints through Aggressive Lipid Lowering (JAMA 2005;294:2437)	8888 men and women with history of MI and qualifying for statin therapy by national guidelines at time of recruitment were randomized to atorvastatin 80 mg/d or simvastatin 20 mg/d. Mean baseline LDL was 121 mg/dL. Median follow-up: 4.8 years.	The primary endpoint of a major coronary event (coronary death, nonfatal MI, resuscitated cardiac arrest) was reduced by 11% with atorvastatin. Atorvastatin also reduced nonfatal MI by 17% and major cardiovascular events by 13%. All-cause mortality was not different between treatment groups. Atorvastatin patients had higher rates of drug discontinuation for adverse events and more liver transaminase elevations (1% vs. 0.1% with simvastatin for ALT; 0.4% vs. 0.04% with simvastatin for AST).

Table 11.1. Clinical Event Trials

Trial	Design	Results
JELIS: Japan EPA Lipid Intervention Study (American Heart Association, November, 2005, Dallas, TX)	18,645 patients (including 3664 with CHD) with total cholesterol ≥ 250 mg/dL were randomized to 1800 mg of highly purified EPA capsules or placebo and followed up for 4.5 years; all patients also received pravastatin 10-20 mg/d or simvastatin 5-10 mg/d. Mean baseline LDL: 180 mg/dL.	Fish oil plus statin significantly reduced the primary endpoint of major coronary events (sudden cardiac death, fatal or nonfatal MI, unstable angina, revascularization) by 19%. Among patients with CHD, combination therapy significantly reduced the risk for the primary endpoint by 19%, but the 18% relative risk reduction among patients without CHD was not statistically significant. LDL was reduced by 26% in both randomized treatment groups.
LIPID: Long-Term Intervention with Pravastatin in Ischaemic Disease (N Engl J Med 1998;339:1349; N Engl J Med 2000:343;317 [stroke]; Lancet 2002;359:1379 [8-year follow-up]; Diabetes Care 2003;26:2713 [diabetes])	9014 men and women with cholesterol ranging from 155 to 271 mg/dL and a history of MI or unstable angina prior to study enrollment were randomized to pravastatin 40 mg/d or placebo. Median LDL was 150 mg/dL. Mean follow-up: 6 years.	CHD death (primary endpoint) was reduced by 24%, CHD death or nonfatal MI by 24%, all-cause mortality by 22%, need for coronary revascularization by 20%, and stroke by 19% in the pravastatin group. Benefit was sustained at 8 years. Pravastatin also reduced risk for cardiovascular events and stroke in patients with diabetes but did not reduce incidence of diabetes.

Table 11.1. Clinical Event Trials

Trial	Design	Results
LIPS: Lescol Intervention Prevention Study (JAMA 2002;287:3215)	1677 patients with total cholesterol 135-270 mg/dL and TG < 400 mg/dL were randomized to fluvastatin 80 mg/d or placebo after successful percutaneous coronary intervention. Primary outcome: survival time free of major adverse coronary events (coronary death, MI, revascularization procedures). Follow-up: 3.9 years (median).	Fluvastatin reduced event rate by 22% (21.4% vs. 26.7%, p = 0.01), which was independent of baseline cholesterol. Risk was reduced by 47% in the 202 patients with diabetics and by 34% in the 614 patients with multivessel coronary disease.
LRC-CPPT: Lipid Research Clinics Coronary Primary Prevention Trial (JAMA 1984;251:351, JAMA 1984;251:365)	3806 men aged 35-59 years without CHD with total cholesterol ≥ 265 mg/dL (mean 292 mg/dL) and LDL ≥ 190 mg/dL (mean 216 mg/dL) were treated with diet and randomized to cholestyramine 24 gm/d or placebo. Follow-up: 7.4 years.	The primary endpoint of CHD death and/or nonfatal MI was reduced by 19% and LDL was reduced by 12% with cholestyramine compared with placebo. Separate analysis of cholestyramine patients indicated that each 11% decrement in LDL was associated with a 19% decrement in CHD risk.
Lyon Diet Heart Study (Lancet 1994;343:1454; Circulation 1999;99:779)	605 men and women with prior MI were randomized to a Mediterranean-type diet (including high monounsaturated fat) or no dietary advice and followed up for 1-4 years (mean 27 months).	The primary endpoint of cardiovascular death or nonfatal MI was significantly reduced by 73% in patients in the diet group; all-cause mortality was significantly reduced by 70%. Protective effect was maintained at 4 years.

Table 11.1. Clinical Event Trials

Trial	Design	Results
MIRACL: Myocardial Ischemia Reduction with Aggressive Cholesterol Lowering (JAMA 2001;285:1711, Circulation 2002;106:1690 [stroke])	3086 men and women within 24-96 hours of admission for acute coronary syndrome were randomized to atorvastatin 80 mg/dL or placebo. Mean LDL 124 mg/dL, mean TG 184 mg/dL, mean HDL 46 mg/dL. Primary endpoint: death, acute MI, cardiac arrest with resuscitation, or recurrent symptomatic ischemia. Follow-up: 16 weeks.	Atorvastatin reduced the primary endpoint by 16% (14.8% vs. 17.4%, p = 0.048), due largely to a 26% reduction in recurrent symptomatic ischemia (6.2% vs. 8.4%, p = 0.02). Atorvastatin reduced the risk for stroke by 51% (0.8% vs. 1.6%, p = 0.04).
PROSPER: Prospective Study of Pravastatin in the Elderly at Risk (Lancet 2002;360:1623)	5804 men and women aged 70-82 years with vascular disease or cardiovascular risk factors were randomized to pravastatin 40 mg/d or placebo. Baseline total cholesterol criterion 155-348 mg/dL. Composite primary endpoint: coronary death, nonfatal MI, or fatal or nonfatal stroke. Mean follow-up: 3.2 years.	Pravastatin reduced the composite primary endpoint by 15% (14.1% vs. 16.2%, p = 0.014). Stroke incidence was similar between treatment groups, but transient ischemic attacks were reduced by 25% with pravastatin (2.7% vs. 3.5%, p = 0.051).
PROVE IT: Pravastatin or Atorvastatin Evaluation and Infection Therapy (N Engl J Med 2004;350;1495)	4162 patients hospitalized for an acute coronary syndrome within the preceding 10 days were randomized to intensive LDL lowering with atorvastatin 80 mg/dL or standard LDL lowering with pravastatin 40 mg/d. Primary endpoint: death, MI, unstable angina requiring hospitalization, revascularization after 30 days, and stroke. Mean follow-up: 2 years.	Atorvastatin reduced the primary endpoint by 16% (22.4% vs. 26.3%, p = 0.005). Benefits were evident as early as 30 days and were consistent over time. Median LDL with atorvastatin was 62 mg/dL (41% decrease from baseline) vs. 95 mg/dL with pravastatin (10% decrease from baseline) (p < 0.001).

Table 11.1. Clinical Event Trials

Trial	Design	Results
4S: Scandinavian Simvastatin Survival Study (Lancet 1994;344:1383; Diabetes Care 1997;20:614 [diabetes]; Arch Intern Med 1999;159:2661 [diabetes or impaired fasting glucose]; Lancet 2004;364: 771 [10-year follow-up])	4444 men and women with CHD and elevated total cholesterol (mean 261 mg/dL) were randomized to simvastatin (mean dosage 27.4 mg/d) or placebo. Mean baseline LDL 188 mg/dL. Median follow-up: 5.4 years. After that, open-label statin therapy was continued for an additional 5 years.	Simvastatin reduced all-cause mortality by 30%, CHD mortality by 42%, and angioplasty, bypass surgery, major coronary events by 30-40%. Benefit was also seen in patient subgroups with diabetes, impaired fasting glucose, low HDL plus high TG, and metabolic syndrome. Survival benefit persisted at 10 years, without an increased risk of cancer.
SPARCL: Stroke Prevention by Aggressive Reduction in Cholesterol Levels (N Engl J Med 2006;355:549-59)	4731 patients with TIA or stroke within preceding 1-6 months, LDL-C 100-190 mg/dL, and no known CHD were randomized to atorvastatin 80 mg/d or placebo. Primary endpoint: first nonfatal or fatal stroke. Median follow-up: 4.9 years.	Atorvastatin reduced the primary endpoint by 16% (p = 0.03), despite a small increase in hemorrhagic stroke. Atorvastatin also reduced major coronary events by 35% (p = 0.003). Mean LDL during the trial was 73 mg/dL (atorvastatin) vs. 128 mg/dL (placebo).
Stockholm Ischaemic Heart Disease Secondary Prevention Study (Acta Med Scand 1988;223:405)	555 men and women aged < 70 years with prior MI were randomized to clofibrate 2 gm/d plus nicotinic acid 3 gm/d or control. Follow-up: 5 years.	Combination therapy reduced all-cause mortality by 26% and CHD mortality by 36%. Mortality benefit only occurred if baseline TG >133 mg/dL and was greatest in patients with ≥ 30% reduction in TG, (CHD mortality reduced by 60% with therapy).

Table 11.1. Clinical Event Trials

Trial	Design	Results
TNT: Treating to New Targets (N Engl J Med 2005;352:1425)	10,001 men and women with CHD and LDL < 130 mg/dL were randomized to atorvastatin 10 mg/d or atorvastatin 80 mg/d. Median follow-up: 4.9 years	Atorvastatin 80 mg reduced the primary endpoint of a first major cardiovascular event (CHD death, nonfatal non-procedure-related MI, resuscitated cardiac arrest, fatal or nonfatal stroke) by 22%. Mean LDL 77 mg/dL with atorvastatin 80 mg/d vs. 101 mg/dL with atorvastatin 10 mg/d. Significantly more patients randomized to atorvastatin 80 mg had persistent ALT and/or AST elevations (1.2% vs. 0.2% of patients randomized to atorvastatin 10 mg) or treatment-related adverse events (8.1% vs. 5.8% of atorvastatin 10 mg patients; 7.2% and 5.3%, respectively, resulted in discontinuation).
VA-HIT: Veterans Affairs HDL Intervention Trial (N Engl J Med 1999;341:410; JAMA 2001;285:1585 [lipids]; Circulation 2001;103:2828 [stroke])	2531 men with CHD (prior MI, angina with ischemia, coronary revascularization, or angiographic evidence), HDL ≤ 40 mg/dL (mean 32 mg/dL), LDL ≤ 140 mg/dL (mean 111 mg/dL), and TG ≤ 300 mg/dL (mean 160 mg/dL) were randomized to slow-release gemfibrozil 1200 mg/d or placebo and followed up for a median of 5.1 years.	MI or cardiac death (primary endpoint) was 22% lower in patients receiving gemfibrozil. The combined endpoint of CHD death, nonfatal MI, and stroke was reduced by 24%. The benefit of gemfibrozil was only partly explained by the change in HDL. Separate analysis of stroke risk indicated a 31% reduction with gemfibrozil.

Table 11.1. Clinical Event Trials

Trial	Design	Results
WHO Cooperative Trial (Br Heart J 1978;40:1069, Lancet 1984;2:600)	15,745 asymptomatic men aged 30-59 years were stratified by total cholesterol, randomized to clofibrate 1.6 gm/d or placebo, and followed up for an average of 5 years.	Clofibrate group had a 20% reduction in CHD incidence (primary endpoint), due to a 25% reduction in nonfatal MI. However, all-cause mortality was increased in the clofibrate group at 5-year follow-up, prompting extended follow-up. At final follow-up of mean 13.4 years, the excess in deaths with clofibrate was no longer statistically significant.
WOSCOPS: West of Scotland Coronary Prevention Study (N Engl J Med 1995;331:1301; Circulation 2001;103:357)	6595 men without prior MI aged 45-64 years with total cholesterol $\geq$ 252 mg/dL (mean 272 mg/dL) were randomized to pravastatin 40 mg/d or placebo. Mean baseline LDL was 192 mg/dL. Mean follow-up: 4.9 years.	Pravastatin reduced CHD death and/or nonfatal MI (primary endpoint) by 31%, all-cause mortality by 22% (p=0.051), and risk for developing diabetes by 30% (p = 0.042).

ATP = Adult Treatment Panel, CHD = coronary heart disease, HDL = high-density lipoprotein cholesterol, LDL = low-density lipoprotein cholesterol, LV = left ventricle, MI = myocardial infarction, TG = triglyceride

Table 11.2. Angiographic and Other Trials

Trial	Design	Results
ACAPS: Asymptomatic Carotid Artery Progression Study (Circulation 1994;90:1679)	919 asymptomatic men and women aged 40-79 years with early carotid atherosclerosis detected by B-mode ultrasonography and LDL between the 60th and 90th percentiles (mean 156 mg/dL) were randomized to lovastatin 20-40 mg/d (goal to reduce LDL to 90-110 mg/dL) or placebo. Ultrasonography was performed at baseline and 3 years.	Patients receiving lovastatin had regression of carotid atherosclerosis as assessed by change in mean maximum IMT across 12 preselected carotid artery segments (primary endpoint): -0.009 mm/year vs. +0.006 mm/year (progression) with placebo.
AFREGS: Armed Forces Regression Study (Ann Intern Med 2005;142:95)	143 retired military personnel with low HDL and CHD were randomized to triple-drug therapy (gemfibrozil, niacin, cholestyramine) or placebo. Follow-up: 30 months.	Focal coronary stenosis decreased by 0.8% in the drug group and increased by 1.4% in the placebo group. Active treatment also reduced a composite clinical endpoint (12.7% vs. 26.4%).
Apo A-1 Milano study (JAMA 2003;290:2292)	123 patients with acute coronary syndrome were randomized to 5 weekly infusions of recombinant Apo A-1 Milano-phospholipid complexes (ETC-216; 15 mg/kg or 45 mg/kg) or placebo.	ETC-216 produced significant regression of atherosclerosis (assessed by intravascular ultrasound). The absolute reduction in atheroma volume was -14 mm^3 (4.2% decrease from baseline).

Table 11.2. Angiographic and Other Trials

Trial	Design	Results
ARBITER: Arterial Biology for the Investigation of the Treatment Effects of Reducing Cholesterol (Circulation 2002;106:2055)	161 patients who met ATP II criteria for drug therapy were randomized to atorvastatin 80 mg/d or pravastatin 40 mg/d and assessed by carotid B-mode ultrasound at baseline and 1 year.	For the primary endpoint of change in mean common carotid IMT at 1 year, the atorvastatin group had regression (−0.038 mm vs. progression of 0.026 mm with pravastatin). Atorvastatin also resulted in greater LDL lowering than pravastatin (48.5% vs. 27.1%).
ARBITER 2 (Circulation 2004;110:3512)	167 patients with CHD and HDL < 45 mg/dL who were on statin therapy were randomized to additional extended-release niacin or placebo and assessed by carotid B-mode ultrasound at baseline and 1 year.	The primary endpoint (change in common carotid IMT at 1 year) was not significantly different between treatment groups, but the placebo group had significant progression compared with baseline, whereas the change from baseline in the niacin group was not statistically significant. Niacin also provided a 21% increase in HDL.

Table 11.2. Angiographic and Other Trials

Trial	Design	Results
ASAP: Atorvastatin vs. Simvastatin on Atherosclerosis Progression (Lancet 2001;357:577)	325 patients with familial hypercholesterolemia were randomized to atorvastatin 80 mg/d or simvastatin 40 mg/d.	For the primary endpoint, change in carotid IMT over 2 years, the atorvastatin group had mean regression (−0.031 mm) as opposed to progression (0.036 mm) with simvastatin. Atorvastatin also resulted in greater LDL lowering than simvastatin (50.5% vs. 41.2%).
AVERT: Atorvastatin vs. Revascularization Treatments (N Engl J Med 1999;341:70)	341 CHD patients with LV ejection fractions ≥ 40% and 1- or 2-vessel coronary disease were randomized to PTCA + usual care (including lipid lowering) vs. atorvastatin 80 mg/dL. Mean LDL 143 mg/dL. Follow-up: 18 months.	LDL was reduced to 77 mg/dL with atorvastatin vs. 119 mg/dL with usual care. The atorvastatin-treated group had a 36% reduction in ischemic events (cardiac death, resuscitated cardiac arrest, nonfatal MI, CVA, PTCA, CABG, worsening angina) compared with patients treated with PTCA + usual care, but the difference was not statistically significant.

Table 11.2. Angiographic and Other Trials

Trial	Design	Results
BECAIT: Bezafibrate Coronary Atherosclerosis Intervention Trial (Lancet 1996;347:849)	92 men with MI before age 45 were randomized to bezafibrate 200 mg tid or placebo. Lipid criteria included total cholesterol ≥ 201 mg/dL and TG ≥ 142 mg/dL on diet. Median LDL 180 mg/dL; median TG 216 mg/dL. Follow-up: 5 years.	For the primary endpoint of median change in mean minimum lumen diameter, the treatment effect was estimated to be 0.13 mm less progression with bezafibrate. The cumulative coronary event rate was significantly lower in bezafibrate patients (6% vs. 23% with placebo).
CCAIT: Canadian Coronary Atherosclerosis Intervention Trial (Circulation 1994; 89:959)	331 men and women with angiographic CHD and total cholesterol 220-300 mg/dL (mean 250 mg/dL) were randomized to lovastatin 40-80 mg/d (titrated to reduce LDL to ≤ 130 mg/dL) or placebo. Mean LDL was 173 mg/dL. Mean lovastatin dosage was 36 mg/d. Quantitative coronary angiography performed at baseline and 2 years was available in 299 patients.	Lovastatin patients had significantly less angiographic progression as assessed by a quantitative coronary change score (primary endpoint), calculated as the per-patient mean of the minimum lumen diameter changes of all lesions (−0.05 mm with lovastatin vs. −0.09 mm with placebo). Significantly fewer lovastatin patients had progression without regression (33% vs. 50% of placebo patients).

Table 11.2. Angiographic and Other Trials

Trial	Design	Results
CLAS: Cholesterol Lowering Atherosclerosis Study (JAMA 1987;257:3233; JAMA 1990;264:3013 [4-year follow-up]; Circulation 1991;83:438 [femoral]; Circulation 1993;88:20 [carotid])	188 hypercholesterolemic (total cholesterol 185-350 mg/dL) middle-aged (40-59 years) nonsmoking men who had undergone coronary bypass surgery were randomized to colestipol 30 gm/d plus nicotinic acid 3-12 gm/d or placebo. 162 completed CLAS I (2 years), 103 completed CLAS II (4 years).	Significantly less progression and fewer new lesions in native vessels and grafts of patients receiving drug therapy. A panel-assessed global change score indicated angiographic regression in 16% of drug patients and 4% of placebo patients at 2 years, and 18% and 6% respectively at 4 years. Benefit was also seen on femoral atherosclerosis assessed by angiography and carotid atherosclerosis assessed by B-mode ultrasound.

Table 11.2. Angiographic and Other Trials

Trial	Design	Results
COMETS: Comparative Study with Rosuvastatin in Subject with Metabolic Syndrome (Eur Heart J 2005;26:2664)	397 statin-naive patients with metabolic syndrome were randomized to rosuvastatin 10 mg/d, atorvastatin 10 mg/d, or placebo for 6 weeks. For an additional 6 weeks, placebo and rosuvastatin patients received rosuvastatin 20 mg/d and atorvastatin patients received atorvastatin 20 mg/d.	At 6 and 12 weeks, rosuvastatin was more effective at lowering LDL and raising HDL. Change from baseline in LDL at 6 weeks (primary endpoint): rosuvastatin 10 mg/d -42.7% vs atorvastatin 10 mg/d -36.6%, $p < 0.001$. More patients achieved ATP III LDL goal with rosuvastatin at 6 and 12 weeks (at 12 weeks: 91% vs. 79% with atorvastatin, $p < 0.001$).
CURVES (Am J Cardiol 1998;81:582)	534 men and women with LDL $\geq$ 160 mg/dL and TG < 400 mg/dL were randomized to atorvastatin, simvastatin, pravastatin, lovastatin, or fluvastatin at various doses. Follow-up: 8 weeks.	Atorvastatin at doses of 10, 20, and 40 mg/dL produced greater reductions in LDL than other statins at milligram-equivalent doses. Persistent elevations in LFTs or CK did not occur with any treatment.

Table 11.2. Angiographic and Other Trials

Trial	Design	Results
DAIS: Diabetes Atherosclerosis Intervention Study (Lancet 2001;357:905)	731 men and women with type 2 diabetes and at least 1 visible coronary lesion were randomized to fenofibrate 200 mg/d or placebo for at least 3 years.	Fenofibrate reduced progression of coronary artery disease (increase in percent diameter stenosis: 2.11% vs. 3.65% for placebo), but the decrease in mean segment diameter was not significantly different between groups (−0.06 mm vs. −0.08 mm).
EASE: Ezetimibe Add-on to Statin for Effectiveness (Mayo Clin Proc 2005;80:587)	3030 patients receiving statin therapy but not at ATP III LDL target were randomized 2:1 to ezetimibe 10 mg/d or placebo in addition to ongoing statin therapy for 6 weeks.	Ezetimibe reduced LDL from statin baseline by 26% and significantly improved LDL goal attainment (71% vs. 21% with placebo). There were also significant improvements in TG, HDL, non-HDL, apo B, and CRP. Combination therapy was safe and well tolerated.
Effect of Cholesteryl Ester Transfer Protein Inhibitor on HDL Cholesterol (N Engl J Med 2004;350:1505)	19 patients with HDL < 40 mg/dL were treated with torcetrapib 120 mg/d x 4 weeks; 9 patients also received atorvastatin 20 mg/d. Torcetrapib 120 mg bid was given to 6 nonatorvastatin subjects for an additional 4 weeks.	Torcetrapib 120 mg/d increased HDL by 61% and 46% in the atorvastatin and nonatorvastatin groups, respectively ($p \leq 0.001$ vs. baseline), and torcetrapib plus atorvastatin reduced LDL by 17% ($p = 0.02$). Torcetrapib 120 mg twice daily increased HDL by 106% ($p < 0.001$).

Table 11.2. Angiographic and Other Trials

Trial	Design	Results
FATS: Familial Atherosclerosis Treatment Study (N Engl J Med 1990;323:1289)	120 men with CHD and apo B ≥ 125 mg/dL completed 2.5-year study; patients received dietary therapy and either lovastatin 40-80 mg/d plus colestipol 30 gm/d, nicotinic acid 4-6 gm/d plus colestipol 30 gm/d, or placebo. Mean LDL 189 mg/dL.	Lesion progression (mean percent change in stenosis in 9 proximal lesions; primary endpoint) was 2.1% in the placebo group vs. −0.9% in the nicotinic acid + colestipol group and −0.7% in the lovastatin + colestipol group. Patients with clinical events: 10/52 in placebo group, 3/46 in lovastatin + colestipol group, and 2/48 in nicotinic acid + colestipol group.
HARP: Harvard Atherosclerosis Reversibility Project (Lancet 1994;344:1182)	91 men and women with angiographic CHD were randomized to placebo or stepwise treatment with pravastatin 40 mg/d, sustained-release nicotinic acid 1.5-3.0 gm/d, cholestyramine 8-16 gm/d, and gemfibrozil 600-1200 mg/d, with the goal of lowering total cholesterol to ≤ 160 and LDL/HDL ratio to <2. Mean baseline LDL was 138 mg/dL. Quantitative coronary angiography performed at baseline and 2.5 years was available in 79 patients.	Angiographic progression, assessed as both decrease in minimum lumen diameter (primary endpoint) and percentage stenosis, did not differ between groups, despite a 41% decrease in LDL in drug patients compared with placebo.

Table 11.2. Angiographic and Other Trials

Trial	Design	Results
HATS: HDL Atherosclerosis Treatment Study (N Engl J Med 2001;345:1583, Am J Cardiol 2004;93:307)	160 men under age 63 and women under age 70 with CHD and isolated low HDL (≤ 35 mg/dL in men; ≤ 40 mg/dL in women) were randomized to simvastatin plus niacin, antioxidants, both, or placebo. Follow-up: 3 years.	First cardiovascular event (death, MI, stroke, revascularization) was reduced by simvastatin plus niacin (3% vs. 21% for antioxidants, 14% for simvastatin plus niacin combined with antioxidants, 24% for placebo). Simvastatin plus niacin lowered LDL by 42%, raised HDL by 26%, and resulted in regression in coronary stenosis by 0.4% vs. progression by 1.8% with antioxidants, 0.7% with simvastatin plus niacin combined with antioxidants, and 3.9% with placebo).
LCAS: Lipoprotein and Coronary Atherosclerosis Study (Am J Cardiol 1997;80:278)	429 men and women aged 35-75 years with angiographic CHD and LDL cholesterol 115-190 mg/dL (mean 146 mg/dL) were randomized to fluvastatin 20 mg BID or placebo. Quantitative coronary angiography performed at baseline and 2.5 years was available in 340 patients.	Angiographic progression, assessed as the mean within-patient per-lesion decrease in minimum lumen diameter (primary endpoint) was significantly reduced with fluvastatin (0.028 mm vs. 0.100 mm with placebo).

Table 11.2. Angiographic and Other Trials

Trial	Design	Results
Lifestyle Heart Trial (Lancet 1990;336:129;JAMA 1998;280:2001)	48 men and women with angiographic CHD were randomized to usual care or extensive lifestyle changes, consisting of very low fat diet, exercise, smoking cessation, and stress management training. Angiographic follow-up was available at 1 year in 41 patients and at 5 years in 35 patients.	Quantitative coronary angiography indicated mean regression (decrease in percent diameter stenosis) in intervention patients and mean progression in controls. Mean change in percent diameter stenosis indicated regression in 82% of intervention patients compared with 42% of controls. At 5 years, intervention patients continued to show regression (8% decrease in percent diameter stenosis) and control patients showed progression (12% increase in stenosis).
MAAS: Multicentre Anti-Atheroma Study (Lancet 1994; 344:633)	381 men and women aged 30-67 years with angiographic CHD and total cholesterol 213-309 mg/dL (mean 246 mg/dL) were randomized to simvastatin 20 mg/d or placebo. Mean baseline LDL was 169 mg/dL. Quantitative coronary angiography performed at baseline and 4 years was available in 345 patients.	Treatment effects with simvastatin included 0.06 mm less progression of diffuse disease (assessed by mean lumen diameter) and 0.08 mm less progression of focal disease (assessed by minimum lumen diameter) compared to placebo.

Table 11.2. Angiographic and Other Trials

Trial	Design	Results
MARS: Monitored Atherosclerosis Regression Study (Ann Intern Med 1993;119:969)	270 men and women aged 37-67 years with angiographic CHD and total cholesterol of 190-295 mg/dL were randomized to lovastatin 80 mg/d or placebo. Coronary angiography performed at baseline and 2 years was assessed in 247 patients.	Quantitative coronary angiographic assessment of per-patient change in percent diameter stenosis (primary endpoint) indicated an increase (progression) of 1.6% in the lovastatin group and 2.2% in the placebo group (p > 0.2). For lesions causing ≥ 50% at baseline, average percent diameter stenosis decreased 4.1% in the lovastatin group and increased 0.9% in the placebo group (p = 0.005). The panel-assessed global change score indicated significantly less progression with lovastatin (+0.4) than placebo (+0.9). Global change scores indicated regression were assessed in 28 lovastatin and 13 placebo patients.

Table 11.2. Angiographic and Other Trials

Trial	Design	Results
MERCURY I: Measuring Effective Reductions in Cholesterol Using Rosuvastatin Therapy (Am Heart J 2004;147:705)	3140 adults with CHD or at high risk of CHD were randomized to initial treatment for 8 weeks to rosuvastatin 10 mg/d, atorvastatin 10 or 20 mg/d, simvastatin 20 mg/d, or pravastatin 40 mg/d. Patients either remained on these treatments for another 8 weeks or switched treatments.	At 8 weeks, rosuvastatin 10 mg brought 80% of patients to target LDL levels vs. 63% for atorvastatin 10 mg, 74% for atorvastatin 20 mg, 54% for simvastatin 20 mg, and 45% for pravastatin 40 mg. At 16 weeks, patients switched to rosuvastatin were again more likely to achieve LDL treatment goals.
MERCURY II (Am Heart J 2006;151:975.e1-9)	1993 patients with CHD or CHD risk equivalents and LDL 130-249 mg/dL were randomized to receive rosuvastatin 20 mg/d, atorvastatin 10 mg/d, atorvastatin 20 mg/d, simvastatin 20 mg/d, or simvastatin 40 mg/d for 8 weeks, then either remained on the same treatment or switched to lower or milligram-equivalent doses of rosuvastatin for 8 more weeks	At 16 weeks, significantly more patients achieved LDL goals by switching to rosuvastatin 10 mg than remaining on atorvastatin 10 mg (66% vs. 42%) or simvastatin 20 mg (73% vs. 32%), and significantly more patients achieved LDL goals by switching to rosuvastatin 20 mg than remaining on atorvastatin 20 mg (79% vs. 64%) or simvastatin 40 mg (84% vs. 56%). Also, more very high risk patients achieved the optional LDL goal of < 70 mg/dL by switching to rosuvastatin.

Table 11.2. Angiographic and Other Trials

Trial	Design	Results
NHLBI Type II Coronary Intervention Study (Circulation 1984;69:313, Circulation 1984;69:325)	143 men and women with type II hyperlipidemia (LDL in the upper 10th percentile) and CHD were randomized to either cholestyramine 24 gm/d or placebo. Mean LDL was 252 mg/dL. Baseline and 5-year coronary angiography were available for 116 patients.	Panel assessment of angiograms indicated CHD progression in significantly fewer cholestyramine patients (32%) than placebo patients (49%) overall and for lesions causing $\geq$ 50% stenosis at baseline (progression in 12% of cholestyramine vs. 33% of placebo patients).
ORION: Outcome of Rosuvastatin Treatment on Carotid Artery Atheroma: a Magnetic Resonance Imaging Observation (Eur Heart J 2005;26 [suppl]:626)	35 patients with LDL 100-250 mg/dL (mean 156 mg/dL) and carotid atherosclerosis were randomized to either rosuvastatin 5 mg/d or rosuvastatin 40 mg/d and assessed by magnetic resonance imaging. Follow-up: 2 years	LDL was reduced by 39% with rosuvastatin 5 mg/d and by 58% with rosuvastatin 40 mg/d. Neither treatment significantly reduced progression of carotid atherosclerosis, with mean (median) changes in carotid artery wall volume of +0.5% (–1.2%) and –1.4% (+1.1%), respectively. Patients who did have regression, however, also had an LDL reduction of 56% and a mean LDL of 69 mg/dL on treatment.

Table 11.2. Angiographic and Other Trials

Trial	Design	Results
PLAC I: Pravastatin Limitation of Atherosclerosis in the Coronary Arteries (J Am Coll Cardiol 1995;26:1133)	408 men and women with CHD and LDL 130-189 mg/dL were randomized to pravastatin 40 mg/d or placebo. Follow-up angiography at 3 years was obtained in 320 patients.	Change in quantitatively assessed mean lumen diameter of 10 prospectively defined segments (primary endpoint) was not significantly different between groups: annual progression rate was 0.02 mm/year with pravastatin vs. 0.4 mm/year with placebo. However, minimum lumen diameter was reduced less with pravastatin; annual progression rates were 0.03 mm/year with pravastatin and 0.05 mm/year with placebo (p = 0.04).
PLAC II: Pravastatin, Lipids, and Atherosclerosis in the Carotid Arteries (Am J Cardiol 1995;75:455)	151 men and women with CHD, ultrasound evidence of carotid atherosclerosis, and LDL between the 60th and 90th percentile for age and sex (mean 167 mg/dL) were randomized to pravastatin 40 mg/d or placebo and followed up for 3 years.	Change in mean maximum IMT of 12 carotid artery segments (primary endpoint) indicated significantly less progression with pravastatin: 0.059 mm/year vs. 0.068 mm/year with placebo.

Dyslipidemia Essentials

Table 11.2. Angiographic and Other Trials

Trial	Design	Results
POSCH: Program on the Surgical Control of the Hyperlipidemias (N Engl J Med 1990;323:946)	838 men and women aged 30-64 years with previous MI and total cholesterol ≥ 220 mg/dL (or total cholesterol 200–219 mg/dL and LDL ≥ 140 mg/dL) despite diet were randomized to partial ileal bypass surgery or control. Mean LDL was 179 mg/dL. Coronary angiography was performed at baseline and 3 years (696 patients), 5 years (634 patients), 7 years (361 patients), and 10 years (175 patients).	All-cause mortality (primary endpoint) was not significantly different between groups, but the incidence of CHD death or nonfatal MI was reduced by 35% in surgery patients. Panel assessment of angiograms indicated CHD progression in 28% of surgery patients vs. 41% of controls at 3 years, 38% vs. 65% at 5 years, 48% vs. 77% at 7 years, and 55% vs. 85% at 10 years.
Post-CABG: Post Coronary Artery Bypass Graft Trial (N Engl J Med 1997;336:153 Circulation 2000;102:157 [7.5-year follow-up])	1351 men and women aged 21-74 years, 1-11 years post CABG, with LDL 130-175 mg/dL (mean 155 mg/dL) were randomized to aggressive (40-80 mg/d) or moderate (2.5-5 mg/d) lovastatin therapy with respective LDL goals of < 85 mg/dL and <140 mg/dL. Angiography was performed at baseline and mean 4.3 years.	LDL was reduced to 93-97 mg/dL with aggressive therapy and 132-136 mg/dL with moderate therapy. The mean per-patient percent of grafts with ≥ 0.6 mm decrease in lumen diameter was improved with aggressive therapy (27% vs. 39% with moderate therapy). Revascularization rate was 29% lower with aggressive therapy (not statistically significant by study criteria). Long-term follow-up at 7.5 years showed significant reductions in revascularization procedures (30%) and the composite clinical event endpoint (24%).

Table 11.2. Angiographic and Other Trials

Trial	Design	Results
PQRST: Probucol Quantitative Regression Swedish Trial (Am J Cardiol 1994;74:875)	303 asymptomatic or symptomatic men and women aged < 71 years with total cholesterol > 265 mg/dL, LDL > 175 mg/dL, and angiographic evidence of femoral atherosclerosis were randomized to probucol 1 gm/d or placebo; all patients also received cholestyramine 8-16 gm/d. Femoral angiography performed at baseline and at 3 years was available in 274 patients.	Change in atheroma volume in femoral segments (primary endpoint) was not significantly different between treatment groups, nor was change in arterial edge roughness (a measure of arterial wall irregularity) or amount of aortofemoral atherosclerosis. However, in placebo patients, lumen volume was significantly increased from baseline, and roughness of the femoral artery significantly decreased.
PRINCE: Pravastatin Inflammation/ CRP Evaluation (JAMA 2001;286:64)	1702 men and women with no prior CHD were randomized to pravastatin 40 mg/d or placebo; 1182 patients with CHD received pravastatin 40 mg/d. Endpoint: change in CRP at 24 weeks.	Pravastatin reduced CRP levels by a median of 17% in the primary prevention cohort and 13% in the secondary prevention cohort.
REGRESS: Regression Growth Evaluation Statin Study (Circulation 1995;91:2528)	885 men with total cholesterol 155-310 mg/dL (mean 232 mg/dL) and angiographic CHD were randomized to pravastatin 40 mg/d or placebo. Mean LDL was 166 mg/dL. Quantitative coronary angiography performed at baseline and 2 years was available in 778 patients.	Both primary endpoints showed less progression with pravastatin: median minimum lumen diameter decreased by 0.03 mm with pravastatin and 0.09 mm with placebo, and average mean lumen diameter decreased by 0.06 mm with pravastatin and 0.10 mm with placebo.

Table 11.2. Angiographic and Other Trials

Trial	Design	Results
REVERSAL: Reversal of Atherosclerosis with Aggressive Lipid Lowering (JAMA 2004;291:1132)	654 patients with symptomatic CHD and a baseline stenosis ≥ 20% on coronary angiography were randomized to intensive lipid lowering with atorvastatin 80 mg/d or moderate lipid lowering with pravastatin 40 mg/d. Intravascular ultrasound was available at baseline and 18 months in 502 patients. Primary endpoint: percent change in atheroma volume.	Pravastatin resulted in a 2.7% progression in atheroma volume at 18 months; net progression did not occur in the atorvastatin group (p = 0.001). Mean LDL with atorvastatin was 79 mg/dL (46% decrease from baseline) vs.110 mg/dL with pravastatin (25% decrease from baseline) (p < 0.001).
STARS: St. Thomas' Atherosclerosis Regression Study (Lancet 1992;339:563)	90 men aged < 66 years with CHD and total cholesterol > 232 mg/dL (mean 280 mg/dL) were randomized to diet, diet plus cholestyramine 16 gm/d, or usual care. Angiography performed at baseline and 39 months was evaluable in 74 patients.	Change in mean lumen diameter (primary endpoint) and change in minimum lumen diameter indicated progression in usual-care patients (–0.201 mm and –0.232 mm, respectively) and regression in diet patients (0.003 mm and 0.030 mm) and diet-plus-cholestyramine patients (0.103 mm and 0.117 mm). Overall progression occurred in 46% of usual-care, 15% of diet-only, and 12% of diet-plus-cholestyramine patients; regression occurred in 4%, 38%, and 33% of the respective groups.

Table 11.2. Angiographic and Other Trials

Trial	Design	Results
STELLAR: Statin Therapies for Elevated Lipid Levels Compared Across Doses to Rosuvastatin (Am J Cardiol 2003;92:152)	2431 patients with LDL 160-249 mg/dL and TG < 400 mg/dL were randomized to 1 of 15 open-label treatment arms for 6 weeks: rosuvastatin 10, 20, 40, or 80 mg; atorvastatin 10, 20, 40, or 80 mg; simvastatin 10, 20, 40, or 80 mg; or pravastatin 10, 20, or 40 mg.	Rosuvastatin 10-80 mg reduced LDL by a mean of 8% more than atorvastatin 10-80 mg, 26% more than pravastatin 10-40 mg, and 12-18% more than simvastatin 10-80 mg (all p < 0.001). Mean increase in HDL was 7.7-9.6% with rosuvastatin vs. 2.1-6.8% in all other groups. ATP III LDL goals were achieved by 82-89% of patients receiving rosuvastatin 10-40 mg vs. 69-85% of patients receiving atorvastatin 10-80 mg.
VYVA: Vytorin vs. Atorvastatin (Am Heart Journal 2005;149:464)	1902 patients with LDL above ATP III goal were randomized to ezetimibe/simvastatin (10/10, 10/20, 10/40, or 10/80 mg) vs. atorvastatin (10, 20, 40, or 80 mg). Study duration: 6 weeks.	Ezetimibe/simvastatin was more effective at lowering LDL reductions at each dose comparison and provided greater increases in HDL at the 40- and 80-mg statin doses. More high-risk patients reached NCEP ATP III LDL goal < 100 mg/dL and optional goal < 70 mg/dL with ezetimibe/ simvastatin 10/80 mg vs. atorvastatin 80 mg.

ATP = Adult Treatment Panel, CABG = coronary artery bypass grafting, CHD = coronary heart disease, CRP = C-reactive protein, CVA = cardiovascular accident, HDL = high-density lipoprotein cholesterol, IMT = intima-media thickness, LDL = low-density lipoprotein cholesterol, LV = left ventricle, MI = myocardial infarction, PTCA = percutaneous transluminal coronary angioplasty, TG = triglyceride

Notice Regarding Dyslipidemia Drug Summaries

Pages 147-162 contain prescribing information pertinent to the clinical use of lipid-modifying drugs, as compiled from a variety of sources. The information provided is not exhaustive, and the reader is referred to other drug information references, including the manufacturer's product literature, which may be found at the website identified at the end of each drug summary. The use of any drug should be preceded by careful review of the package insert, which provides indications and dosing approved by the U.S. Food and Drug Administration.

Clinical use of the information provided and any consequences that may arise from its use are the responsibilities of the prescribing physician. The authors, editors, and publisher do not warrant or guarantee the information contained in this section, and do not assume and expressly disclaim any liability for errors or omissions or any consequences that may occur from such.

Chapter 12

Dyslipidemia Drug Summaries (see notice, p. 146)

Atorvastatin (Lipitor)

Class: HMG-CoA reductase inhibitor
Mechanism of Action: Atorvastatin competitively inhibits the enzyme HMG-CoA reductase, which is the rate-limiting step in cholesterol synthesis. Enzyme inhibition results in decreased intracellular cholesterol production in the liver, which upregulates intrahepatic LDL receptor activity and facilitates LDL cholesterol clearance from the circulation. HMG-CoA reductase inhibitors increase HDL and decrease LDL, VLDL, and triglycerides.
Indications: (1) Adjunct to diet to reduce elevated total and LDL cholesterol, apo B, and triglycerides and to increase HDL cholesterol in primary hypercholesterolemia (heterozygous familial and nonfamilial) and mixed dyslipidemia (Types IIa and IIb); (2) Adjunct to diet in treatment of elevated serum triglyceride (Type IV); (3) Treatment of primary dysbetalipoproteinemia (Type III) not responding to diet; (4) To reduce total and LDL cholesterol in patients with homozygous familial hypercholesterolemia as an adjunct to other lipid-lowering treatments (e.g., LDL apheresis) or if such treatments are unavailable; (5) Adjunct to diet to reduce total and LDL cholesterol and apoB levels in boys and postmenarchal girls, ages 10-17 years, with heterozygous familial hypercholesterolemia, if after adequate trial of diet therapy LDL cholesterol remains ≥ 190 mg/dL, or ≥ 160 mg/dL with 2 or more other CHD risk factors or a family history of premature cardiovascular disease.
Dosage: Recommended starting dose is 10-20 mg once daily or 40 mg when LDL reduction > 45% is required. Dosage range is 10-80 mg/d administered as a single dose.
Renal Impairment: No dosage adjustment necessary.
Hepatic Impairment: Use with caution.
Contraindications: Hypersensitivity, active liver disease, unexplained persistent elevations of serum transaminases, pregnancy, lactation.
Adverse Effects: Headache, flatulence, dyspepsia, myalgia, rash, elevated liver enzymes, pharyngitis, rhinitis. Rhabdomyolysis with renal dysfunction has occurred with some agents from this class.
Monitoring: LFTs, lipid panel.
Drug Interactions: Coadministration with cyclosporine, erythromycin, fibric acid derivatives, nicotinic acid, or azole antifungals may increase the risk of myopathy or rhabdomyolysis. Discontinue HMG-CoA reductase inhibitor while on azole antifungal

therapy. May increase serum digoxin levels (monitor) and oral contraceptive levels (norethindrone, ethinyl estradiol). Separate administration from bile acid sequestrants by 2-4 hours.

Comments: Can be taken at any time of the day. May decrease triglycerides to a greater extent than other HMG-CoA reductase inhibitors. Instruct patients to report promptly any muscle pain, tenderness, or weakness, especially if accompanied by fever or malaise.

Dosage Forms: Tablet (10 mg, 20 mg, 40 mg, 80 mg)

Website: www.lipitor.com

Cholestyramine (Questran, Prevalite, Questran Light)

Class: Bile acid sequestrant

Mechanism of Action: Cholesterol is a precursor of bile acids, which are secreted via the bile from the liver and gallbladder to emulsify intestinal fats and lipids in foods. Cholestyramine binds bile acids in the intestine and decreases their reabsorption, resulting in increased bile acid production in the liver; LDL receptors are upregulated to meet the increased need for cholesterol, facilitating clearance of LDL cholesterol from the circulation. This agent may increase triglycerides, VLDL, and HDL.

Indications: Adjunct to diet for reduction of elevated serum cholesterol in primary hypercholesterolemia.

Dosage: Usual starting dose is 4 gm 1-2 times daily. Maximum recommended dose: 24 gm/d in up to 6 divided doses.

Renal Impairment: No dosage adjustment needed.

Contraindications: Hypersensitivity, complete biliary obstruction.

Adverse Effects: Constipation, fecal impaction, abdominal pain/distention, GI bleeding, N/V/D, flatulence, dysphagia, headache, fatigue, urticaria, rash, muscle/joint pain, increased PT, hyperchloremic acidosis.

Monitoring: Serum cholesterol and triglycerides.

Drug Interactions: May interfere with absorption of vitamins A, D, E, K, and folic acid. May decrease the effects of warfarin, mycophenolate, thyroid hormone, digoxin, and amiodarone by interfering with their absorption.

Comments: To prevent decreased absorption of other medications, separate concomitant administration of bile acid sequestrants by 2-4 hours.

Dosage Forms: Questran (4 gm anhydrous resin/9 gm packets and 378 gm cans); Questran light (4 gm anhydrous resin/5 gm packets and 210 gm cans); Prevalite (4 gm anhydrous resin/5.5 gm packets)

Website: www.pdr.net

Colesevelam (WelChol)

Class: Bile acid sequestrant

Mechanism of Action: Cholesterol is a precursor of bile acids, which are secreted via the bile from the liver and gallbladder to emulsify intestinal fats and lipids in foods. Colesevelam binds bile acids in the intestine and decreases their reabsorption, resulting in increased bile acid production in the liver; LDL receptors are upregulated to meet the increased need for cholesterol, facilitating clearance of LDL cholesterol from the circulation. This agent may increase triglycerides, VLDL, and HDL.

Indications: Alone or in combination with a statin as an adjunct to diet and exercise for reduction of elevated LDL cholesterol in patients with primary hypercholesterolemia (Type IIa).

Dosage: *Monotherapy:* Usual starting dose is 3 tablets twice daily with meals or 6 tablets once daily with a meal. The dose can be increased to 7 tablets. *Combination therapy:* Doses of 4 to 6 tablets per day have been shown to be safe and effective when coadministered with a statin or when the two drugs are dosed apart. For maximal therapeutic effect, the recommended dose is 3 tablets taken twice daily with meals or 6 tablets taken once daily with a meal.

Contraindications: Bowel obstruction, hypersensitivity.

Adverse Effects: Constipation, N/V/D, abdominal pain, flatulence, headache, fatigue, myalgia, flu syndrome.

Monitoring: Serum cholesterol and triglycerides.

Drug Interactions: This agent may interfere with absorption of vitamins A, D, E, K, and folic acid. No significant effect on bioavailability of digoxin, metoprolol, quinidine, lovastatin, valproic acid, or warfarin.

Dosage Forms: Tablet (625 mg)

Website: www.welchol.com

Colestipol (Colestid)

Class: Bile acid sequestrant

Mechanism of Action: Cholesterol is a precursor of bile acids, which are secreted via the bile from the liver and gallbladder to emulsify intestinal fats and lipids in foods. Colestipol binds bile acids in the intestine and decreases their reabsorption, resulting in increased bile acid production in the liver; LDL receptors are upregulated to meet the increased need for cholesterol, facilitating clearance of LDL cholesterol from the circulation. This agent may increase triglycerides, VLDL, and HDL.

Indications: Adjunct to diet for reduction of elevated serum cholesterol in primary hypercholesterolemia.

Dosages: *Granules:* Starting dose is 5 gm once or twice daily mixed with liquids. Usual dose is 5-30 gm/d in 2-4 divided doses. *Tablets:* Starting dose is 2 gm once or twice daily, then increased by 2 gm once or twice daily at 1-2 month intervals. Usual dose is 2-16 gm/d given once or in divided doses.

Renal Impairment: No dosage adjustment needed.

Contraindications: Hypersensitivity, complete biliary obstruction.

Adverse Effects: Constipation, fecal impaction, abdominal pain/distention, GI bleeding, N/V/D, flatulence, dysphagia, headache, fatigue, urticaria, rash, muscle/joint pain, increased PT, hyperchloremic acidosis.

Monitoring: Serum cholesterol and triglycerides.

Drug Interactions: May interfere with absorption of vitamins A, D, E, K, and folic acid. May decrease the effects of warfarin, mycophenolate, thyroid hormone, digoxin, and amiodarone by interfering with absorption.

Comments: To prevent decreased absorption of other medications, separate administration of bile acid sequestrants by 2-4 hours. Swallow tablets whole; do not crush, chew, cut.

Dosage Forms: Tablet (1 gm); granule (5 gm colestipol/7.5 gm powder in 300 gm and 500 gm bottles, and 5 gm and 7.5 gm packets)

Website: www.pdr.net

Ezetimibe (Zetia)

Class: Cholesterol absorption inhibitor

Mechanism of Action: Ezetimibe reduces blood cholesterol by inhibiting the absorption of cholesterol and phytosterols such as sitosterol from the small intestine. Intestinal cholesterol is derived primarily from cholesterol secreted in the bile and from dietary cholesterol. By inhibiting cholesterol absorption, ezetimibe reduces the delivery of intestinal cholesterol to the liver, which causes a reduction of hepatic cholesterol stores and an increase in cholesterol clearance from the blood. This mechanism is complementary to that of statins.

Indications: Adjunct to diet for (1) primary hypercholesterolemia (heterozygous familial and nonfamilial), either as monotherapy or in conjunction with statins to reduce elevated total cholesterol, LDL cholesterol, and apo B; (2) homozygous familial hypercholesterolemia, combined with

atorvastatin or simvastatin, as an adjunct to other lipid-lowering treatments (e.g., LDL apheresis) or if such treatments are unavailable; (3) homozygous sitosterolemia, as adjunctive therapy to diet for the reduction of elevated sitosterol and campesterol levels (only agent with this indication).

Dosage: 10 mg once daily, with or without food. Can be given at the same time as statins. No dosage adjustment is needed in the elderly or in patients with renal or mild hepatic insufficiency.

Contraindications: Hypersensitivity. The combination of ezetimibe and statins is contraindicated in active liver disease or unexplained persistent transaminase elevations, pregnancy, lactation. Due to unknown effects, ezetimibe is not recommended in moderate or severe hepatic insufficiency.

Adverse Effects: Fatigue, abdominal pain, diarrhea, pharyngitis, sinusitis, viral infection, arthralgia, back pain, coughing.

Monitoring: Baseline LFTs when used in conjunction with statins, lipid panel.

Drug Interactions: The safety and effectiveness of ezetimibe has not been established with fibrates. Carefully monitor patients receiving cyclosporine. Cholestyramine may reduce the effectiveness of ezetimibe. Ezetimibe should be given > 2 hours before or > 4 hours after bile acid sequestrants.

Dosage Forms: Tablet (10 mg)

Website: www.zetia.com

Ezetimibe with simvastatin (Vytorin)

Class: Combination of cholesterol absorption inhibitor and HMG-CoA reductase inhibitor

Mechanism of Action: See ezetimibe (p. 150) and simvastatin (p. 161)

Indications: (1) Adjunct to diet for primary (heterozygous familial and nonfamilial) hypercholesterolemia or mixed hyperlipidemia, to reduce elevated total cholesterol, LDL cholesterol, apo B, triglycerides and non-HDL cholesterol, and to increase HDL cholesterol; (2) For the reduction of elevated total cholesterol and LDL cholesterol in homozygous familial hypercholesterolemia, as an adjunct to other lipid-lowering treatments (e.g., LDL apheresis) or if such treatments are unavailable.

Dosage: Taken as a single daily dose in the evening, with or without food. Usual starting dose is 10/20 mg/d; 10/10 mg/d may be considered when less aggressive LDL cholesterol reduction is required, and 10/40 mg/d may be considered when larger (> 55%) LDL cholesterol reductions are required. Dosage range is 10/10 mg to 10/80 mg once daily. No dosage adjustment is needed in the elderly. Do not start in patients taking cyclosporine unless the patient has already tolerated treatment with simvastatin 5 mg/d or higher and do not exceed 10/10 mg/d; monitor closely. For patients taking amiodarone or verapamil, do not exceed 10/20 mg/d.

Renal Impairment: No dosage adjustment is required for mild or moderate renal insufficiency. For severe renal insufficiency, do not start unless the patient has already tolerated treatment with simvastatin 5 mg/d or higher; monitor closely.

Hepatic Impairment: No dosage adjustment is required for mild hepatic insufficiency. Not recommended in moderate or severe hepatic insufficiency due to unknown effects.

Contraindications: Hypersensitivity, active liver disease, unexplained transaminase elevations, pregnancy, lactation.

Adverse Effects: See ezetimibe (p. 150) and simvastatin (p. 161).

Monitoring: Baseline LFTs, lipid panel.

Drug Interactions: See ezetimibe (p. 150) and simvastatin (p. 161). Give ≥ 2 hours before or ≥ 4 hours after bile acid sequestrants.

Comments: Administer in the evening. Instruct patients to report promptly any muscle pain, tenderness, or weakness, esp. if accompanied by fever or malaise.

Dosage Forms: Tablet (10/10 mg, 10/20 mg, 10/40 mg, 10/80 mg)

Website: www.vytorin.com

Fenofibrate (Tricor)

Class: Fibric acid derivative

Mechanism of Action: Fenofibrate decreases triglycerides and increases HDL cholesterol. The exact mechanism of action is not known, but may include: (1) increasing triglyceride clearance by enhancing lipoprotein lipase activity; (2) PPAR-α–mediated transcriptional induction of apo A-I, apo A-II, and lipoprotein lipase synthesis; decreased hepatic transcription of apo C-III.

Indications: Adjunct to diet for (1) primary hypercholesterolemia or mixed dyslipidemia (Types IIa and IIb) to reduce total cholesterol, LDL cholesterol, triglycerides, and apo B; (2) hypertriglyceridemia (Types IV and V).

Dosage: Initial dose: 160 mg/d with meals for primary hypercholesterolemia or mixed hyperlipidemia; 54-160 mg/d with meals for hypertriglyceridemia. Adjust at 4-8 week intervals. Maximum dose: 160 mg/d.

Adverse Effects: Abnormal LFTs, abdominal pain, back pain, headache, asthenia, flu syndrome, diarrhea, nausea, constipation, increased CK, respiratory disorder, rhinitis.

Monitoring: Lipid profile, LFTs, periodic blood counts.

Drug Interactions: Rhabdomyolysis, severe myopathy, acute renal failure may occur when administered with statins. Potentiates oral anticoagulants (reduce anticoagulant dose). Allow at least 1 hour before or 4-6 hours after concomitant bile acid sequestrants. Caution with immunosuppressants (e.g., cyclosporine), other nephrotoxic drugs, statins.

Dosage Forms: Tablet (48 mg, 145 mg)

Website: www.tricortablets.com

Fluvastatin (Lescol, Lescol XL)

Class: HMG-CoA reductase inhibitor

Mechanism of Action: Fluvastatin competitively inhibits the enzyme HMG-CoA reductase, which is the rate-limiting step in cholesterol synthesis. This enzyme inhibition results in decreased intracellular cholesterol production in the liver, which upregulates intrahepatic LDL receptor activity and facilitates LDL cholesterol clearance from the circulation. HMG-CoA reductase inhibitors increase HDL and decrease LDL, VLDL, apo B, and triglycerides.

Indications: Adjunct to diet (1) to reduce elevated total and LDL cholesterol, apo B, and triglycerides and to increase HDL cholesterol in primary hypercholesterolemia (heterozygous familial and nonfamilial) and mixed dyslipidemia (Types IIa and IIb); (2) to slow the progression of coronary atherosclerosis in patients with CHD; (3) to reduce the risk of undergoing coronary revascularization procedures in patients with CHD.

Dosage: Initial dose is 40-80 mg/d at bedtime, 20 mg/d in patients requiring < 25% LDL cholesterol reduction. Usual dosage range is 40-80 mg/d. Administer 80 mg dose in two doses of 40-mg immediate-release capsules or one 80-mg extended-release tablet.

Renal Impairment: Use with caution in severe renal impairment.

Hepatic Impairment: Use with caution.

Contraindications: Hypersensitivity, active liver disease, pregnancy, lactation.

Adverse Effects: Headache, insomnia, N/V/D, flatulence, dyspepsia, myalgia, back pain, arthralgia, upper respiratory tract infection, rhinitis, pharyngitis, rash, fatigue. Rhabdomyolysis with renal dysfunction has occurred with some agents from this class.

Monitoring: LFTs, lipid panel.

Drug Interactions: Coadministration with cyclosporine, erythromycin, clofibrate, gemfibrozil, or nicotinic acid may increase the risk of severe myopathy or rhabdomyolysis. Itraconazole may increase HMG-CoA reductase inhibitor levels; discontinue HMG-CoA reductase inhibitor administration while on azole antifungal therapy. HMG-CoA reductase inhibitors may increase anticoagulant effect of warfarin (monitor PT/INR). Monitor digoxin. May inhibit endogenous steroid production; use with caution with spironolactone, cimetidine, ketoconazole. May be potentiated by cimetidine, ranitidine, omeprazole, and antagonized by rifampicin. Separate administration of bile acid sequestrants from HMG-CoA reductase inhibitors by 2-4 hours.

Comments: Administer single dose at bedtime. Instruct patients to promptly report any muscle pain, tenderness, or weakness, especially if fever or malaise.

Dosage Forms: Capsule (20 mg, 40 mg); extended-release tablet (80 mg)

Website: www.lescol.com

Gemfibrozil (Lopid)

Class: Fibric acid derivative

Mechanism of Action: Gemfibrozil decreases triglycerides and increases HDL cholesterol. The exact mechanism of action is not known; possible mechanisms include: (1) increasing triglyceride clearance by enhancing lipoprotein lipase activity; and (2) PPAR-α–mediated transcriptional induction of apo A-I, apo A-II, and lipoprotein lipase synthesis; decreased hepatic transcription of apo C-III.

Indications: Adjunct to diet for (1) severe hypertriglyceridemia in patients who are at risk for pancreatitis (Type IV and Type V hyperlipidemia); (2) to reduce risk of CHD in Type IIb patients without CHD and with low HDL in addition to elevated LDL and triglycerides.

Dosage: Usual dose is 600 mg twice daily 30 minutes before breakfast and the evening meal.

Contraindications: Hepatic dysfunction, severe renal dysfunction, gallbladder disease, hypersensitivity.

Adverse Effects: N/V/D, abdominal pain, acute appendicitis, atrial fibrillation, constipation, headache, fatigue, increased incidence of gallstones, elevated LFTs, elevated CK, rarely severe anemia, leukopenia, thrombocytopenia, myalgias, rash, blurred vision.

Monitoring: Lipid profile, LFTs, periodic blood counts.

Drug Interactions: May potentiate anticoagulant effect of warfarin (monitor PT/INR). Risk of myopathy may be increased when given with HMG-CoA reductase inhibitors.

Dosage Forms: Tablet (600 mg)

Website: www.pdr.net

Lovastatin (Mevacor)

Class: HMG-CoA reductase inhibitor

Mechanism of Action: Lovastatin competitively inhibits the enzyme HMG-CoA reductase, which is the rate-limiting step in cholesterol synthesis. This enzyme inhibition results in decreased intracellular cholesterol production in the liver, which upregulates intrahepatic LDL receptor activity and facilitates LDL cholesterol clearance from the circulation. HMG-CoA reductase inhibitors increase HDL and decrease LDL, VLDL, apo B, and triglycerides.

Indications: Adjunct to diet (1) to reduce elevated total and LDL cholesterol in primary hypercholesterol-emia and mixed dyslipidemia (Types IIa and IIb); (2) to slow progression of atherosclerosis in patients with CHD; (3) to reduce risk of MI, unstable angina, and coronary revascularization procedures in patients without cardiovascular disease who have average to moderately elevated total and LDL cholesterol and below-average HDL cholesterol; (4) to reduce total cholesterol, LDL cholesterol, and apo B levels in adolescent boys and postmenarche ($\geq$ 1 year) girls, aged 10-17 years, with heterozygous FH if after adequate trial of diet therapy LDL cholesterol remains > 189 mg/dL, or > 160 mg/dL with $\geq$ 2 other cardio-vascular risk factors or a family history of premature cardiovascular disease.

Dosage: Start with 20 mg/d with evening meal. If patient is on immunosuppressant therapy or requires < 20% LDL reduction, start with 10 mg/d. Adjust dosage at 4-week intervals. Usual dosage is 10-80 mg/d in 1 dose or 2 divided doses. Maximum recommended dose for patients on fibrates, niacin, or immunosuppressants is 20 mg/d.

Renal Impairment: For creatinine clearance < 30 ml/min, doses above 20 mg/d should be used with caution.

Hepatic Impairment: Use with caution.

Contraindications: Hypersensitivity, active liver disease, pregnancy, lactation.

Adverse Effects: Headache, insomnia, N/V/D, flatulence, dyspepsia, leg pain, myalgia, arthralgia, rash. Rhabdo-myolysis with renal dysfunction has occurred with some agents in this class.

Monitoring: LFTs, lipid panel.

Drug Interactions: Coadministration with cyclosporine, erythromycin, clofibrate, gemfibrozil, or nicotinic acid may increase the risk of severe myopathy or rhabdomyolysis. Itraconazole may increase HMG-CoA reductase inhibitor levels; discontinue HMG-CoA reductase inhibitor administration while on azole antifungal therapy. HMG-CoA reductase inhibitors may increase anticoagulant effect of warfarin (monitor PT/INR). Caution with spironolactone, cimetidine, steroid hormone suppressive drugs, HIV protease inhibitors. Separate administration from bile acid sequestrants by 2-4 hours.

Comments: Administer with the evening meal. Instruct patients to report promptly any muscle pain, tenderness, or weakness, especially if accompanied by fever or malaise.

Dosage Forms: Tablet (10 mg, 20 mg, 40 mg)

Website: www.pdr.net

Niacin, extended-release (Niaspan)

Class: Nicotinic acid derivative

Mechanism of Action: Niacin decreases total and LDL cholesterol, lipoprotein(a), apo B, and triglycerides and increases HDL cholesterol. The exact mechanism of action is not known. Several explanations have been offered as possible mechanisms: (1) decreased VLDL production and release; (2) decreased release of free fatty acids from adipose tissue into the circulation, thus decreasing triglyceride synthesis. Mechanism by which niacin increases HDL cholesterol is unknown.

Indications: Adjunct to diet (1) to reduce elevated total cholesterol, LDL cholesterol, apo B, and triglycerides, and to increase HDL cholesterol in primary hypercholesterolemia and mixed dyslipidemia (Types IIa and IIb); (2) to reduce risk of recurrent nonfatal MI in patients with a history of MI and hypercholesterolemia; (3) in combination with a bile acid sequestrant to slow progression or promote regression of atherosclerosis in patients with CHD and hypercholesterolemia; (4) in combination with a bile acid sequestrant to reduce elevated total cholesterol and LDL cholesterol in primary hypercholesterolemia when diet or diet plus monotherapy has been inadequate; (5) as adjunctive therapy in patients with very high serum triglycerides (Types IV and V) who are at risk for pancreatitis when dietary measures are inadequate; (6) in combination with lovastatin for treatment of primary hypercholesterolemia and mixed dyslipidemia (Types IIa and IIb) in patients receiving lovastatin who require additional triglyceride reduction or HDL cholesterol increase and in patients receiving niacin who require additional LDL cholesterol reduction.

Dosage: Initial dose: 500 mg once daily for 4 weeks, then 1 gm once daily for weeks 5-8. May increase by up to 500 mg every 4 weeks to usual range of 1-2 gm daily: max 2 gm/d. Retitrate if restarting after an extended time. Women may need lower dose. Swallow whole; do not crush, chew, or divide. Take at bedtime with low-fat snack. Avoid concomitant alcohol and hot beverages. May pretreat with aspirin or another NSAID 30 minutes before dose.

Contraindications: Hepatic dysfunction, unexplained elevations of serum transaminases, active peptic ulcer disease, arterial bleeding.

Adverse Effects: Flushing, dizziness, tachycardia, palpitations, shortness of breath, sweating, chills, edema, headache, GI upset, pain, rhinitis, rash, pruritus, glucose intolerance, peptic ulcer, abnormal LFTs, jaundice.

Monitoring: Lipid profile, LFTs, blood glucose, serum phosphorus in patients at risk for hypophosphatemia.

Drug Interactions: Avoid alcohol. Monitor for any symptoms of

rhabdomyolysis with HMG-CoA reductase inhibitors. May potentiate antihypertensives, other vasoactive drugs (e.g., ganglionic or adrenergic blockers, nitrates, calcium channel blockers). Caution with anticoagulants (monitor PT and platelet counts). Antidiabetic agents may need adjustment. Avoid other products with high amounts of niacin or nicotinamide. Separate dosing of bile acid sequestrants by 4-6 hours.
Dosage Forms: Extended-release tablet (500 mg, 750 mg, 1 gm)
Website: www.niaspan.com

Niacin, immediate-release (Niacor) and sustained-release (Slo-Niacin) (various OTC preparations)

Class: Nicotinic acid derivative
Mechanism of Action: Niacin decreases total and LDL cholesterol, lipoprotein(a), apo B, and triglycerides and increases HDL cholesterol. The exact mechanism of action is not known. Several explanations have been offered as possible mechanisms: (1) decreased VLDL production and release; (2) decreased release of free fatty acids from adipose tissue into the circulation, thus decreasing triglyceride synthesis. Mechanism by which niacin increases HDL cholesterol is unknown.
Indications: Adjunct to diet for (1) reduction of elevated total and LDL cholesterol in primary hypercholesterolemia (Types IIa and IIb); (2) treatment of adults with very high serum triglyceride (Types IV and V) with risk of pancreatitis and inadequate response to diet.
Dosage: Initiate at 250 mg after evening meal; increase frequency and daily dose every 4-7 days until LDL and/or triglyceride goal is achieved or dose is 1.5-2 gm/d. With immediate-release niacin, if hyperlipidemia is not controlled at this dosage, increase at 2- to 4-week intervals to 3 gm/d (1 gm tid); dosage generally should not exceed 6 gm/d. Maximum daily dose of sustained-release niacin is 2 gm/d.
Contraindications: Hepatic dysfunction, hypersensitivity, arterial hemorrhage, active peptic ulcer.
Adverse Effects: Flushing, nausea, flatulence, headache, pruritus, skin tingling, heartburn, hypotension, dizziness, tachycardia, vasovagal attacks, blurred vision, wheezing, abnormal LFTs, glucose intolerance.
Monitoring: Lipid profile, LFTs, blood glucose.
Drug Interactions: Additive hypotensive effect with ganglionic blocking agents and vasoactive drugs. Decreased efficacy of oral hypoglycemic agents. Increased risk of myopathy with concurrent use of HMG-CoA reductase inhibitors.
Comments: Aspirin or NSAIDs taken 30-60 minutes prior to niacin can help with adverse effects (e.g. flushing, tingling, headache).
Dosage Forms: Immediate-release tablet (500 mg), and various OTC preparations.
Website: www.pdr.net

Niacin, extended-release, with lovastatin (Advicor)

Class: Combination of nicotinic acid and HMG-CoA reductase inhibitor in a single preparation.

Mechanism of Action: See niacin (p. 155) and lovastatin (p. 154).

Indications: Adjunct to diet in treatment of primary hypercholesterolemia (heterozygous familial and nonfamilial) and mixed dyslipidemia (Types IIa and IIb) in (1) patients receiving lovastatin who require further reduction in triglycerides or increases in HDL cholesterol who may benefit from niacin added to their regimen; (2) patients receiving niacin who require further reduction in LDL cholesterol who may benefit from lovastatin added to their regimen.

Dosage: (1) The usual recommended starting dose for extended-release niacin is 500 mg at bedtime, which must be titrated by not more than 500 mg every 4 weeks up to a maximum dose of 2000 mg/d, to reduce the incidence and severity of side effects. Patients already receiving a stable dose of extended-release niacin may be switched directly to a niacin-equivalent dose of extended-release niacin/lovastatin. Patients receiving immediate-release or sustained-release niacin should be started on extended-release niacin at 500 mg and titrated by the schedule described above. (2) The usual recommended starting dose of lovastatin is 20 mg once a day; dose adjustments should be made at intervals of 4 weeks or more. Patients already receiving a stable dose of lovastatin may receive concomitant dosage titration with extended-release niacin, then switched to extended-release niacin/lovastatin once a stable dose of extended-release niacin has been reached. Extended-release niacin/lovastatin should be taken at bedtime with a low-fat snack; tablets should be taken whole and should not be broken, crushed, or chewed. Doses > 2000 mg/40 mg are not recommended.

Contraindications: Hypersensitivity, active liver disease or unexplained persistent elevations in serum transaminases, active peptic ulcer disease, arterial bleeding, pregnancy, lactation. Use with caution in patients with unstable angina or acute MI, renal dysfunction, or predisposition to gout.

Adverse Effects: Flushing, asthenia, flu syndrome, headache, infection, abdominal pain, back pain, diarrhea, dyspepsia, nausea, vomiting, hyperglycemia, myalgia, pruritus, rash, elevations in serum transaminases, CK, and fasting glucose, reductions in phosphorus. May reduce platelet count and increase prothrombin time; evaluate carefully patients undergoing surgery.

Monitoring: Lipid profile, LFTs, blood glucose; serum phosphorus in patients at risk for hypophosphatemia. Use with close observation in patients with history of jaundice, hepatobiliary disease, or peptic ulcer.

Drug Interactions: May potentiate the effects of ganglionic blocking agents and vasoactive drugs, resulting in postural hypotension. Binds to cholestyramine and colestipol; separate administration by at least 4-6 hours.

Concomitant alcohol may increase flushing and pruritus. Vitamins or other nutritional supplements containing large doses of niacin or related compounds such as nicotinamide may potentiate adverse effects. Myopathy and rhabdomyolysis have been reported with concomitant therapy of HMG-CoA reductase inhibitors with cyclosporine, itraconazole, ketoconazole, gemfibrozil, niacin, erythromycin, clarithromycin, nefazodone, or HIV protease inhibitors. May increase prothrombin time and/or bleeding; in patients taking anticoagulants, determine prothrombin time before initiation of extended-release niacin/lovastatin and monitor frequently during early therapy and if extended-release niacin-lovastatin dosage is changed.

Comments: Flushing may be reduced by pretreatment with aspirin (approximately 30 minutes before extended-release niacin/lovastatin) or other NSAIDs; flushing, pruritus, and gastrointestinal distress are also reduced by increasing the dose slowly and avoiding administration on an empty stomach. Concomitant alcohol or hot drinks may increase flushing and pruritus and should be avoided around the time of administration.

Dosage Forms: Tablet (500 mg/20 mg, 750 mg/20 mg, 1000 mg/20 mg)

Website: www.advicor.com

Omega-3 acid ethyl esters (Omacor)

Class: Omega-3 fatty acid

Mechanism of Action: Omega-3 fatty acids reduce VLDL synthesis, possibly because EPA and DHA are inefficient substrates for enzymes involved in triglyceride synthesis and because EPA and DHA inhibit esterification of other fatty acids. Other possible mechanisms include inhibition of acyl-coenzyme A:cholesterol acyltransferase and increased hepatic peroxisomal β-oxidation.

Indications: Adjunct to diet to reduce very high triglycerides (≥ 500 mg/dL) in adults.

Dosage: Daily dose is 4 gm daily; may be taken as a single dose or two 2-gm doses.

Contraindications: Hypersensitivity. Use with caution in patients allergic or sensitive to fish. May prolong bleeding time; monitor patients receiving anticoagulants.

Adverse Effects: Eructation, taste perversion, dyspepsia, flu syndrome, back pain, infection, rash.

Monitoring: LFTs, lipid panel

Drug Interactions: May prolong bleeding time; monitor patients receiving anticoagulants.

Dosage Forms: Capsule (1 g)

Website: www.omacorrx.com

Pravastatin (Pravachol)

Class: HMG-CoA reductase inhibitor

Mechanism of Action: Pravastatin competitively inhibits the enzyme HMG-CoA reductase, which is the rate-limiting step in cholesterol synthesis. This enzyme inhibition results in decreased intracellular cholesterol production in the liver, which upregulates intrahepatic LDL receptor activity and facilitates LDL cholesterol clearance from the circulation. HMG-CoA reductase inhibitors increase HDL and decrease LDL, VLDL, apo B, and triglycerides.

Indications: Adjunct to diet (1) to reduce elevated total cholesterol, apo B, LDL cholesterol, and triglycerides and increase HDL cholesterol in primary hypercholesterolemia and mixed dyslipidemia (Types IIa and IIb); (2) for treatment of patients with elevated triglycerides (Type IV) or primary dysbetalipoproteinemia (Type III); (3) to reduce risk of MI, reduce risk of undergoing myocardial revascularization procedures, and reduce risk of cardiovascular mortality with no increase in death from noncardiovascular causes in hypercholesterolemic patients without clinically evident CHD; (4) to slow progression of coronary atherosclerosis, reduce risk of total mortality by reducing coronary death, reduce risk of MI, reduce risk of undergoing myocardial revascularization procedures, and reduce risk of stroke or transient ischemic attack (TIA) in patients with clinically evident CHD.

Dosage: Starting dose is 40 mg once daily at bedtime. Usual range is 20-80 mg daily at bedtime.

Renal Dysfunction, Hepatic Impairment, Concomitant Cyclosporine Use: Start with 10 mg/d at bedtime.

Contraindications: Hypersensitivity, active liver disease, pregnancy, lactation.

Adverse Effects: Headache, N/V/D, flatulence, heartburn, localized pain, myalgia, common cold, rhinitis, cough, chest pain, rash, fatigue, urinary abnormality. Rhabdomyolysis with renal dysfunction has occurred with some agents from this class.

Monitoring: LFTs, lipid panel.

Drug Interactions: Coadministration with cyclosporine, erythromycin, clofibrate, gemfibrozil, and nicotinic acid may increase the risk of severe myopathy or rhabdomyolysis. Itraconazole may increase HMG-CoA reductase inhibitor levels; discontinue HMG-CoA reductase inhibitor administration while on azole antifungal therapy. Separate administration of bile acid sequestrants from HMG-CoA reductase inhibitors by 2-4 hours.

Comments: Administer at bedtime. Most patients on immunosuppressant therapy are maintained with doses of 20 mg or less. Instruct patients to report promptly any muscle pain, tenderness, or weakness, especially if accompanied by fever or malaise.

Dosage Forms: Tablet (10 mg, 20 mg, 40 mg, 80 mg)

Website: www.pravachol.com

Rosuvastatin (Crestor)

Class: HMG-CoA reductase inhibitor

Mechanism of Action: Rosuvastatin competitively inhibits the enzyme HMG-CoA reductase, which is the rate-limiting step in cholesterol synthesis. Enzyme inhibition results in decreased intracellular cholesterol production in the liver, which upregulates intrahepatic LDL receptor activity and facilitates LDL cholesterol clearance from the circulation. HMG-CoA reductase inhibitors increase HDL and decrease LDL, VLDL, apo B, and triglycerides.

Indications: (1) As an adjunct to diet to reduce elevated total cholesterol, LDL cholesterol, apo B, non-HDL cholesterol, and triglycerides and to increase HDL cholesterol in patients with primary hypercholesterolemia (heterozygous familial and nonfamilial) and mixed dyslipidemia (Types IIa and IIb); (2) As an adjunct to diet for the treatment of patients with elevated triglycerides (Type IV); (3) To reduce LDL cholesterol, total cholesterol, and apoB in patients with homozygous familial hypercholesterolemia as an adjunct to other lipid-lowering treatments (e.g., LDL apheresis) or if such treatments are unavailable.

Dosage: Dose range is 5-40 mg once daily for patients with hypercholesterolemia or mixed dyslipidemia. The usual starting dose is 10 mg/d. Initiation with 5 mg/d may be considered for patients requiring less aggressive LDL cholesterol reductions or who have predisposing factors for myopathy. For patients with marked hypercholesterolemia (LDL > 190 mg/dL) and aggressive lipid targets, a 20-mg starting dose may be considered. The 40-mg dose should be reserved for those who have not achieved goal LDL cholesterol at 20 mg. After initiation and/or upon titration of rosuvastatin, lipid levels should be analyzed within 2-4 weeks and dosage adjusted accordingly. For patients with homozygous FH, the recommended starting dosage is 20 mg/d and the maximum recommended dose is 40 mg/d. For patients taking cyclosporine, rosuvastatin should be limited to 5 mg/d. For patients taking gemfibrozil, rosuvastatin should be limited to 10 mg/d; combination therapy with gemfibrozil should generally be avoided. A dosage reduction should be considered for patients receiving 40-mg therapy who have unexplained persistent proteinuria during routine urinalysis testing. For patients of Japanese or Chinese ancestry, dosage reductions may be considered; pharmacokinetic studies showed ~ 2-fold elevation in median exposure in Japanese subjects residing in Japan and in Chinese subjects residing in Singapore compared with Caucasians residing in North America and Europe.

Renal Impairment: For severe renal impairment (CrCl < 30 mL/min/1.73m^2), start with 5 mg/d and do not exceed 10 mg/d.

Hepatic Impairment: Use caution.

Contraindications: Hypersensitivity, active liver disease, unexplained transaminase elevations, pregnancy, lactation.

Adverse Effects: The most frequent adverse effects include myalgia, constipation, asthenia, abdominal pain, nausea. Rare cases of rhabdomyolysis with acute renal failure secondary to myoglobinuria have occurred with some agents from this class.

Monitoring: LFTs, lipid panel.

Drug Interactions: Rosuvastatin clearance is not dependent on metabolism by cytochrome P450 3A4 to a clinically significant extent (confirmed in studies with ketoconazole, erythromycin, itraconazole). Coadministration with cyclosporine or other lipid-lowering therapies (e.g., fibrates, niacin) may increase the risk of myopathy or rhabdomyolysis. Coadministration with warfarin may increase INR (monitor). When antacids (aluminum/magnesium combination) are needed, administer antacid 2 hours after rosuvastatin. Separate statins from bile acids by 2-4 hours.

Comments: Instruct patients to report promptly any muscle pain, tenderness, or weakness, esp. if accompanied by fever or malaise. Temporarily withhold therapy in patients with suspected myopathy or a serious condition predisposing to the development of renal failure secondary to rhabdomyolysis (e.g., sepsis, hypotension, major surgery, trauma).

Dosage Forms: Tablet (5 mg, 10 mg, 20 mg, 40 mg)

Website: www.crestor.com

Simvastatin (Zocor)

Class: HMG-CoA reductase inhibitor

Mechanism of Action: Simvastatin competitively inhibits the enzyme HMG-CoA reductase, which is the rate-limiting step in cholesterol synthesis. Enzyme inhibition results in decreased intracellular cholesterol production in the liver, which upregulates intrahepatic LDL receptor activity and facilitates LDL cholesterol clearance from the circulation. HMG-CoA reductase inhibitors increase HDL and decrease LDL, VLDL, apo B, and triglycerides.

Indications: (1) Adjunct to diet for primary hypercholesterolemia (heterozygous familial and nonfamilial) and mixed dyslipidemia (Types IIa and IIb), to reduce elevated total cholesterol, LDL cholesterol, apo B, and triglycerides, and to increase HDL cholesterol; (2) Adjunct to diet for hypertriglyceridemia (Type IV) or primary dysbetalipoproteinemia (Type III); (3) Adjunct to other lipid-lowering treatments (such as LDL apheresis) for homozygous familial hypercholesterolemia, or if such treatments are not available, to reduce total cholesterol and LDL cholesterol; (4) To reduce risk of total mortality by reducing coronary death, reduce risk for nonfatal MI and stroke/TIA, and reduce need for revascularization procedures in patients with CHD, diabetes, peripheral arterial disease, or history of stroke or other cerebrovascular disease; (5) Adjunct to diet to reduce total cholesterol, LDL cholesterol, and apo B levels in adolescent boys and postmenarche (≥ 1 year) girls, aged 10-17 years, with heterozygous FH if after adequate trial of diet therapy LDL cholesterol remains ≥ 190 mg/dL, or ≥ 160 mg/dL with ≥ 2 other cardio-vascular risk factors or a family history of premature cardiovascular disease..

Dosage: Initial dose is 20-40 mg once daily in the evening, or 40 mg for those at high risk of coronary events because of CHD or other vascular disease or diabetes. Adjust dose at 4-week intervals. Dosage range is 5-80 mg/d. For patients with homozygous FH, recommended dosage is 40 mg/d in the evening or 80 mg/d in divided doses of 20 mg, 20 mg, and 40 mg in the evening. For patients on cyclosporine, initial dosage is 5 mg/d (max. 10 mg/d). For patients taking amiodarone or verapamil, max. dosage is 20 mg/d.

Renal Impairment: Start with 5 mg/d.

Hepatic Impairment: Use caution.

Contraindications: Hypersensitivity, active liver disease, unexplained transaminase elevations, pregnancy, lactation.

Adverse Effects: Headache, abdominal pain, constipation. Rhabdomyolysis with renal dysfunction has occurred with some agents from this class.

Monitoring: LFTs, lipid panel.

Drug Interactions: Coadministration with cyclosporine, itraconazole, ketoconazole, erythromycin, clarithromycin, HIV protease inhibitors, nefazodone, clofibrate, gemfibrozil, nicotinic acid, and with higher-dose simvastatin, amiodarone or verapamil may increase the risk of myopathy or rhabdomyolysis. Itraconazole may increase HMG-CoA reductase inhibitor levels; discontinue statin while on azole antifungal therapy. May increase warfarin effect (monitor PT/INR). Monitor digoxin. Separate statins from bile acids by 2-4 hours.

Comments: Administer in the evening. Instruct patients to report promptly any muscle pain, tenderness, or weakness, esp. if accompanied by fever or malaise.

Dosage Forms: Tablet (5 mg, 10 mg, 20 mg, 40 mg, 80 mg)

Website: www.zocor.com

Appendices

Appendix 1. Primary (Genetic) Dyslipidemias

Dyslipidemia	Description	Treatment/Comments
Heterozygous familial hyper-cholesterolemia (FH)	LDL cholesterol twice normal (190-350 mg/dL). Tendon xanthomas, corneal arcus. Premature atherosclerosis. Prevalence: 1/500 in US.	Treated with high-dose statins initiated simultaneously with therapeutic lifestyle changes. Bile acid sequestrants ± niacin may also be required.
Homozygous familial hyper-cholesterolemia (FH)	Extremely high LDL cholesterol (400-1000 mg/dL). Multiple xanthomas (cutaneous, tendinous, tuberous), corneal arcus. Severe, diffuse atherosclerosis. Prevalence: 1/1,000,000 in US.	High-dose statins and niacin are somewhat effective. Diet, bile acid sequestrants, ileal bypass surgery are ineffective. LDL apheresis may be required.
Familial defective apo B-100	Similar phenotype to FH, with severely elevated LDL cholesterol and clinical findings that can include tendinous xanthomas and corneal arcus. Prevalence: 1/1000.	High-dose statin therapy, combined as necessary with bile acid sequestrants or nicotinic acid.
Polygenic hyper-cholesterolemia	Cholesterol elevation generally less than in heterozygous FH. LDL cholesterol ≥ 190 mg/dL. Xanthomas very rare. High prevalence: approximately 1/20. Risk of CHD increased 3-fold.	Treatment depends on sex, age, LDL cholesterol level, and CHD risk status. Severe cases should be treated as in heterozygous FH.
Familial combined hyperlipidemia	Elevated cholesterol (250-350 mg/dL), triglyceride (250-500 mg/dL), or both. No unique clinical features.	Treat with appropriate agents—statins, fibrates, niacin—to normalize lipid elevations.

Appendix 1. Primary (Genetic) Dyslipidemias

Dyslipidemia	Description	Treatment/Comments
Type III hyperlipidemia (familial dysbeta-lipoproteinemia)	Elevated cholesterol (300-600) mg/dL and triglycerides (400-800 mg/dL, but may be higher). Xanthomas, xanthelasmas, corneal arcus. Premature atherosclerosis. Expression may result from hypothyroidism, obesity, estrogen deficiency, glucose intolerance.	Low saturated fat diet and weight control, supplemented as needed with statins/fibrates to decrease remnant particles. Niacin may be helpful (caution in patients with impaired glucose metabolism).
Familial hyper-triglyceridemia	Triglyceride typically 200-500 mg/dL in type IV phenotype, > 1000 mg/dL in type V phenotype; total cholesterol only moderately elevated; LDL/HDL reduced. Abdominal pain, CHD, pancreatitis, eruptive xanthomas, hepatosplenomegaly, glucose intolerance, hyperuricemia.	Treat as described for elevated triglyceride (pp 23-26).
Familial low HDL cholesterol (hypoalphali-poproteinemia)	Very rare. HDL cholesterol may be < 10 mg/dL. Manifestations may include corneal opacities, xanthomatosis, tonsil anomalies, neuropathy, hepatospleno-megaly, amyloidosis.	Patients should be referred to a lipid specialist for treatment.
Familial chylomicronemia	Rare. Autosomal recessive (consanguinity common). Recurrent acute pancreatitis, eruptive xanthomas, retinal lipemia, hepatosplenomegaly, psychoneurologic manifestations (e.g., paresthesias of the hands, memory loss). In heterozygotes, triglyceride may be normal or mildly elevated. In homozygotes, triglyceride may > 1000 mg/dL.	Diet low in simple carbohydrates and < 10% fat; medium-chain triglyceride intake helpful. Avoid alcohol. Control body weight. Drugs usually do not improve triglyceride levels in these patients.

Appendix 2. Common Causes of Secondary Dyslipidemias

Cause	Effect on Plasma Lipids			Comments
	Total-C	TG	HDL	
Diabetes *Type 1*	None	None or ↑	None, ↓, or ↑	Lipid values vary greatly and are dependent on glycemic control, ranging from ↑ TG and ↓ HDL with poor control to ↓ TG and ↑ HDL with very tight control. Hyperchylomicronemia is due to LPL deficiency, which is insulin dependent.
Type 2	None or ↑	↑	↓	Although poor glycemic control leads to ↑ TG and ↓ HDL, even optimal glycemic control will usually not normalize dyslipidemia.
Hypo-thyroidism	↑	↑	None or ↑	Receptor-mediated clearance of LDL is partly dependent on thyroid hormone activity. Increases in VLDL and TG are due to decreased LPL activity. Effects on HDL are inconsistent.
Obesity	None	↑	↓	High waist/hip ratio associated with insulin resistance and poor prognosis.
Primary biliary cirrhosis	↑	↑	↑ in early stages, ↓ in late stages	Increased fraction of free cholesterol. Abnormal lipoprotein (lipoprotein X), an immature form of HDL that accumulates with decreased LCAT activity, is present.
Obstructive liver disease	↑↑	None	↑	Mildly increased LFTs, particularly increased GGT, may be secondary to hyperlipidemia rather than causative.

Appendix 2. Common Causes of Secondary Dyslipidemias

Cause	Effect on Plasma Lipids			Comments
	Total-C	TG	HDL	
Cushing's syndrome	↑	↑↑	None or ↑	Rare, but consider diagnosis if suggested by exam and history. Lipid abnormalities similar to exogenous glucocorticoids.
Cigarette smoking	None	None	↓	Lowers HDL cholesterol by an average of 5-10 mg/dL
Nephrotic syndrome	↑ (usually > 350 mg/dL)	↑ – ↑↑	None or ↓	Mechanisms of hyperlipidemia probably include increased hepatic production of VLDL and decreased LDL catabolism. Low or normal cholesterol levels suggest a poor prognosis.
Uremia	Usually none	↑	None or ↓	Increased TG is due to decreased VLDL catabolism secondary to reduced LPL activity. Improved HDL cholesterol and triglyceride levels are often noted after renal transplantation.
Drugs *Thiazide diuretics*	None or ↑	None or ↑	None	Dose-dependent effects, particularly in individuals with insulin-resistance syndrome.
Beta-blockers	None	↑	↓	Beta-blockers with intrinsic sympathomimetic activity may increase HDL levels. Cardioselective agents appear to affect lipid levels less.
Estrogens	↓	↑	↑	Transcutaneous preparations have minimal effect on lipids.
Progestins	↑	↓	↓	Effects are generally opposite those of estrogen.

Appendix 2. Common Causes of Secondary Dyslipidemias

| Cause | Effect on Plasma Lipids | | | Comments |
	Total-C	TG	HDL	
Androgens	↑	↓	↓	Very low HDL cholesterol levels suggest anabolic steroid abuse.
Gluco-corticoids	↑	↑	↑	Direct relation between total cholesterol and prednisone dose.
Cyclo-sporine	↑↑	None or ↑	None	May increase risk of myositis with statin therapy.
Alcohol	None	↑↑	↑	May dramatically increase triglyceride, particularly in binge consumption.
Protease inhibitors	↑	↑↑	None or ↓	May dramatically increase triglycerides. Effects more prominent with some protease inhibitors (ritonavir).

HDL = high-density lipoprotein, LCAT = lecithin cholesterol acyl transferase, LDL = low-density lipoprotein, LFT = liver function test, LPL = lipoprotein lipase, TG = triglycerides, TC = total cholesterol, VLDL = very low density lipoprotein

Appendix 3. Fredrickson Classification of Hyperlipidemia

Pheno-type	ICD-9 code	Lipoprotein(s) elevated	Plasma TC	Plasma TG	Athero-genicity	Relative frequency
I	272.3	Chylomicrons	Normal to ↑	↑↑↑↑	Rare	<1%
IIa	272.0	LDL	↑↑	Normal	+++	10%
IIb	272.2	LDL and VLDL	↑↑	↑↑	+++	40%
III	272.2	IDL, β-VLDL	↑↑	↑↑↑	+++	<1%
IV	272.1	VLDL	Normal to ↑	↑↑	+	45%
V	272.4	VLDL and chylomicrons	↑ to ↑↑	↑↑↑↑	+	5%

IDL = intermediate-density lipoprotein, LDL = low-density lipoprotein, TG = triglycerides, TC = total cholesterol, VLDL = very low density lipoprotein

References and Suggested Readings

(see Clinical Trials, pp. 113-145, for additional references)

American Diabetes Association. Standards of medical care in diabetes. Diabetes Care 2006;29(suppl I):S4-S42.

American Diabetes Association. Management of dyslipidemia in adults with diabetes. Diabetes Care 2003;26:S83–S86.

Antiplatelet Trialists' Collaboration. Collaborative overview of randomized trials of antiplatelet therapy, I: prevention of death, myocardial infarction, and stroke by prolonged antiplatelet therapy in various categories of patients. BMJ 1994;308:81-106.

Antiplatelet Trialists' Collaboration. Secondary prevention of vascular disease by prolonged antiplatelet treatment. Br Med J (Clin Res Ed) 1988;296:320-331.

Ariyo AA, Thach C, Tracy R. Lp(a) lipoprotein, vascular disease, and mortality in the elderly. N Engl J Med 2003;349:2108-2115.

Ballantyne CM. Hyperlipoproteinemias. In: Rakel RE, Bope ET (eds). Conn's Current Therapy. Philadelphia: W.B. Saunders, 2002:572–577.

Ballantyne CM, Rangaraj GR. The evolving role of high-density lipoprotein in reducing cardiovascular risk. Prev Cardiol 2001;4:65–72.

Ballantyne CM, Olsson AG, Cook TJ, et al. Influence of low high-density lipoprotein cholesterol and elevated triglyceride on coronary heart disease events and response to simvastatin therapy in 4S. Circulation 2001;104:3046–3051.

Ballantyne CM, Andrews TC, Hsia JA, et al. Correlation of non-high-density lipoprotein cholesterol with apolipoprotein B: effect of 5 hydroxymethylglutaryl coenzyme A reductase inhibitors on non-high-density lipoprotein cholesterol levels. Am J Cardiol 2001;88:265–269.

Ballantyne CM. Development and assessment of antiatherosclerotic therapies beyond low-density lipoprotein cholesterol and blood pressure. Curr Atheroscler Rep 2000;2:281–283.

Ballantyne CM, Grundy SM, Oberman A, et al. Hyperlipidemia: diagnostic and therapeutic perspectives. J Clin Endocrinol Metab 2000;85:2089–2112.

Ballantyne CM, Corsini A, Davidson MH, et al. Risk for myopathy with statin therapy in high-risk patients. Arch Intern Med 2003;163:553-564.

Blair SN, Goodyear NN, Gibbons LW, Cooper KH. Physical fitness and incidence of hypertension in healthy normotensive men and women. JAMA 1984;252:487-490.

Brown BG, Zhao XQ, Chait A, et al. Simvastatin and niacin, antioxidant vitamins, or the combination for the prevention of coronary disease. N Engl J Med 2001;345:1583-1592.

Brown G, Albers JJ, Fisher LD, et al. Regression of coronary artery disease as a result of intensive lipid-lowering therapy in men with high levels of apolipoprotein B. N Engl J Med 1990;323:1289-1298.

Brown WV. Cholesterol absorption inhibitors: Defining new options in lipid management. Clin Cardiol 2003;26;259-264.

Brown WV (ed.). Reaching goal: Conquering the treatment gaps in dyslipidemia management. Clin Cardiol [supplement] 2003;26:III-1-III-44.

Burr ML, Fehily AM, Gilbert JF, et al. Effects of changes in fat, fish, and fibre intakes on death and myocardial reinfarction: Diet and Reinfarction Trial (DART). Lancet 1989;2:757-761.

Canner PL, Berge KG, Wenger NK, et al. Fifteen year mortality in Coronary Drug Project patients: long-term benefit with niacin. J Am Coll Cardiol 1986;8:1245-1255.

Cannon CP, Braundald E, McCabe CH, et al., for the Pravastatin or Atorvastatin Evaluation and Infection Therapy–Thrombolysis in Myocardial Infarction 22 Investigators. Comparison of intensive and moderate lipid lowering with statins after acute coronary syndromes. N Engl J Med 2004;350:1495-1504.

CAPRIE Steering Committee. A randomised, blinded, trial of clopidogrel versus aspirin in patients at risk of ischaemic events (CAPRIE). Lancet 1996;348:1329-1339.

Chobanian AV, Bakris GL, Black HR, et al. The seventh report of the Joint National Committee on Prevention, Detection, Evaluation, and Treatment of High Blood Pressure: the JNC 7 report. JAMA 2003;289:2560-2572.

Cholesterol Treatment Trialists' (CTT) Collaborators. Efficacy and safety of cholesterol-lowering treatment: prospective meta-analysis of data from 90 056 participants in 14 randomised trials of statin. Lancet 2005;366:1267-1278.

Coronary Drug Project Research Group. Clofibrate and niacin in coronary heart disease. JAMA 1975;231:360-381.

de Lorgeril M, Renaud S, Mamelle N, et al. Mediterranean alpha-linolenic acid-rich diet in secondary prevention of coronary heart disease. Lancet 1994;343:1454-1459.

Downs JR, Clearfield M, Weis S, et al, for the AFCAPS/TexCAPS Research Group. Primary prevention of acute coronary events with lovastatin in men and women with average cholesterol levels: results of AFCAPS/TexCAPS. JAMA 1998;279:1615-1622.

Dunn AL, Marcus BH, Kampert JB, et al. Comparison of lifestyle and structured interventions to increase physical activity and cardiorespiratory fitness: a randomized trial. JAMA 1999;281:327-334.

Durrington P. Dyslipidaemia. Lancet 2003;362:717-731.

Farmer JA, Gotto AM Jr. Dyslipidemia and the vulnerable plaque. Prog Cardiovasc Dis 2002;44:415-528.

Farmer JA. Pleiotropic effects of statins. Curr Atheroscler Rep 2000;2:208–217.

Faxon DP, Creager MA, Smith SC, et al. Atherosclerotic vascular disease conference. Circulation 2004;109:2595-2650.

Fedder DO, Koro CE, L'Italien GJ. New National Cholesterol Education Program III guidelines for primary prevention lipid-lowering drug therapy: projected impact on the size, sex, and age distribution of the treatment-eligible population. Circulation 2002;105:152-156.

Fonarow GC, French WJ, Parsons LS, et al., for the National Registry of Myocardial Infarction 3 Participants. Use of lipid-lowering medications at discharge in patients with acute myocardial infarction: data from the National Registry of Myocardial Infarction 3. Circulation 2001;103:38–44.

Ford ES, Giles WH, Mokdad AH. The distribution of 10-year risk for coronary heart disease among U.S. adults. J Am Coll Cardiol 2004;43:1791-1796.

Freeman DJ, Norrie J, Sattar N, et al. Pravastatin and the development of diabetes mellitus: evidence for a protective treatment effect in the West of Scotland Coronary Prevention Study. Circulation 2001;103:357-362.

GISSI-Prevenzione Investigators. Dietary supplementation with n-3 polyunsaturated fatty acids and vitamin E after myocardial infarction: results of the GISSI-Prevenzione trial. Lancet 1999;354:447-455.

Gotto AM Jr, Brinton EA. Assessing low levels of high-density lipoprotein cholesterol as a risk factor in coronary heart disease. J Am Coll Cardiol 2004;43:717-724.

Gotto AM Jr. Treating hypercholesterolemia: looking forward. Clin Cardiol 2003;26(suppl 1):I21-I28.

Gotto AM Jr. High-density lipoprotein cholesterol and triglycerides as therapeutic targets for preventing and treating coronary artery disease. Am Heart J 2002;144(6 suppl):S33-S42.

Gotto AM Jr. Statins and C-reactive protein: considering a novel marker of cardiovascular risk. Prev Cardiol 2002;5:200-203.

Gotto AM Jr. Lipid management in diabetic patients: lessons from prevention trials. Am J Med 2002;112(suppl 8A):19S-26S.

Gotto AM Jr. Management of dyslipidemia. Am J Med 2002;112(suppl 8A):10S-18S.

Gotto AM Jr, Kuller LH. Eligibility for lipid-lowering drug therapy in primary prevention: how do the Adult Treatment Panel II and Adult Treatment Panel III guidelines compare? Circulation 2002;105:136-139.

Gotto AM Jr, Farmer JA. Reducing the risk for stroke in patients with myocardial infarction: a Myocardial Ischemia Reduction with Aggressive Cholesterol Lowering (MIRACL) substudy. [editorial] Circulation 2002;106:1595-1598.

Gotto A, Pownall H. Manual of Lipid Disorders. 3rd ed. Philadelphia, PA: Lippincott Williams & Wilkins; 2003. 482 pp.

Gotto AM, Whitney E, Stein EA, et al. Relation between baseline and on-treatment lipid parameters and first acute major coronary events in the Air Force/Texas Coronary Atherosclerosis Prevention Study (AFCAPS/TexCAPS). Circulation 2000;101:477-484.

Grundy SM, Vega GL, McGovern ME, et al. Efficacy, safety, and tolerability of once-daily niacin for the treatment of dyslipidemia associated with type 2 diabetes: results of the Assessment of Diabetes Control and Evaluation of the Efficacy of Niaspan Trial. Arch Intern Med 2002;162:1568–1576.

Grundy SM, Cleeman JI, Bairey Merz CN, et al. Implications of recent clinical trials for the National Cholesterol Education Program Adult Treatment Panel III guidelines. Circulation 2004;110:227-239.

Grundy SM. Non–high-density lipoprotein cholesterol level as potential risk predictor and therapy target. Arch Intern Med 2001;161:1379-1380.

Haffner SM. Metabolic syndrome, diabetes and coronary heart disease. Int J Clin Pract Suppl 2002;132:31-37.

Hambrecht R, Neibauer J, Marburger C, et al. Various intensities of leisure time physical activity in patients with coronary artery disease: effects on cardiorespiratory fitness and progression of coronary atherosclerotic lesions. J Am Coll Cardiol 1993;22:468-477.

Heart Outcomes Prevention Evaluation Study Investigators. Effects of an angiotensin-converting-enzyme inhibitor, ramipril, on cardiovascular events in high-risk patients. N Engl J Med 2000;342:145-153.

Heart Outcomes Prevention Evaluation Study Investigators. Effects of ramipril on cardiovascular and microvascular outcomes in people with diabetes mellitus: results of the HOPE study and MICRO-HOPE substudy. Lancet 2000;355:253-259.

Heart Protection Study Collaborative Group. MRC/BHF Heart Protection Study of cholesterol lowering with simvastatin in 20,536 high-risk individuals: a randomised placebo-controlled trial. Lancet 2002;360:7-22.

Hennekens CH, Dyken ML, Fuster V. Aspirin as a therapeutic agent in cardiovascular disease: a statement for healthcare professionals from the American Heart Association. Circulation 1997;96:2751-2753.

Hirsch J, Guyatt G, Albers G, et al. The seventh ACCP conference on antiplatelet and thrombolytic therapy. Chest 2004;126:172S-178S.

Hu FB, Bronner L, Willett WC, et al. Fish and omega-3 fatty acid intake and risk of coronary heart disease in women. JAMA 2002;287:1815-1821.

Iso H, Rexrode KM, Stampfer MJ, et al. Intake of fish and omega-3 fatty acids and risk of stroke in women. JAMA 2001;285:304-312.

James WPF, Astrup A, Finer N, et al. Effect of sibutramine on weight maintenance after weight loss: a randomised trial. Lancet 2000;356:2119-2125.

Jenkins DA, Kendal CWC, Marchie A, et al. Effects of a dietary portfolio of cholesterol-lowering foods vs lovastatin on serum lipids and C-reactive protein. JAMA 2003;290:502-510.

Jones PH. Diet and pharmacologic therapy of obesity to modify atherosclerosis. Curr Atheroscler Rep 2000;2:314-320.

Katan MB, Grundy SM, Jones P, et al. Efficacy and safety of plant stanols and sterols in the management of blood cholesterol levels. Mayo Clin Proc 2003;78:965-978.

Knopp RH. Drug treatment of lipid disorders. N Engl J Med 1999;341:498-511.

Krauss RM, Eckel RH, Howard B, Appel LJ, et al. AHA dietary guidelines: revision 2000: a statement for healthcare professionals from the Nutrition Committee of the American Heart Association. Circulation 2000;102:2284-2299.

Kris-Etherton P, Eckel RH, Howard BV, et al. Lyon Diet Heart Study. Benefits of a Mediterranean-style, National Cholesterol Education Program/American Heart Association Step I dietary pattern on cardiovascular disease. Circulation 2001;103:1823-1825.

Libby P, et al. Vascular effects of statins. Circulation (supplement) 2004;21:II-1-II-48.

Lipid Research Clinics Program. The Lipid Research Clinics Coronary Primary Prevention Trial results. I. Reduction in incidence of coronary heart disease. JAMA 1984;251:351-364.

Lipid Research Clinics Program. The Lipid Research Clinics Coronary Primary Prevention Trial results. II. The relationship of reduction in incidence of coronary heart disease to cholesterol lowering. JAMA 1984;251:365-374.

Long-Term Intervention with Pravastatin in Ischaemic Disease (LIPID) Study Group. Prevention of cardiovascular events and death with pravastatin in patients with coronary heart disease and a broad range of initial cholesterol levels. N Engl J Med 1998;339:1349-1357.

Maron DJ, Fazio S, Linton MF. Current perspectives on statins. Circulation 2000;101:207-213.

Mori TA, Beilin LJ, Burke V, et al. Interactions between dietary fat, fish, and fish oils and their effects on platelet function in men at risk of cardiovascular disease. Arterioscler Thromb Vasc Biol 1997;17:279-286.

Mosca L, Appel LJ, Benjamin EJ, et al. Evidence-based guidelines for cardiovascular disease prevention in women. J Am Coll Cardiol 2004;43:900-921.

Mosca L, Collins P, Herrington DM, et al. Hormone

replacement therapy and cardiovascular disease: a statement for healthcare professionals from the American Heart Association. Circulation 2001;104:499–503.

National Cholesterol Education Program. Third Report of the National Cholesterol Education Program (NCEP) Expert Panel on Detection, Evaluation, and Treatment of High Blood Cholesterol in Adults (Adult Treatment Panel III) final report. Circulation 2002;106:3143-3421.

Nissen SE, Tuzcu EM, Schoenhagen P, et al., for the REVERSAL Investigators. Effect of intensive compared with moderate lipid-lowering therapy on progression of coronary atherosclerosis: a randomized controlled trial. JAMA 2004;291:1071-1080.

Obesity Education Initiative. Executive summary of the clinical guidelines on the identification, evaluation, and treatment of overweight and obesity in adults. Arch Intern Med 1998;158:1855–1867.

O'Keefe JH, Cordain L, Harris WH. et al. Optimal low-density lipoprotein is 50 to 70 mg/dl. J Am Coll Cardiol 2004;43:2142-6.

Pasternak RC, Smith SC Jr, Bairey-Merz CN, et al. ACC/AHA/NHLBI clinical advisory on the use and safety of statins. J Am Coll Cardiol 2002;40:568–73.

Pearson TA, Blair SN, Daniels SR, et al. AHA guidelines for primary prevention of cardiovascular disease and stroke: 2002 update: consensus panel guide to comprehensive risk reduction for adult patients without coronary or other atherosclerotic vascular diseases. Circulation 2002;106:388–391.

Pearson TA, Mensah GA, Alexander RW, et al. Markers of inflammation and cardiovascular disease. Circulation 2003;107:499-511.

Pearson TA, Laurora I, Chu H, Kafonek S. The Lipid Treatment Assessment Project (L-TAP): a multicenter survey to evaluate the percentages of dyslipidemic patients receiving lipid-lowering therapy and achieving low-density lipoprotein cholesterol goals. Arch Intern Med 2000;160:459–467.

Rifai N, Ridker PM. Inflammatory markers and coronary heart disease. Curr Opin Lipidol 2002;13:383–389.

Ridker PM, Rifai N, Clearfield M, et al. Measurement of C-reactive protein for the targeting of statin therapy in the primary prevention of acute coronary events. N Engl J Med 2001;344:1959-1965.

Ridker PM. Rosuvastatin in the primary prevention of cardiovascular disease among patients with low levels of low-density lipoprotein cholesterol and elevated high-sensitivity C-reactive protein. Circulation 2003;108:2292-2297.

Robins SJ, Collins D, Wittes JT, et al. Relation of gemfibrozil treatment and lipid levels with major coronary events: VA-HIT: a randomized controlled trial. JAMA 2001;285:1585-1591.

Rubins HB, Robins SJ, Collins D, et al., for the Veterans Affairs High-Density Lipoprotein Cholesterol Intervention Trial Study Group. Gemfibrozil for the secondary prevention of coronary heart disease in men with low levels of high-density lipoprotein cholesterol. N Engl J Med 1999;341:410-418.

Sacks FM, Pfeffer MA, Moye LA, et al., for the Cholesterol and Recurrent Events Trial investigators. The effect of pravastatin on coronary events after myocardial infarction in patients with average cholesterol levels. N Engl J Med 1996;335:1001-1009.

Scandinavian Simvastatin Survival Study Group. Randomised trial of cholesterol lowering in 4444 patients with coronary heart disease: the Scandinavian Simvastatin Survival Study (4S). Lancet 1994;344:1383-1389.

Sever PS, Dahlöf B, Poulter NR, et al. for the ASCOT Investigators. Prevention of coronary and stroke events with atorvastatin in hypertensive patients who have average or lower-than-average cholesterol concentrations, in the Anglo-Scandinavian Cardiac outcomes Trial—Lipid Lowering Arm (ASCOT-LLA): a multicentre randomised controlled trial. Lancet 2003;361:1149-1158.

Shepherd J, Cobbe SM, Ford I, et al., for the West of Scotland Coronary Prevention Study Group. Prevention of coronary heart disease with pravastatin in men with hypercholesterolemia. N Engl J Med 1995;333:1301-1307.

Sjostrom L, Rissanen A, Andersen T, et al. Randomised placebo-controlled trial of orlistat for weight loss and prevention of weight regain in obese patients. Lancet 1998;352:167-173.

Smith SC Jr, Allen J, Blair SN, et al. AHA/ACC guidelines for secondary prevention for patients with coronary and other atherosclerotic vascular disease: 2006 update. Circulation 2006;113:2363-2372.

Smith SC Jr, Greenland P, Grundy SM. Prevention conference V: Beyond secondary prevention: Identifying the high-risk patient for primary prevention: executive summary. Circulation

2000;101:111–116.

Smith SC Jr, Blair SN, Bonow RO, et al. AHA/ACC guidelines for preventing heart attack and death in patients with atherosclerotic coronary disease: 2001 update: a statement for healthcare professionals from the American Heart Association and the American College of Cardiology. Circulation 2001;104:1577–1579.

Stewart KJ. Exercise training and the cardiovascular consequences of type 2 diabetes and hypertension: plausible mechanisms for improving cardiovascular health. JAMA 2002;288:1622-1631.

Tobacco Use and Dependence Clinical Practice Guideline Panel, Staff, and Consortium Representatives. A clinical practice guideline for treating tobacco use and dependence: a US Public Health Service report. JAMA 2000;283:3244–3254.

UK Prospective Diabetes Study Group. Tight blood pressure control and risk of macrovascular and microvascular complications in type 2 diabetes: UKPDS 38. BMJ 1998;317:703-713.

U.S. Department of Health and Human Services. Physical Activity and Health: A Report of the Surgeon General. Atlanta, GA: U.S. Department of Health and Human Services, Centers for Disease Control and Prevention, National Center for Chronic Disease Prevention and Health Promotion, 1996.

U.S. Department of Health and Human Services and U.S. Department of Agriculture. Dietary Guidelines for Americans, 6th ed. Washington, DC: U.S. Government Printing Office, 2005.

U.S. Preventive Services Task Force. Aspirin for the primary prevention of cardiovascular events: recommendation and rationale. Ann Intern Med 2002;136:157–160.

Waters DD, Schwartz GG, Olsson AG, et al. Effects of atorvastatin on stroke in patients with unstable angina or non-Q-wave myocardial infarction: a Myocardial Ischemia Reduction with Aggressive Cholesterol Lowering (MIRACL) substudy. Circulation 2002;106:1690-1695.

Williams MA, Fleg JL, Ades PA, Chaitman BR, et al. Secondary prevention of coronary heart disease in the elderly (with emphasis on patients > 75 years of age): an American Heart Association scientific statement from the Council on Clinical Cardiology Subcommittee on Exercise, Cardiac Rehabilitation, and Prevention. Circulation 2002;105:1735–1743.

Xydakis AM, Ballantyne CM. Combination therapy for combined dyslipidemia. Am J Cardiol 2002;90:21K–29K.

Yancy WS Jr, Westman EC, French PA, Califf RM. Diets and clinical coronary events: the truth is out there. Circulation 2003;107:10–16.

Yusuf S, Wittes J, Friedman L. Overview of results of randomized clinical trials in heart disease. I. Treatments following myocardial infarction. JAMA 1988;260:2088-2093.

Index

DYSLIPIDEMIA ESSENTIALS — ORDERING INFORMATION

Price (U.S. dollars)
1–9 copies:	$17.95 each
10–49 copies:	$16.95 each
50–100 copies:	$15.95 each
> 100 copies:	call

Shipping
USA: UPS Ground delivery (call for next day, 2-day, or 3-day express delivery charges):
1–3 copies:	add $5
4–10 copies:	add $7
10–49 copies:	add $12
> 50 copies:	call

Outside USA: Call, fax, or e-mail for delivery charges

Michigan residents: add 6%

4 Ways to Order:
By Phone:	(248) 616-3023
By Fax:*	(248) 616-3003
By Mail:*	Physicians' Press
	620 Cherry Avenue
	Royal Oak, Michigan 48073
By Internet:	www.physicianspress.com

* Please print or type name, mailing address, credit card number and expiration date or purchase order number (if applicable), telephone number (important), fax number, and e-mail address. We accept VISA, MasterCard, and American Express.

Be sure to visit www.physicianspress.com

- Acute Coronary Syndrome (ACS) Essentials
- Dyslipidemia Essentials
- Hypertension Essentials
- Diabetes Essentials
- Handbook of Diabetic Hypertension
- Stroke Essentials

- Antibiotic Essentials
- HIV Essentials
- Pneumonia Essentials
- The Complete Guide to ECGs
- The ECG Criteria Book
- Cardiometabolic Essentials
- Essentials of Cardiovascular Medicine

PHYSICIANS' PRESS

Innovative Medical Publishing